WOMEN WHO STAY
WITH
MEN WHO STRAY

WOMEN WHO STAY WITH MEN WHO STRAY

What Every Woman

Needs To Know

About Men and Infidelity

DEBBIE THEN, PH.D.

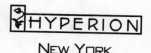

HYPERION

NEW YORK

Library of Congress Cataloging-in-Publication Data

Then, Debbie.
　Women who stay with men who stray : what every woman needs to know about men and infidelity / Debbie Then.—1st ed.
　　　p.　cm.
　Includes bibliographical references.
　ISBN 0-7868-6524-5
　　1. Adultery.　2. Man-woman relationships.　3. Marriage—Psychological aspects.　I. Title.
　HQ806.T48　1999
　306.73'6—dc21
98-48827
CIP

FIRST EDITION

10　9　8　7　6　5　4　3　2　1

The people and situations described in this book are real, but the names and other identifying details have been altered. Any similarity between an individual or situation described in the book and a specific real person or event is purely coincidental.

CONTENTS

PART THREE
THRIVING IN LIFE AFTER A HUMILIATING
BETRAYAL 181

We can't change the wind, but we can adjust our sails.

—ANONYMOUS

Acknowledgments

Writing this book was a very solitary process, but the development of the ideas and the accumulation of materials that led me to it has involved many people. Even as adultery rates are rising, infidelity is still a taboo topic of conversation. As such, this book required the input of many people who wish to remain anonymous. I am indebted to the men and women who told me their stories of infidelity. I could not have written the book without them. While their names and personal details have been altered to protect the guilty and the innocent, I thank them all for sharing their most intimate experiences with me. I also thank the writer Nora Ephron, whose novel and movie, *Heartburn*, provided the inspirational seed which blossomed into this book.

I am very blessed to have many wonderful colleagues and friends who regularly offer me insightful suggestions and encouragement. My deep appreciation goes out to all of them: John, Gerri, Judy, Jane, Margaret, Tom, Barry, Phil, Richard, Wendy, the Seattle gang, and, especially, Howard.

My thanks also go to the many editors and journalists at magazines, newspapers, and television shows who have been so kind and helpful to me for many years. And I am especially grateful to Barrie for believing in my work, and for taking that initial chance on me. Also I thank Angelo, James, Belinda, Katrina, Christine, Robyn, Wanda, and Meg, who have all worked so hard on my behalf. My great debt goes to Maureen O'Brien, my talented editor at Hyperion, as well as to Jennifer Morgan, John Marius, Jennifer Landers, Brittany Zucker, and Adrian C. James; to Jennifer Gates, my extraordinary agent—for her cheerfulness, enthusiasm, and professionalism; and to Lane Zachary, Todd Shuster, and Esmond Harmsworth at the Zachary Shuster Literary Agency for taking good care of me. Thanks also to Harry Langdon, a kind man and a talented photographer.

A very special note of gratitude, appreciation, and love to my husband. It's . . . MAGIC!

Introduction

There were three of us in this marriage, so it was a bit crowded.
— DIANA, PRINCESS OF WALES

What does Hillary Rodham Clinton have in common with Princess Diana and millions of other women? Each has reportedly suffered the personal pain and public humiliation of an allegedly philandering husband.

That's what this book is about—women staying with men who stray. It tells the details of men's affairs and reveals why so many women stand by their cheating men. Most of all, this book is about the importance trust plays in marriage. Infidelity is about illicit sex, but at its most basic, infidelity is about lying and deception, and it wreaks havoc on a marriage.

What is it that makes wives stay with men who are unfaithful to them? This is a dilemma facing many women today, and this book is the first to investigate the controversial issue.

One of the most visible cases of infidelity has lived itself out in the media over the last year or so. Unless one were living under a rock, it would be hard not to be aware of what has come to be known as "zippergate" or "Monicagate." Certainly Bill Clinton's televised confession that he "had an inappropriate relationship" is one of the more dramatic examples of a man caught with his pants down. Still, Hillary remains committed to her man and her marriage—at least for now.

She is not alone in her dedication—some might say blind devotion, or delusional denial—in the wake of hearing about the philandering of her husband. Like Hillary, millions of women, for a variety of personal, social, and financial reasons, decide to stand by their man when confronted with his infidelity.

As the September 1998 issue of *Ladies' Home Journal* reported in their study on the "Amazing American Woman," 46 percent of women responding said they would forgive their man for a one-night stand. Another 46 percent said they couldn't forgive. The women were least likely to forgive if they found out about the affair from someone else first. Only 10 percent of women said they would forgive their husband if he had a long-term affair.

Since affairs — and forgiveness — are never cut-and-dried issues, research about how a woman reacts to a straying husband often varies. The September 7, 1998, issue of *People* reported on a survey the magazine conducted in the wake of President Clinton's relationship with Monica Lewinsky. Sixty percent of the women said their reaction to their cheating husband would depend on the circumstances of his affair; 17 percent said they would leave the marriage; and 21 percent said they would find a way to save their marriage.

While many women can't say exactly how they will react to infidelity if it touches their marriage, a *Time*/CNN poll entitled "How We Really Feel About Fidelity" reported in an article in the August 31, 1998, issue of *Time* magazine said that women are clear on one thing: If their husband, on the eve of leaving for a vacation together, admitted to having sex with a twenty-one-year-old intern, 68 percent of the women said they would not go along on the vacation!

Whether to stay with a man who strayed — and who will possibly continue to stray — or choose to leave a marriage is a question confronting more and more women these days. And there is no easy answer to the situation. Whether the woman involved is the first lady or a first-grade teacher, a man's infidelity causes her pain and concern.

In a 1995 BBC television interview broadcast around the globe, Princess Diana talked about the breakdown of her marriage to Prince Charles — a marriage, she said, that she "desperately wanted to work." Her "woman's instinct," as she called it, led her to suspect Charles of having an affair with the then married Camilla Parker Bowles. She confided that Charles's infidelity was "pretty devastating," and that having "a husband who loved someone else" gave her "a feeling of being no good at anything, [of] being useless and hopeless, and [of having] failed in every direction." Yet even after Prince Charles's own televised confession in 1994 of his infidelity, Diana still did not want to divorce.

If one of the richest and most beautiful women in the world was devastated by her husband's affair, what about the rest of us women? An unfaithful, adulterous, cheating, lying, philandering husband is *every* woman's worst nightmare. Yet most men believe that adultery is no big deal. Having sex with a woman other than their wife? "So what, it's just sex, it isn't love," they argue. Women, on the other hand, believe that infidelity is a very big deal—and a very bad deal. The majority of women don't want to share their husband with another woman. Illustrating this great divide between men and women are the four words most feared by women and those most feared by men. Women dread hearing from their husband: "I'm having an affair." For men, the most feared four words are: "I'll tell your wife."

No woman is ever happy that her partner strays, and no one is immune to the trauma infidelity brings. Famous or not, women suffer, and often in silence. Too many women waste precious years of their lives trying to figure out how to "cheat-proof" their marriage, or how to win back their husband from the "Other Woman."

Women need to know that they cannot change their partner's behavior. All they can change is how they choose to deal with a man who strays. "The only time a woman really succeeds in changing a man is when he is a baby," the late actress Natalie Wood once said.

A man who strays wreaks untold damage on a woman's self-confidence, emotional well-being, physical health, and sense of stability and security in the world. No woman wants to imagine her husband sharing sex and pillow talk with another woman. Most women fear abandonment, loss of love, and sexual and emotional betrayal by a partner. Therefore, an unfaithful husband unravels even the most competent woman's self-esteem.

"What do women want?" asked Sigmund Freud, the father of psycho-analysis. Women want, and worry about, fidelity. Few women would vow on their wedding day to stand by their husband while he has sexual and emotional involvements with other women. In order to carry on illicit, ex-tramarital affairs, men have to lie. Such deceptions can erode the trust and foundation of even a rock-solid marriage.

UNFAITHFULLY YOURS

When a man strays, a woman almost always assumes it is because some-thing is wrong with *her*. She blames herself and assumes that she is lacking in some fundamental way. She worries that she is not pretty enough, not thin enough, not rich enough, not young enough, not successful enough.

Not enough of *something*—something that her husband is seeking elsewhere.

Much of the time, however, a man strays because he feels that, as a man, having affairs is his birthright, and that they have nothing to do with his feelings for his wife. Many men have a sense of arrogant entitlement and believe they aren't "real" men if they don't continue to bed other women. Yet a woman blames herself when her husband strays, and often, society blames her too. "Why can't she just accept that it's just how men are?" is the view often taken.

Whether we approve of infidelity or not, extramarital sex figures largely in society today. The sad fact is, many women will be cheated on—and sometimes repeatedly. Society all too frequently condones men's affairs and simultaneously praises a woman who stands by her man, while at the same time looking down on her and questioning her self-respect.

Infidelity is such a controversial issue because it strikes a chord with so many people. Talk about infidelity has long been taboo, even as we read all about it, displaying our voyeuristic interest in other people's sex lives. Infidelity may be more common today than ever before; but that doesn't make it the right thing to do to a marriage. In the August 1998 poll on "How We Really Feel About Fidelity," *Time* magazine reported that 69 percent of men and 60 percent of women know someone who has committed adultery. Many things in life occur with frequency; that does not mean they are good for us or our relationships.

Most women say they feel deeply hurt and emotionally abandoned when their partner is sexually involved with another woman. They struggle to find answers to difficult questions they ask themselves when faced with an unfaithful husband. *Should I stay with the man I love even though he continues to cheat on me, betray me, and possibly expose me to sexually transmitted diseases?*

Women everywhere wonder, at one time or another, if their husband may be involved with another woman. No woman likes to enter a room and wonder how many women present have had sex with her husband. Yet this is a situation many women confront whenever they attend a social function.

Most women develop a kind of radar that enables them to sniff out their husband's philandering. When they see their partner talking to another woman at a party, they may wonder why he is being so attentive to her.

Women's imagination, intuition, and anxiety level surge into overdrive. Often, they are correct in their assumption that sparks are flying and an affair may be waiting to ignite. Whether or not a woman wants to acknowledge her husband's infidelity, she "just knows" when her husband is straying.

Research suggests that when a wife suspects that her husband is having an affair, she is usually correct. Many women say they have a sort of "infidelity radar," and that they "feel it in their bones" when their husband is being unfaithful.

It is little surprise that women often mistrust other women where men are concerned. I encountered just such a woman recently at a party where I was speaking to an exceedingly attractive and interesting man. Not long into our conversation, a woman appeared at my new friend's side. She looked at him briefly before shifting her gaze to me. She looked me up and down, looked back at my friend, then departed in a huff and headed for the bar.

Immediately I knew that this woman was the man's wife. Her silence, sad eyes, and not-so-subtle glances to check my finger for a wedding ring gave her away instantly. She was trying to assess whether I was a possible partner in play for her philandering husband. Her discomfort signaled to me in an instant that the man I was speaking with must have strayed in the past, and that she suffered through his philanderings.

MAN SHARING

Every woman worries about losing her lover to another woman. And in many cases, they have good reason to worry, for not only do they have to be concerned about their man seeking out other women, but they must also contend with the ever-increasing numbers of women who purposely try to lure away other women's partners. The "good man shortage" is a reality. More and more women are looking to borrow or steal other women's husbands.

Helen Gurley Brown, former longtime editor of *Cosmopolitan* magazine, wrote a book in which she advised women to "borrow other women's husbands for sex." In *The Late Show: A Practical, Semiwild Survival Guide for Every Woman in Her Prime or Approaching It* (1993), she says: "Consider the man who is mildly or seriously unhappy in his marriage or simply bored with it. . . . Don't go moral on me. We're talking dalliance here, not a permanent husband snatch." This type of attitude gives a lot of women real grief, especially since Ms. Gurley Brown does not want her own husband to be "borrowed" by a woman in search of a mere "dalliance." Even the sexy septuagenarian gets her feathers ruffled when she thinks about *her* husband straying.

Gurley Brown confides: "Having your man fancy other women in bed and *do* something about it has got to be the most ego-destroying happiness-basher there is and I don't believe I could stand it." This aged *Cosmo* girl urges you to do as she says—but not with *her* husband!

STAND BY YOUR MAN, OR SPLIT?

So, how do women stand it? Exactly how do women stay with a man who strays? How do they live through long-term infidelity, and why do they choose to stay with a philandering mate rather than leave him? These questions are the subject of this book. I will tell you the truth about men's affairs—why and how they stray, and why so many women stay with men who stray. The book tells the intimate stories of men's affairs, how women find out about them, the personal, social, and financial reasons many women decide to stay with a man who strays, how women's own extramarital affairs can help them cope with a philandering husband, and the emotional costs a woman pays for standing by her man.

Unfortunately, infidelity is a side effect of many marriages—and that is unlikely to change in the years ahead. Adultery is etched in society and will not disappear just because we wish it away. To focus only on "getting your man back" from the Other Woman is a futile pursuit for women, as many men simply will never give up philandering.

Many, many women stay with men who stray. In fact, if all marriages touched by infidelity broke up, the divorce rate would probably double. The truth is, men and women will always be attracted to one another, and many will act on that attraction, even if one or both of them are married. For many marriages, infidelity is a way of life. Not a *happy* way of life, but all too common nonetheless.

HAVING THEIR CAKE AND EATING IT TOO

Many men simply refuse to give up having affairs. They want the comfort of marriage and the excitement of a bit on the side. They know that their philandering offends and hurts their wives, yet they either try to enforce a "don't ask, don't tell" policy, or they simply continue the affair more discreetly. Even though most men realize that their extramarital affair upsets their wife and creates trouble in their marriage, some of the men simply refuse to give up their philandering. Under these circumstances, a woman must decide if she can stand by and tolerate her husband being intimately involved with another woman. Such a situation confronted Princess Diana. According to Richard Kay, a noted reporter on the royals for the *Daily Mail* in London, and co-author of *Diana: The Untold Story* (1998), Prince Charles once said to Diana: "Do you seriously expect me to be the first Prince of Wales in British history *not* to have a mistress?" Such an attitude is bound to create tension between a couple.

One man I spoke with while researching this book confided that he is aware that his serial philandering with women at his office hurts his wife tremendously. He also confessed that he wouldn't stop seeing other women. He believes he has been able to maintain a long and reasonably stable marriage *because* he has sex outside his primary relationship. While his wife occasionally finds out about his dalliances, he tries hard to protect her feelings and not cause her undue humiliation.

Women have varying reactions to their partner's philandering. Some seem resigned to it; others refuse to accept it and fight it every day of their life. Most people can't handle a sexually open marriage, so a man lies to his wife and has "discreet" affairs. This causes women untold grief and humiliation. As one woman told me, "It's easier for me to sleep fifteen hours a day than to admit that my husband is sleeping with other women." Another woman said, "My one glass of wine at lunch became a bottle—then two, then three, and a piece of candy suddenly became several boxes" after she learned that her husband was having an affair.

Infidelity is a topic that fascinates people, yet few want to talk about it publicly. Few husbands and wives talk to each other about infidelity, as if talking about it will lead to suspicions and accusations. The topic is threatening to women in particular, because they worry that any talk of the issue will lead to divorce.

Women don't know who to turn to in the wake of infidelity, and they often receive little support from friends, family, or society. Instead, they are encouraged to stand by their man, regardless of the personal toll this takes on them. The traditional thinking has been that if a man is sober, employed, and doesn't beat his wife, then she should overlook his infidelities. Women deserve more than this from a man—and from a marriage. Life is valuable; too valuable for a woman to waste on a philandering husband.

SHATTERED FAIRYTALES

*I*nfidelity may make for an exciting plot in reel life, but in real life even Princess Diana was unnerved by her unfaithful prince. When she revealed, in the 1995 interview on the BBC's *Panorama*, her distress over Prince Charles's affair with Camilla Parker Bowles, the program became the most watched show in British television history—until Diana's funeral service in August 1997, which also set viewing records around the world.

Like the princess, many women today are confronted with a husband who will not give up his extramarital liaisons. Yet most women don't want to end their marriage, so they see staying with a man who strays as their only alternative to divorce. But this is not an easy circumstance to live with, and the women's stories in this book elucidate exactly what life is like in a marriage to a philanderer.

One woman, the wife of a perpetual philanderer, told me she is so distraught over her husband's cheating that she regularly approaches women at parties and asks, "Are you screwing my husband?" This is not your usual cocktail-party conversation, but for a woman who is fed up with the public charade of a happy marriage to a closet serial adulterer, it is altogether understandable behavior.

Another woman who was tiring of staying with her straying husband now tells women she meets at parties to stay away from her husband. In doing so, she reveals to the world that she is married to a player and displays her deep despair over his behavior.

Even glamorous celebrity wives express turmoil over their man's dalliances. The very beautiful Diandra Douglas, ex-wife of actor Michael Douglas, told W magazine in August 1998 that "women my son's age are throwing themselves at Michael on a daily basis. So it must be very difficult for him, putting myself in his shoes, because you're saying, 'no, no, my marriage, my family.'"

When a woman chooses to stay with a partner who strays, what emotional cost do they pay? This book reveals the answers and offers hope to women whose marriages are rocked by infidelity. Regardless of how a husband behaves, a woman must learn to live her life to the fullest and be guided by her own inner compass. I intend to show women how to "get a life" apart from their partner. Infidelity may devastate women, but it doesn't have to destroy them.

In order to fully understand why men stray and so many women stay, one must first look at the double standards of sex, looks, aging, and marriage in our society. Looks, lust, love, sex, and money all have an enormous impact on infidelity—and on why women stay with men who stray.

I don't judge a woman as a saint or a sucker for staying with a straying mate. Infidelity is simply a part of life today. This book looks realistically at a problem that will touch many marriages and that places an enormous burden on women. Women have choices and a lot more control over their lives than they imagine. Once a woman realizes it is futile to try to "cheat-proof" her marriage, she can funnel her energy into constructing a life on her own terms—a life that makes her happy regardless of the state of her marital union.

STORIES OF STRAYERS
AND STAYERS

To gather information for this book, I requested women to write to me about their philandering husbands, and men to tell me about their affairs. In addition, I put the word out through colleagues, friends, and the media that I was researching men's affairs and how women cope. The voices heard in this book represent interviews, phone calls, and letters with men and women from around America, who range in age from twenty to seventy. The majority are white, mostly middle-class or higher, married, and have children.

Though not based on a large-scale scientific study of infidelity, the stories contained here are critically important as they represent the voices of women who have decided to stand by a philandering man. This is the first book to document why, and how, women make a controversial and difficult decision to stay married in the face of infidelity, and what their lives are like, day by day, when continuing to live with a philandering man. As such, the material can offer men and women information about the realities of coping with adultery.

Although the information is also relevant to singles and people in live-in relationships, I interviewed only married men and women. I believe there is a fundamental difference between a live-in relationship and a marriage. When a couple marries, they publicly pledge to forsake all others and promise fidelity, and they become *legally* joined. Having made such a commitment, it may be more difficult to end a marriage after infidelity.

The stories of more than a hundred men and women, including intimate details of their marriages, sex lives, and infidelities, are shared on these pages. I spoke with or heard from straying men, betrayed women, "other women," straying wives, and cuckolded husbands. While the book does not represent a scientific random sample, the information gleaned from men who stray and the women who stay with them is an important first step in understanding this very common and unfortunate predicament that millions of women confront. The majority of people who participated in my research believed that there are no happy endings for *anyone* involved in an extramarital affair.

No one ever really knows what goes on between two people; what draws them together, and what keeps them together despite all odds. But one thing is certain: marriage is the only relationship in our lives where we can hope to drop our guard and find love, acceptance, stability, and trust. Infidelity—and the duplicity that it involves—is the enemy of a happy marriage.

If you are a woman married to a man who is sexually and/or emotionally involved with other women, or to a man who thinks safe sex is paying for a tryst in a hotel with cash instead of a credit card, then you are in for a miserable life. Only you can make the very important decision of whether to stay with such a man.

Every woman must examine her personal priorities in her marriage and her life. For some women, companionship and the identity of being married outweigh the desire for sexual exclusivity. Yet, for many other women, fidelity is the most important aspect of their marriage and a priority they won't compromise. The key is knowing what matters most to *you*—what *you* are willing and able to tolerate in your marriage.

If you are concerned about infidelity touching your marriage, this book will help you to understand how society encourages men to stray, and women to stay with them. The book is divided into three parts. Part 1 (chapters 1–6) discusses the social foundations of infidelity. Part 2 (chapters 7–10) presents stories of women who have chosen to stay with straying husbands, and discusses why they have done so and how they cope from day to day. Part 3 (chapters 11–15) describes the consequences of living with a philandering husband, and tells tales of infidelity among the rich and famous. These chapters also offer advice to women who are trying to regain their self-confidence and develop a new life.

Many men stray. Many women stay with men who stray. Whether you will be one of them is up to you. This book shows you what life is like for women who are married to unfaithful men, and it explains how to build a new dream if such a life is not for you. Living well is the best revenge!

WOMEN WHO STAY
WITH
MEN WHO STRAY

Part One

The Social Foundations of Men's Infidelities

Chapter 1

INFIDELITY UNVEILED: WHO STRAYS AND WHY

*W*oman wants monogamy;
man delights in novelty—
with this the gist and sum of it,
what earthly good can come of it?

—Dorothy Parker

WHAT IS INFIDELITY, ANYWAY?

Infidelity is, first and foremost, a violation of sexual exclusivity between a man and woman who are married. Infidelity occurs when a married person has intimate sexual contact with someone other than their spouse. Regardless of their religious orientation, most people understand that their marriage vows entail "forsaking all others."

As clear and simple as the basic definition of infidelity is, some people try to "bend" the definition to suit their situation so that they can rationalize their unfaithful behavior to themselves. For example, some people wonder if "an affair of the heart," otherwise known as "emotional adultery," *really* counts as infidelity. Emotionally close relationships between men and women who aren't married to each other can cause difficulty in marriages. However, this is not infidelity. The cornerstone of infidelity and adultery is the presence of *sexual intimacy* between two people, one of whom is married to someone else.

When Is Sex Really Sex?

Many people have their own definitions of what constitutes infidelity to them. One man considered that only an *ongoing* sexual relationship with a woman other than his wife constituted infidelity. Another believed that sex with a prostitute didn't count as infidelity. And many men dismissed one-night stands with women in towns away from where they live with their wife. For such men, infidelity means *involvement*—not just sex—with another woman. Amazingly, many men say that oral sex is *not* adultery—because penetration does not occur. One man told me that having sex while wearing a condom does not count as infidelity.

This issue of "when is sex not really sex" came to public attention when the media jumped all over President Bill Clinton's now-famous January 1998 televised claim that "I did not have sexual relations with *that* woman, Ms. Lewinsky." Many people interpreted this as semantic hair-splittting and stonewalling over the issue of oral sex not *really* being sex at all. It was a nice attempt to reinvent the definition of sexual relations. Most adults, however, disagree with Mr. Clinton's definition of what is and is not sex. According to a *Time* magazine/CNN poll, "When Is Sex Not 'Sexual Relations'?" quoted in *Time*, August 24, 1998, 87 *percent of adults believe that oral sex is sex*. Oral sex *is* sex—sex is even part of the expression.

In "How We Really Feel About Fidelity," *Time* reported in its August 31, 1998, issue that 75 percent of married women believe kissing someone other than one's spouse constitutes cheating in a marriage; only 59 percent of men believe this; and 74 percent of women and 64 percent of men think that a sexually explicit phone conversation constitutes cheating. Once again, clear evidence showing men's and women's polarized views on infidelity.

When men's "oral sex is not really sex" argument is taken to the extreme, women could claim that "sex is only sex if they had an orgasm." Using this definition, millions of women could say they have never had sex! Not surprisingly, women tend to have stricter definitions of infidelity than many men do. Several women I spoke with said that when a man pays another woman more attention than he pays his wife, he is being unfaithful. Where many women are concerned, men don't even have to have sex with a woman other than their wife to be considered a philanderer; all they have to do is show intense interest in another female.

An Israeli joke from Tel Aviv's *Ma'ariv* newspaper was cited in *Newsweek*: "According to the polls, 12 percent of the American public thinks that oral sex isn't sex. I'm sure they're just doing it wrong."

Emotional and physical displays of affection by men toward a woman other than their wife are seen by most women as a violation of fidelity. For the purposes of this book, the term "infidelity" is used to describe a *sexual* encounter or ongoing sexual relationship with a person other than one's spouse. Common terms used to describe infidelity by men and women interviewed for this book include:

- extramarital affair

- cheating

- adultery

- fooling around

- playing around

- betraying

- a bit on the side
- exploring options
- affectionate accommodation
- sexual variety
- sexual novelty
- liaison
- rendezvous
- tryst
- afternoon delight
- matinee
- inappropriate relationship

By whatever name you call it, infidelity complicates lives, is detrimental to marriage, and infuriates women—and it is one of the leading factors implicated in divorce.

Are We Naturally Unfaithful?

Monogamy is not a natural human condition.
— SHIRLEY MACLAINE

Infidelity has long been a part of the marital landscape. However, Dr. Lana Staheli, in her book *Triangles: Understanding, Preventing and Surviving an Affair* (1997), says that the number of men and women engaging in extramarital sex is increasing. Surprisingly, more married women than ever before are indulging in affairs, and both men and women are being unfaithful earlier in their marriages.

Not all this bed-hopping is going undetected. Recent reports indicate that most betrayed wives suspect their partner's infidelity. While they may try to deny to themselves that their mate is philandering, most women feel it is their gut and report "just knowing." However, fewer men are equipped with the finely tuned emotional sensitivity that women bring to their marriages, and they are therefore slower to discover their wives' extramarital affairs.

With so much adultery going on, one might question whether men and women are really meant to be monogamous. Anthropologist Dr. Helen Fisher reports in her *Anatomy of Love: A Natural History of Mating, Marriage, and Why We Stray* (1992) that adultery is a major factor in divorce and family disruptions in the U.S. and other countries.

So, does this mean we aren't monogamous by nature? Is infidelity *really* in our genes, as many men claim? Not necessarily. While many men rationalize their philandering in this way, what they are really referring to is motivation and opportunity.

Given the right social situation, and a selection of people to stray with, both men and women exhibit a desire to stray, and many ultimately indulge their urges. Motivation to stray and the opportunity to do so are factors in both male and female infidelity.

While some men will continue to argue that a genetic predisposition encourages men—and some women—to cheat, it is really social circumstances that are of paramount importance in determining who strays—and who stays.

WHO STRAYS?

Recent research by sex experts William Masters and Virginia Johnson, *The Janus Report on Sexual Behavior* by Drs. Samuel and Cynthia Janus, *The Hite Report on Male Sexuality* and *Women in Love* by Shere Hite, and the University of Chicago's study, *Sex in America* (1994), all indicate that anywhere from 25 to 90 percent of men have been unfaithful to their wives. The same research claims that 20 to 60 percent of women have had or are having extramarital affairs.

The 1993 *Janus Report on Sexual Behavior* bills itself as "The First Broad-Scale Scientific National Survey Since Kinsey." Its research concludes that one in three married men, and one in four married women have had at least one extramarital affair. This amounts to a lot of people engaging in infidelity.

There is a broad range of percentages documented in infidelity research studies detailing who strays because, where sexual behavior is concerned, many people tend to be less than truthful. When researchers question men and women face-to-face about their sexual activities, as the researchers did in the 1994 *Sex in America* study, people are less likely to be as truthful as they would be when promised anonymity.

Whatever the true percentages of infidelity, the number of married people involved in affairs is large, and anecdotal evidence indicates that adultery is increasing. Much more important than statistics citing rates of adultery is the impact that infidelity has on a marriage and the subsequent relationship between the two partners. Stories of individual men's affairs and how women cope are critical because they can guide individuals and couples in dealing with their own situation. Stories and details of infidelity are more important than the exact number of people who are straying.

If you count the number of married men and women who have either had an affair, are currently involved in one, or are anticipating cheating on their spouse, the amount of adultery-prone people is staggering. With so much infidelity around, there is a very good chance that an extramarital affair will touch many marriages.

In *Triangles*, Dr. Staheli claims that 60 percent of all marriages are touched by extramarital affairs; similarly, the psychologist Dr. Bonnie Eaker Weil in her book *Adultery: The Forgivable Sin* (1994) estimates that 85 percent of all marriages will be touched by infidelity.

The research done for *The Janus Report*, for the University of Chicago's *Sex in America*, by Shere Hite, and by the psychologist Shirley Glass, all indicate that men stray primarily for sexual variety and novelty; a woman strays for emotional reasons rather than for pure sexual experimentation.

According to the psychologist Jan Halper's book on successful men, *Quiet Desperation: The Truth About Successful Men* (1988), the higher a man's income, the more likely he is to cheat on his wife. Dr. Halper argues that men tend to cheat for sexual and ego reasons, whereas women seek affairs for emotional nourishment first; sexual adventure is a secondary interest.

What the surveys and articles also underscore is the very basic differences in *why* men and women stray. Men are primarily seeking "extra" sex, while a majority of women are searching for an emotional connection *along with* sex. Sure, a minority of women will be after pure sex, but sexual variety and experimentation is not the motivating factor in their extramarital affairs. What drives most women to affairs is not having their emotional needs met in their marriage, and the need to feel desirable.

Infidelity in Britain and France

America is not yet France, but neither is it Monogamydonia.
—QUOTED IN *TIME*, AUGUST 31, 1998

The Great British Sex Survey, conducted by and reported in the *Sunday Mirror* (London) (April 1, 1996), revealed that British men and women lag behind their American contemporaries in the extramarital affairs sweepstakes. Sixteen percent of British men who participated in the survey said they had had an affair, while 14 percent of the women respondents had cheated on their husband. Does this indicate the stiff upper lip (manifested in a lack of passion and lust) for which Britons are known? Or does it imply a closed upper lip, with Britons hesitant to discuss their adulterous liaisons? Only they know for sure!

Across the Channel, Frenchwomen tend to stay with husbands who stray. According to a study on infidelity around the world conducted in March 1996 by *Cosmopolitan* magazine, France boasts the largest number of unfaithful wives: 87 percent. While women may be betraying their husbands, they are also likely to suffer their men's infidelity, as only 22 percent said they would divorce their mate for straying. It could be that the notoriously lovely Frenchwoman simply gives her man a dose of his own medicine in the affairs game. Perhaps Frenchwomen have affairs of their own as a way of coping with a philandering mate.

When a woman stays with a man who strays, it doesn't necessarily mean that she approves of her husband's cheating. She may disapprove of infidelity but realizes that marriage, like most things in life, is a trade-off, and she may tolerate his adultery while reaping other benefits of the union.

Though there are some universal truths about sex, marriage, and infidelity, some cultural differences are very real. For example, in the European and aristocratic styles of marriage, men are virtually expected to take a mistress—and to stay married. As long as the wife is cared for and respected, and his infidelity is discreet, everything is supposed to work smoothly (at least on the surface!). Wives of British Parliamentarians are humiliated regularly by sex scandals, yet they remain silent and stand by their man.

In America, younger women are becoming somewhat less likely stoically to accept infidelity than older women, although many still do, especially if they are financially dependent on their husband. Among the many women interviewed for this book, the general sentiment is: "I don't want to know about it—what I don't know can't hurt me." Thus, many women adopt a head-in-the-sand denial for as long as they can when dealing with infidelity. Unfortunately, what many of these women ultimately learn is that ignoring something they don't want to acknowledge won't make it disappear.

Whether the culture is British, French, or American, most people marry, some divorce, most expect love and loyalty in marriage, and many men and women either stray or live with a straying spouse.

INFIDELITY AND DIVORCE

According to *The Janus Report on Sexual Behavior*, extramarital affairs account for fewer than 25 percent of all divorces. While discovery of infidelity may not lead immediately to divorce, extramarital affairs erode trust and, over time, are likely to figure prominently in an eventual divorce.

Divorce still means personal failure to many people, and the stigma associated with being seen as a "loser" in the marriage game keeps many people from divorcing. This may be one reason why the divorce rate has slowed somewhat in recent years, hovering around 50 percent in America, and somewhat lower in Britain and France. At the same time, adultery is increasing, which means that more couples are living with ongoing infidelity as a thorn in their marriage. One can only wonder whether these affairs will lead to an increase in divorces down the line.

It is interesting to note that the marriages with the highest household incomes are the least likely couples to divorce. However, Jan Halper in *Quiet Desperation* says that high-income men are most likely to stray; thus, women married to successful men are likely to confront the "stand by your man" question at some point in their marriage.

Research cited by the sociologist Annette Lawson in her book, *Adultery: Analysis of Love and Betrayal* (1988), and by Dr. Lana Staheli in her book, *Triangles*, shows that a wife's infidelity is cited as the leading cause of men divorcing women. Some studies indicate that as many as 25 percent of divorces are related to a wife's infidelity. Women are likely to stay when a man strays, but men are unlikely to stay when a woman strays. The sexual double standard is alive and well, and evident in most households!

In recent years, it is women who initiate most divorces. This is surprising, since most women still lack significant financial and social clout in society, and marriage has long been one of the ways women could ensure their financial security. Women's trade-offs in marriage have long been predicated on tolerating men's infidelity in return for financial stability for themselves and their children. Perhaps more women are deciding that this previously accepted "arrangement" is no longer viable, and they are striking out on their own regardless of the obstacles.

Quite simply, women's opportunities for career advancement and financial gain still lag behind those for men, yet some women are braving the odds and deciding that staying with a philandering husband is too high a cost for them to pay. Nevertheless, the majority of women married to philandering men stay married to them. As Dr. Eaker Weil says in *Adultery: The Forgivable Sin*, "Infidelity, by one or both partners, touches over 80 percent of all marriages." With such large numbers of marriages affected by adultery, it is clear there are still many women choosing to stay with men who stray.

DO AS I SAY, NOT AS I DO

While ever-increasing numbers of men and women are involved in extra-marital affairs, most of them espouse a wholehearted belief in monogamy. Essentially, more people say they believe in monogamy than actually practice it. Many people even say they think adultery is always wrong even as they are engaged in an adulterous liaison. In this regard, monogamy can be viewed in the same light as eating and exercising. Most people say they strive to eat a nutritionally balanced diet and to exercise daily. The number of people who actually follow through with their behaviors is another matter entirely. While monogamy might be espoused as the ideal, in reality it is hard for many people, but especially men, to practice.

The *Time* magazine/CNN poll done in August 1998, *"How We Really Feel About Fidelity,"* reported that 86 percent of adults feel men having sexual relations with someone other than their spouse are always wrong; and 85 percent of respondents say adultery is morally wrong for women. Similarly, a March 1998 NBC/*Wall Street Journal* poll found that 74 percent of adults believe that adultery is always wrong.

Practice What You Preach?

A survey by the *American Journal of Public Health*, and reported in *USA Today* on September 3, 1998, indicated that American men and women are less tolerant of sexual straying than their British counterparts, yet are much more likely to have had more sexual partners. This study reported that 89 percent of American men and 94 percent of American women believe that "sex outside marriage is always wrong." However, 76 percent of British men and 83 percent of women Britons said affairs are always wrong.

The discrepancy between both American and British men and women is also striking. More women in both countries are more strongly against sex outside marriage than men are. Quite simply, many people have one set of sexual standards for others and a different one for themselves. "Do as I say, not as I do" prevails, it seems, where sexual behaviors, especially extramarital affairs, are concerned.

These studies of the acceptability of extramarital affairs also underscore the polarizing attitudes men and women have toward infidelity. More men engage in adultery than women and less men than women believe extramarital affairs are wrong. Perhaps a way to rationalize their own behavior? The men's differing attitudes and behavior regarding infidelity emphasize the major headache a man's philandering causes his spouse.

According to research by Annette Lawson cited in her book *Adultery*, nearly 90 percent of marriages are "closed"—meaning marital partners do not condone one another having sexual relations with other people. "Open marriages" simply are not popular, and more than half of them end in divorce. Infidelity *always* involves lying and deception because most people having extramarital affairs are not honest with their spouse about their behavior. Not many men will say to their wife, "Darling, hold dinner for me, I'll be stopping by my mistress for sex before heading home." Instead, they will lie outright or filter their facts, all of which undermines communication and trust in a marriage.

Many people the world over condemn adultery even as they practice it; yet it is interesting to note that having more than one sex partner doesn't necessarily mean that a person is actually having more sex. According to Dr. Edward Laumann and his colleagues of the University of Chicago, when a man is faithful to one partner, he has more sex in a year than a man who has two, three, four, or more partners. The reason is simple: juggling more than one sex partner means more time is spent *planning* for sex than actually having it!

CASUAL SEX

People don't like to talk about sex, they just like to do it.
—FRANK MANKIEWICZ, DEMOCRATIC POLITICAL CONSULTANT,
CITED IN *NEWSWEEK*

What is the likelihood of a man participating in casual sex? Pretty high, according to evolutionary psychologist Dr. David Buss. Dr. Buss and his colleagues at the University of Texas tested how willing men would be to have sex with a woman they had just met. The researchers had men pose the following question to women: "Hi, I've been noticing you around town lately, and I find you attractive. Would you go to bed with me?" All the women who were asked this question said no. But when women posed the question to men, 75 percent of the men said yes and added that they were very flattered by the woman's request.

Dr. Buss's research supports other studies which indicate that many men will rarely turn down a sexual advance from a woman. Research and casual observation support the view that many more men than women engage in opportunistic sex—one-night stands—even when they have no interest in having a relationship, or even further contact, with the person. This finding doesn't bode well for married men who receive propositions from women, nor for their wives, who could be cheated on repeatedly.

Research by the renowned sex researchers Masters, Johnson, and Kolodny, reviewed in their book *Heterosexuality* (1994), claims that men would be promiscuous throughout their lives if there were no social consequences for their behavior. Even when there are real repercussions for their infidelity, men may still risk all and cheat on their wives.

Men's desire for a variety of sexual partners is also salient in their fantasies. Men's sexual fantasies are dominated by images of strangers and multiple sexual partners. Beautiful women showing lots of skin who offer sex without strings are the mainstays of such male fantasies. In contrast, female sexual fantasies most often involve emotions and feelings, and focus on someone with whom the woman is already emotionally involved. As Bruce Ellis and Donald Symons report in their 1990 study on sex differences in sexual fantasy, "The most striking feature of male fantasy is that sex is sheer lust and physical gratification, devoid of encumbering relationships, emotional elaboration, complicated plot lines, flirtation, courtship, and extended foreplay."

Given men's proclivity for sex on the run, it's no surprise that in a *Playboy*-sponsored survey, over one quarter of happily married men said they would have an affair if they wouldn't get caught. The behavior of a prominent media executive is a prime example of men's often casual attitude toward sex and adultery:

I like to have "revolving door" sex. I like to have a lot of women pass through my life and not stay any longer than a casual sexual encounter. In business I am constantly exposed to an array of young, attractive, and sexually willing women, so I'm able to have no-strings flings all the time. I'm careful not to let my wife find out, but since I'm fairly well-known there is always a risk. On some level, I think my wife knows about my double life. I can tell by the way she looks at some of the women we encounter at

parties—women I have slept with tend to give me a knowing look when we
run into each other about town, and that may tip people off.

This man's behavior illustrates the classic "having his cake and eating
it too" scenario. While he may suspect that his wife knows about his flings,
he doesn't seem overly concerned about her; nor does he seem interested
in curtailing his affairs.

ONCE A CHEAT, ALWAYS A CHEAT?

According to a 1994 "Mr. One-Night Stand" poll conducted by and reported in *New Woman* magazine, men who have one-night flings tend to
do so over and over again. It seems that once a cheat, always a cheat. The
poll claimed that "one-night wonders" were still behaving like Don Juans
even after ten years of marriage. Philandering, apparently, leads to more and
more of the same. Dr. Staheli says that 15 percent of women and 25 percent
of men will have more than four affairs during the course of their marriage!

THE SEXUAL DOUBLE STANDARD: WHY MEN STRAY

Even after nearly thirty years of feminism, sexual double standards are alive
and well in most living rooms (and bedrooms!). What many men think is
perfectly acceptable sexual behavior for themselves is often viewed as a no-
no for their wives. Shere Hite reported in *The Hite Report on Male Sexuality*
that 72 percent of men married longer than two years have had an extramarital affair.

Surveys and articles about men's infidelity are staples of all women's
magazines. Women are told how to improve their relationships; how to get
a man to marry them; how to keep their man faithful; and if that doesn't
work, how to win him back from the "Other Woman." At the same time,
men are reading magazines such as *Penthouse*, *Playboy*, and *Hustler*, which
encourage them to explore as many women as possible. Publications also

reinforce sex differences, condoning men who stray for sexual variety while encouraging women to stay and tolerate it, or to have their own affair as revenge.

Although there are certain situations under which men and women will both be likely to engage in extramarital affairs, those affairs are usually motivated by different factors. Men seek attention through sex; women seek attention, then sex. Overall, men and women desire many of the same qualities in a marriage partner; they just go about meeting their emotional and sexual needs in different ways.

Common Reasons Men Give for Their Extramarital Affairs

SEXUAL REASONS

- sexual variety
- more sex, more often
- oral sex

NOVELTY REASONS

- the thrill of a new body
- for fun—no complications or burdensome emotions
- for companionship with someone new
- the excitement of a new challenge
- hearing a different set of moans and groans

EGO-BOOST REASONS

- feeling attractive to a younger woman
- the thrill/possibility of getting caught by wife
- the adventure of the forbidden
- the ego pump

- being the total center of attention
- opportunity too good to pass up
- "She came on to me"
- "If available, why not?"

WIFE-RELATED REASONS

- power over wife
- boredom in marriage
- wife no longer physically/sexually appealing
- to get back at wife
- to transition out of marriage
- to avoid intimacy with wife
- to hurt wife
- wife too involved with children

FANTASY-ROMANCE REASONS

- for a romantic experience
- to get love and affection
- temporary escape from unhappy marriage
- escape to fantasy world
- to prove sexual attractiveness/desirability/virility

The exact reasons *why* men stray are as diverse as the number of men who stray. Many of the men I spoke with for this book offered revealing insights about their extramarital affairs. Their remarks elucidate why they stray, and how their reasons for doing so differ dramatically from women's reasons:

- *Any man who turns down no-strings sex with a woman is a sissy.*
- *I've been married for twenty years because I have stuff on the side.*

- *My wife will never perform oral sex, and I love a good blow job. She's a cold and proper woman. She's my best friend, and a great mother to our daughter, but I can't survive on the kind of limited sex she doles out.*

- *Marriage? It equals suffocation.*

- *I want sex to be like the fireworks I see in the movies. It can't be like that with a woman I share a child with.*

- *How can I possibly turn down a woman if she offers herself to me on a platter? I'd have to be insane.*

- *No woman is going to tell me how to conduct my sex life.*

- *It's just sex. It's no big deal. It's not love. I don't know why women get so upset.*

- *I'm too young to be in sexual prison.*

- *I love and respect my wife, but I need other women in my life.*

- *After you cheat once and get away with it, you never look back.*

As shocking as some of these comments are, they nevertheless reflect what motivates many men to commit adultery.

THE MADONNA-WHORE COMPLEX

A common but little discussed, and seldom understood, reason why so many men stray is the *madonna-whore complex*. If a man has difficulty being sexual with a woman he is emotionally involved with, he may have a madonna-whore complex. Such men view a wife as a mother figure and a "good girl"—the Madonna. They also see "bad women" (prostitutes and one-night stands) as sex objects—or "whores"; and mistresses and girlfriends as someone they can be sexually free with.

One reason why many men begin extramarital affairs while their wife is pregnant, or shortly after she gives birth, is because they have trouble expressing sexuality toward a mother figure. They say that once their wife becomes a mother, she is no longer sexually arousing, and they therefore turn to a "bad girl" for sex. Many men simply find they cannot enjoy uninhibited sex with a woman who shares their bed, sink, mortgage, and children, so they turn to other women to meet their sexual needs.

Several men I interviewed told me they had lost sexual interest in their wives because the women had let their looks "go down the drain after marriage." One man said he started an affair because his wife had become "an eating machine" and wouldn't lose the weight she had gained. He was embarrassed to be seen with her; and because he was no longer sexually turned on by her, he sought sex and companionship elsewhere.

More than a few men complained that their wives "turned into someone else" after a few years of marriage. One man said, "My wife isn't interested in sex anymore, so I found someone who is."

While some men will try to blame their affair on something related to their wife, such as her looks or her interest in home and family, the truth is, when a man strays, he strays because *he chooses to*. A woman never "drives him to it," although way too many men will use this excuse to alleviate their own guilt. *A woman is not responsible for her husband's irresponsible philandering.*

Fear of Intimacy

Another common reason why men stray is their general discomfort with, and distrust of, emotional closeness with one woman. "Commitment-phobic" is the term often used to describe someone who is reluctant to marry because of a fear of closeness. When a man with commitment phobia *does* marry, his fear of closeness doesn't just disappear; it manifests itself differently. Men who have difficulty committing to marriage, or who are afraid to experience emotional intimacy with their wife, very often become philanderers. By "spreading themselves around" sexually, they alleviate their feeling of emotional claustrophobia. Just as the commitment-phobic boyfriend is a bad bet for marriage, a married man who fears intimacy is a good bet to become an unfaithful husband.

TAKE NOTE*

- "Successful," high-income men are more likely than their lower income peers to be unfaithful.

- When businessmen travel, they are twice as likely as a vacation traveler to have sex with someone new while away.

- After two years of marriage, over 70 percent of men stray.

- Once a man has an affair, he is more likely to do so again.

- Eighty-five percent of philandering men don't leave their wives.

MEN'S AND WOMEN'S DIFFERING NEEDS

There are some very basic differences in the way the sexes think about sex, and more importantly, in how they behave sexually when married. Far more men than women view sex as recreation. Women tend to view sex as an extension of an emotional and affectionate alliance. These differences set the stage for difficulties in marriage and explain why so many women end up tolerating men's affairs, whereas men tend to walk out on an unfaithful wife.

Quite simply, men stray because they can. They see it as their birthright. They believe they are entitled to bed as many women as they want, and too often without considering the consequences of their actions. As one man expressed it, he wants to "sample all the smorgasbord has to offer without getting indigestion." He wants lobster *and* filet mignon!

What Men Want . . . What Women Want . . . *

- Men's favorite activity in bed, other than sleeping: sex.

- Women's favorite activity in bed, other than sleeping: reading.

*Sources: Shere Hite; Lana Staheli; Janus and Janus; Jan Halper; *Glamour* magazine.
*Sources: *Glamour* magazine; Janus and Janus; Annette Lawson; Jan Halper; Shere Hite.
*Sources: Ellis and Symons.

- The majority of couples kiss for only one minute before breaking contact.

- The average amount of time a woman needs to go from arousal to climax is 13 minutes; it takes a man just 2 1/2 minutes.

- Eighty-nine percent of women say that love is more important to them than sex, power, or wealth.

- Sixty-five percent of men say love is more important to them than sex, power, or wealth.

- Eighty-six percent of men fantasize about having sex with two women.

- Fifty-seven percent of men have had intercourse in the presence of other people.

- Twenty-eight percent of all men have paid for sex with a prostitute.

- How often do people think about sex? Men: on average, 203 times a day.

- Women's number one sexual fantasy: sex in a public place.

- Men's number one sexual fantasy: sex with a stranger.

- Men's number two sexual fantasy: sex with two women.

Many men think life is too short to be monogamous. Extramarital affairs offer them thrills, while their marriage offers them a home base. This illustrates the needs that vacillate within so many people: excitement and adventure versus stability and security. Two needs alternate—one for connection, the other for freedom. Men accommodate their needs by getting married and then straying. Many women meet their needs by marrying and then nurturing children, and possibly by having a supplemental affair of their own.

Some men don't even need a reason to have illicit sex; they just need to find a place to have it. For actor Hugh Grant, that place was a BMW parked off Los Angeles's famed Sunset Strip. After the actor was arrested for "lewd behavior" with prostitute Divine Brown in June 1995, he appeared on *The Tonight Show with Jay Leno*, where the host asked him: "What the hell were you thinking?" Grant apologized profusely to his longtime girlfriend Elizabeth Hurley, saying publicly that he "did a bad thing—there, you have it."

Not only did men and women forgive Hugh Grant, but most men said the only stupid part of his act was getting caught! The buzz circulating after the incident was "There but for the grace of God go I." More than a few people wondered why Grant needed a prostitute when he could have had his pick of any of the many beautiful women who frequent the bar of the sort of five-star hotel at which he was staying. Newspapers ran polls asking readers if they thought Hurley should stand by her man or kick him out. Publications featured editorials chanting the "stand by your man" mantra, while others advised Hurley to pack her bags as quickly as possible.

When a woman stays with a man who strays, as Elizabeth Hurley chose to do, a man may interpret her behavior as a sign that she will continue to stay with him even if he plays around in the future. If a man thinks he will have nothing to lose by straying, why should he stop his philandering? When there are no consequences for their infidelity, men will often continue to stray.

They stray, quite simply, because they are motivated to and they often get away with it. Even for the average, run-of-the-mill guy, opportunities for sex are readily available, much more so than they are for married women.

WHY DO WOMEN STRAY?

Many women involved in extramarital affairs say they like who they are when they are with a lover. They say their involvement is as much about the person they *become* when they are with their lover as it is about the person they are cheating with.

Women's primary motivation for affairs is to boost their ego and gain self-confidence and self-esteem, which has often been eroded in their marriage. Women also have affairs to get back at an unfaithful husband and to experience sexual variety. However, research studies and interviews reinforce the claim that the majority of married women have affairs as a way to feel better about themselves and in order to feel an emotional, affectionate connection. While men "supplement" their marriages with outside sex, women "augment" their marriages with emotional nourishment that also includes sex.

Men, more often than women, believe that everything is happy in their marriage, and that they cheat for something extra. Men tell themselves their affairs have nothing to do with their marriage. The following view is shared by many men: "There is a 'firewall' between my home life and my affairs on the road. One side of my life has nothing whatsoever to do with the other side. But I hope the two never meet." Most women would disagree with this, and too often, two separate lives crash into one another unexpectedly.

Over and over again, women told me of their desire for an emotional connection. They said that emotional support—the general feeling of being respected, of being cared for, of being "the one"—was missing from their marriage. I heard accounts of emotionally closed-off men who could not be physically affectionate apart from perfunctory sex. I came away thoroughly drained from interviews with women after hearing tale after tale of loneliness and emotional desolation in their marriages. Add to that the burden of coping with a husband's infidelity and one may wonder how any woman could function under such stress.

Many women complain that men don't invest much time in foreplay and their lovemaking with their wives, but that men with whom women have affairs shower them with attention and affection. As one woman explained, "I can live all week on one of my lover's compliments." People may laugh at this stereotype, but as with most stereotypes, there is a core of truth. It is indicative of how one woman talked about her husband: "His sexual skills are so seriously deficient that I can sum up his repertoire like this—he's in, out, over, and asleep before I even know what's happened. That's because *nothing* ever happens for me."

There are some conditions under which women act as adulterously as men do. When women are financially independent, they are often as motivated as men are to seek multiple sex partners. Shere Hite and the psychologist Carol Tavris both report that wives employed full time have infidelity rates twice as high as for homemakers. A woman with money of her own can call her own shots; she isn't dependent on a man for her livelihood, and therefore is less worried about losing a partner who is her meal ticket in life.

Much anecdotal evidence indicates that when women are employed, especially in professional positions, they are much more likely to become involved in an adulterous liaison than their stay-at-home counterparts. Quite simply, when women interact regularly with desirable men, they have the opportunity and the motivation to stray.

Married, employed women, with money at their disposal and the chance to meet desirable and willing sex partners, are every bit as unfaithful as men. Frankly, many women are monogamous out of fear—fear that if they stray, their husband, on whom they are financially dependent, will dump them. Financially dependent women are less likely to cheat than are women who earn their own wages. When a woman has everything to lose—her husband and her lifestyle—she is unlikely to stray for sex or even an emotional connection.

A double standard of sex and infidelity operates in a majority of marriages, whereby a woman's infidelity is met with harsher repercussions than a man's philandering. This means that most women don't betray their marriage vows lightly.

THE TRUTH ABOUT OPEN MARRIAGE

Open marriages and "key parties," or mate swapping, were popular during the 1960s and 1970s, which were times of sexual experimentation for many. But these lifestyles never really caught on, as open infidelity caused difficulty for many people. Adultery, whether overt or covert, is hard for many men and women to cope with. The fantasy of the open marriage may thrive, but the reality of such an arrangement rarely works and seldom fulfills the parties involved.

Most people who have extramarital affairs lie about their activities rather than seek acceptance from their spouse. Whichever way you look at it— open marriages or secret affairs—multiple sex partners usually pose a problem for marriages, and particularly so for wives.

THE FUTURE OF INFIDELITY

When men and women pair up, they don't become hermetically sealed off from one half of the human race. Our needs for flirtation and sexual attraction, for attention, for passion, will always be with us, and therefore so will infidelity. I often hear people say, "Men will be men and women will be women." What this means, based on all sorts of research findings, is that men will continue to cheat on their wives; many wives will stay with a husband who strays; and some women will have affairs of their own.

TAKE NOTE

- More men stray than women.

- Employed women have more affairs than stay-at-home wives.

- Men tend to have extramarital affairs for sexual variety — to supplement their marriage, not replace it.

- Women generally seek emotional connection, rather than pure sexual experimentation, in their affairs.

- Adulterous sexual activities are likely to take place in the marital bed.

- Infidelity statistics are not really important. The impact infidelity has on the marriage is what matters.

- A man cheats because he wants to. A man will only stop cheating when he wants to.

- Infidelity is common — but *all men don't stray*.

Chapter 2

THE TWO SIDES OF EVERY MARRIAGE: HIS AND HERS

*N*obody talks about this, but marriage is not the haven for women that it is for men.

—*Author Dalma Heyn*

THE DOUBLE STANDARD
OF MARRIAGE

*Women are still socialized to believe that marriage is the most important
life transition they will make. It is not the same for men. So when the
marriage isn't perfect, it may be a bigger disappointment for women
than men.*

— SOCIOLOGIST GARY LEE

Every marriage is a disappointment.
— PSYCHIATRIST AND AUTHOR DR. FRANK PITTMAN

*P*erhaps nowhere is the double standard between the sexes more evident
than in marriage. Little girls play "weddings" with their Barbie and Ken
dolls. As they mature, they dress up in bridal attire; before you know it, they
are reading bridal magazines. Society cultivates the idea that marriage is
extremely important for the adult identity of a woman. Even the most career-
oriented women admit they wish to marry, and marry they eventually do.

Although marriage rates have been on a slight decline in recent years,
and the average age at first marriage has increased, most men and women—
about 95 percent—still marry at some point in their lives. In every union,
however, there are really two marriages, *his* and *hers*. According to research
in her classic book *The Future of Marriage* (1982), sociologist Jessie Bernard
writes that many wives are more depressed, frustrated, and dissatisfied in their
marriages than men are; women shoulder most of the child-care and household responsibilities, even when they work full time outside the home, and
they report many negative feelings about married life. Married men, despite
their protests that they were pressured into marriage, display the best mental
health out of the following groups: married men, single men, married
women, single women. Married men are happiest and healthiest in a marriage. These same differences in the lives of married women and married
men are discussed by Regina Barreca in her humorous book, *Perfect Husbands (And Other Fairy Tales)* (1993).

"*Women must, men should*" is, even in the last years of the twentieth
century, the prevailing attitude toward marriage. Society rewards women

who possess the ultimate status symbols for a female: a man on her arm and a ring on her finger. If the man is successful, all the better.

To this day, marriage is promoted as a way in which women can attain "true womanhood," social status, and financial stability. Therefore, the pressure on women to marry, and to stay married no matter what, is enormous. According to a book by the psychiatrist Julian Hafner entitled *The End of Marriage: Why Monogamy Isn't Working* (1993), a woman's desire for children is what often drives her to marry, and the longing for children is often stronger than her need for a husband's social status, financial resources, and companionship. Yet, when a woman marries, she dramatically curtails her options for career progress and social opportunities. These factors put women at great risk when their husband strays.

More often than not, when a woman marries, she marries a lifestyle. This is a fact that escapes few women. A woman marries *his* way of life, for even if a woman is professionally oriented, a man's life often takes priority over a married woman's. For example, more women relocate to follow their husband's career than vice versa.

These days, a man and a woman are both likely to be employed when they marry. The usual scenario is for the couple to have children a few years after marriage, and at that time, many women will return to work, but often in a position requiring less commitment, working part time or retreating to the home to care for the children until they are in school. This tends to be the pattern even for professionally qualified women, although more and more women with young children are using child care and working full time.

According to numerous reports, when both husband and wife work outside the home, women still spend twice as much time on housework as men do. It seems that a woman's work is never ever done. Even when she brings home some of the bacon, she still shops for it, cooks it, and cleans up afterward.

With the arrival of children, the marriage begins to split dramatically into *hers* and *his*, with the woman more and more inwardly focused, even if she is also employed outside the home. Men, on the other hand, are still externally focused on the workforce and on the myriad of social opportunities they encounter on the job. Men can work late and socialize with their friends, and possibly women, afterward; most women must rush home to care for house and family, leaving little chance for networking, or for meeting men with whom to have an affair.

Careers and Marriage: His versus Hers

When husband and wife begin leading such disparate lives, trouble often ensues. While the woman is busy raising kids, the husband is gaining economic power and being exposed to new people, places, and ideas. He is often meeting desirable women, too. This may be the time when infidelity first begins. After two years of marriage, 70 percent of men are unfaithful, according to Hite.

The challenge for a marriage at this point is for the husband and wife to continue to grow as individuals, while continuing to grow together as a couple. It can be a daunting one. Still, a woman is fulfilling what is expected of her in society, and what she has grown to expect of herself: being a wife and mother. But her career as a wife and mother is all too often a tenuous one, with few benefits should the marriage explode.

For the majority of women worldwide, home and family are the priorities, even if they are employed for pay outside the home. Regardless of whether a woman is a career professional or works part time, she herself usually considers that her most important role is that of wife and mother. Quite simply, women are still seen as the keeper of the relationship and the family. Men see women this way, and the majority of women see themselves this way. Unfortunately, this scenario sets women up for a vast array of emotional and financial difficulties ranging from depression to a husband's infidelity.

While marriage and motherhood are very valuable choices, it is often the women who put marriage and children first, and who are, unfortunately, left holding the proverbial bag, with little or no money and atrophied job skills with which to support themselves and their children should their husband leave them. Men usually give work priority over family life. Their emphasis on career has implications for women and for infidelity. Since more women seek happiness in relationships as well as in success at work, they often end up with limited career advancement and financial accomplishments. This may be fine if a marriage survives; but for many women, their independence is affected by relying on a husband's income. If a woman decides to leave her marriage for any reason, it will be harder to do so if she has no money of her own.

The Pressure on Women to Marry—and Stay Married

Regardless of the strides women have made in education and the workforce over the last decade or so, there is still pressure for a woman to marry in order to be perceived as "complete." The subtle and often not so subtle pressure for women to "couple up and settle down" creates undue stress for many women who enjoy their independent state. The abundance of "marriage-push" books that have proliferated in the last few years are a clear sign that women are still expected to marry before some imaginary "use-by date."

An April 1997 survey in *Glamour* magazine reported that 80 percent of people believe society is biased against single women. The survey "Is Society biased against Single Women?" also found that people find it hard to believe singlehood could actually be a choice. The majority of respondents said it is easier for a man to be single than a woman. One woman thought it was better to be divorced than never married. "At least if you are divorced," she said, "it means a man wanted to marry you—that you were chosen once."

The survey also reported that 72 percent of people believe the ceiling of acceptable singlehood has risen—to thirty. However, the majority of people believe society still assumes that most women would prefer to be married. The survey seems to align with popular sentiment, where the average person thinks women somewhat strange if they are single beyond a certain age. Men don't face such a stigma. The double standard of sex and marriage, unfortunately, lives on in many ways.

In spite of delayed marriages, live-in relationships, and some single-for-life folks, many people still believe marriage is the best way to spend their life, and they look down on singles—especially on single women "of a certain age." Everyone has heard derogatory comments about single women, such as: "Single women over forty are the bottom of the barrel, single men are the cream of the crop."

Even professionally successful, financially independent women would like to share their life with a man. As the actress Frances Fisher told *USA Today* in August 1998, "The c-word — commitment . . . isn't that what every woman wants?" Whatever women achieve in terms of work and other interests, many also want a companion in life with whom they can create a family.

These days, it seems, divorce holds less stigma than being single. Being single due to a failed marriage is more socially condoned than having never been married. The idea of "being chosen" looms large in women's minds, as it conveys social acceptance to them. This idea also has ramifications for women once they marry. A woman is much more likely to worry about losing her husband to another woman if she believes she was almost "left on the vine" to remain unchosen.

The more opportunities a woman has to date, and the more suitors interested in marrying her, the more secure she feels in her sexuality. A woman who never dated much before marrying may be overly concerned about her man straying because she worries that since she barely snagged him, she would have real trouble trying to land a second husband. This type of thinking reinforces in women the notion that they need to stay married at any cost — even through their husband's infidelity.

In the view of some men and women, a successful woman is one wearing a wedding ring. Yet women who are professionally employed and financially independent show less interest in marriage and children, although many still want a partner and companion to share their lives. Most high-flying women still marry at some stage, but usually later than their less educated peers.

According to 1996 data from the U.S. Census Bureau reported in *USA Today* in September 1998 — "Practice What We Preach?" — women at all education levels from high school diploma through those holding a doctoral degree earn less money than men. The majority of employed women aren't economically independent, and at best earn only seventy-five cents to every dollar a man earns. Women rarely earn as much money as men, so many women look to marriage for financial stability as well as love and companionship.

The persistent economic inequality in the workplace and in marriage sets the stage for men to have more opportunities for almost everything than their wives do. Men generally have more financial resources than women, and this enables them more easily to pursue infidelity. With more financial resources at their disposal, men can splurge on two women, pay for hotels, and travel more often, thus helping to conceal overnight stays with another woman.

There is a real push toward married life for women, as well as for men. Whether it is society in general, parents, or a religious group inflicting the pressure, most people feel some nudging toward marriage. In the 1950s, marriage was about the only way a woman could attain a decent standard of living. Today, it often takes a wife and husband working to attain and maintain a middle-class standard of living. Nowadays, women are not only seeking a marital partner with whom they can create and raise a family; they also want a man with whom emotional and sexual fulfillment will be possible.

The double standard of looks and aging makes it more difficult for women to find suitable marriage partners as they age. Men have a ready supply of available women, whether the man is eighteen or eighty. Since men tend to "marry down" in age, they have a huge pipeline of women to choose from. Women, however, tend to "marry up"—in age, status, and income. But this becomes increasingly more difficult to do as the woman ages. A woman of fifty finds few available men fifty and over, and the men who are available often prefer to partner with a woman younger than themselves rather than one their own age.

In addition, many men don't want to marry a woman who is their educational or professional equal. Such men don't want to be upstaged or have their masculinity threatened by a savvy, successful woman. So, for example, a bank manager marries a secretary, while a female banking executive will find her pool of eligible men more limited because her executive peer group of men will tend to "marry down" in status.

This discrepancy in numbers of available men and women affects how a woman thinks about an unfaithful husband and divorce. She realizes her opportunities in the dating market are not in her favor. Even if she is unhappily married, she may decide to stay with her partner because she figures her chances of finding *any* man, let alone an adequate replacement for her husband, are slim to none.

The "marriage push" in turn affects single women, and the married women who must contend with them. Married women realize how in de-

mand desirable men are and often cling to an unhappy marriage to a philandering husband just because they are thankful they have a man at all.
Some married women stay with a man who strays because they don't want
to be thrown back into the shark-infested dating waters, especially when they
are no longer considered of "dating age."

Several recent books have been hugely popular because of their realistic portrayal of modern single women. One example is Helen Fielding's
Bridget Jones' Diary (1998). Her descriptions of Bridget's dating life and
her obsession with calories, as well as her humorous descriptions of "sin-
gletons" vs. "smug marrieds," struck a chord with women readers. Similarly, Candace Bushnell's *Sex and the City* (1997) charts the goings-on of
four single women about town in Manhattan. Both of these fabulous
books document the trials and tribulations of contemporary women in
their search for the right man.

Wedding Bell Blues

For many women, disappointment and disillusionment with marriage
hit them like a ton of bricks. After all the effort some women exert to find
a suitable husband, they are very often startled at the many changes marriage
brings to their lives. One woman told me she felt as if she had been placed
in a glass jar, with the top screwed on tightly. She could still see the world,
but could no longer participate in it in the same way she had done in the
past. Another woman said she couldn't understand what all the fuss was
about. She had been married for four years and wished she were still single.
She says she is basically single anyway, as her husband never pays her any
attention. She is excruciatingly lonely, because other men ignore her as a
married woman:

*Marriage isn't what it's cracked up to be. It's the biggest ruse going. Women
get the short end of the stick. The joke is on women. Single women—wake
up before it's too late. Enjoy your life on your own.*

Still another attractive and well-educated woman commented:

I was never keen on marriage anyway, but it's worse than I ever could have imagined. I loved having my own place. Now, I share one half of a home, one half of a bed, and for what? Regular sex? What a joke. I had more "regular" sex when I was single. Nothing — nothing — is worse than going to bed at night with a husband who stays so far to his side of the bed that he almost falls out on the floor. Some nights he puts his pillow between us so he doesn't have to be near me. I can't believe I gave up a decent single life for this boring and passionless existence.

For all the effort of playing bridal Barbie, reading bridal magazines, and dreaming of Mr. Right, many women are less enthused with the marital state than they had anticipated. And this is even before they have children or their husband starts fooling around on them!

A Band — or Brand? — of Gold

The double standard of marriage is especially evident where wedding rings are concerned. Almost all women wear an engagement or wedding ring, while less men seem to do so these days. A wedding ring immediately signals to other people that a woman is "taken." Women are branded; men can still appear to be bachelors. Occasionally, women are even more attracted to a man with a wedding band because they see him as the ultimate challenge to be lured away from another woman.

Imagine you are a man in a bar, and you spot an attractive woman. Chances are, you will look at her finger to see if she is sporting a wedding ring. If she isn't, you may deem her acceptable to approach. Now, if you were a woman and you spotted a handsome man, the lack of a wedding ring wouldn't necessarily tell you the entire story of the man's marital status.

Women can hardly wait to "get the ring," but until they wear it, they don't realize they are often discriminated against by potential male friends because of it. Women are considered "off-limits" when they are married — and an obvious sign of this, such as a ring, really sends a negative message. This message limits women from even meeting men as friends. Married men don't face the same restrictions.

What's a Name Got to Do with It?

Some people tend to think that women who keep their own names after marriage are less committed to the marriage. However, a 1996 survey by the American Sociological Association reports that women who keep their own names are just as happily married as women who take their husband's name. Women who retain their own names tend to be better educated, better employed, hold more liberal views on sex, and are likely to be marrying for the first time. A divorced woman who remarries is more likely than a first-time married to take her new husband's name.

When you keep your own name, people are often confused by why you have done so. They often assume you don't love your husband, because if you did, then you would take his name. Wrong! It is critical for women to maintain their own identity in a marriage, and keeping one's own name is one important way of doing so.

While more women these days are keeping their own name when they marry, it is still largely professional women who do so. However, it may be the women who *aren't* career-minded who could benefit most by keeping their own name, for at least then they would have some visible part of their identity intact in their marriage. It is so easy for women to be swallowed up and overshadowed in marriage; the more ways they can preserve their own identity and stature, the better off they will be.

By retaining her name, a woman signals that *her* identity and contribution to the marriage are every bit as valuable as that of the man she married. Women are important in their own right. They have an identity, and it doesn't change when they marry. Just because they marry, they don't change their fundamental being; they have merely added a man to their personal life. However, married women are widely perceived to be extensions of their husband. Women who have professional lives of their own are particularly sensitive to being seen as an appendage to their husband. As one has said: "How dare the media call me 'Wife of Mr. So-and-So.'"

In Sickness and in Health . . .

Over 57 percent of married people suffer from chronic heartburn, reports the Opinion Research Corporation. It is no surprise that the married state induces physical symptoms. We usually assume that marriage is good for women and bad for men. Not so. According to Bowling Green University sociologist Gary Lee, quoted in *USA Today* (April 22, 1997), "Men benefit more from marriage than women." Without a doubt, marriage is a better deal for men than for women.

Several other studies over the years have documented that married women suffer the worst mental health, and often suffer from double the rates of depression experienced by men. A report published by the American Psychological Association, entitled *Women and Depression* (1990), claims that women suffer higher rates of depression because of socioeconomic, biological, and emotional factors. Married women are most likely to be depressed, and the more children in the family, the greater their frequency of depression. Low economic status for women is also highly related to increased rates of depression.

Research conducted by the psychologist and author Dr. Susan Nolen-Hoeksema (1990) indicates that women have significantly higher rates of depression than men do; in fact, the ratio is 2:1. For the last thirty years in America, and internationally, women have suffered depression twice as frequently as men. Some researchers even cite a 3:1 ratio for female-to-male depression rates. Women's depression is clearly linked to marital status; married women have the highest rates of depressive symptoms, according to a landmark study by Ellen McGrath and colleagues published by the American Psychological Association in 1990.

> *Marriage protects men from depression and makes women more vulnerable.*
> —PSYCHOLOGIST AND MARRIAGE RESEARCHER DR. NEIL JACOBSON

Depression is also linked to poverty. Since women universally earn less money than men, their unemployment or underemployment is directly linked to their high depression rates. Employed women almost universally earn less money than men do, and when women are employed, they often receive little domestic help from their husbands.

In a 1989 article published by the *Journal of the American Medical Association* entitled "Increasing Rates of Depression," two mental health researchers, G. Klerman and M. M. Weissman, concluded after reviewing numerous studies on depression that the prime factors influencing female depression are low social status and marriage. Low social status means limited financial resources, which causes distress; marriage also causes tension and stress, with few outlets from child care.

Dalma Heyn reports in her book *Marriage Shock: The Emotional Transformation of Women into Wives* (1997) that even independent, self-confident women stop speaking up as much and hide their opinions more after they marry. In general, the married women she interviewed for her book felt that marriage robbed them of an essential aspect of their individual identity.

Women suffer more depression in marriage when they are not employed, because they feel dependent on their husband and their marriage to meet their emotional, financial, and social needs. This is asking a lot, particularly if a woman is married to a cold, emotionally remote man. In fact, a March 1997 CNN/*USA Today*/Gallup poll on "Family Values," indicates that over one third of women believe they are dominated and controlled by their husband. Feeling a lack of control over one's activities or environment has long been cited as a major contributor to depression.

How Women's Life Priorities Set the Stage for Staying with a Man Who Strays

Women's marriage, work, and career priorities are critical in understanding how women's and men's life experiences differ. Married men and women are basically on different tracks throughout life, with married men focused externally and, by and large, married women focused internally on the family. These differences affect the motivation and opportunities for extramarital affairs. They also have a dramatic influence on how a woman reacts when her husband is unfaithful.

Women who lack self-confidence and are financially dependent on their marriage are less likely to leave an adulterous husband. Women need to learn that multiple roles—such as wife, mother, and employed worker—can inoculate them against depression and give them more options if confronted with a straying husband. As the photographer Margaret Bourke-White once said, "Work is something you can always count on, a trusted, lifelong friend who never deserts you."

Lacking her own financial resources, and often lacking in education and/or current career skills, a woman faces a difficult dilemma when confronted with a husband's philandering. Her options are more limited when she is not in the labor force. She doesn't have opportunities to regularly interact with men, and she doesn't have activities in her life to keep her self-esteem high and ward off depression. A woman without a life of her own apart from her marriage is a woman without much of a life!

Due to the choices that women make—to marry, bear children, and take time off to raise them—many women are just one man away from poverty should their husband leave them. When women have their own interests, friends, and money, they are less devastated if their man strays. They will also have infinitely more options should they decide not to stay married to a philanderer.

While many women stay with a man who strays, men are less likely to stay when a wife strays. Marriages are much more likely to end when a woman has an affair than when a man does. Many men simply cannot forgive a woman's infidelity, and they leave the marriage. Perhaps because men have a ready-made dating market available to them, they are less likely to try to work out their marriage once their wife has cheated on them. These very same men will say it is okay for them to stray, but that women should not. As one man told me: "I have lovers. If my wife had other men, she would no longer be my wife."

Many women tolerate a philandering husband because they don't want to end up on the divorce heap of abandoned women. As one fifty-year-old woman explained: "I'm not going to let that little slut waltz in here and take away my life." So women stay and put up a good fight against other women.

The message is clear to wives: stay in line and don't complain or you'll be sorry and end up alone.

THE DOUBLE STANDARD OF DIVORCE AND REMARRIAGE

Although the divorce rates have been leveling off in the last several years at about 50 percent, an often-overlooked fact is that women are the ones filing for the majority of divorces. Not only are women waiting longer to marry, but they are also beginning affairs of their own earlier in their marriages and making the choice to end their marriages at rates higher than ever before in history. It has always been true that highly educated, employed women, and women with independent incomes, marry later than their peers, and often, they never marry at all. They also have higher rates of divorce and may decide not to remarry. Once women have tasted the freedom of independence, many of them are reluctant to marry again and take on a man who will contribute more negatives than positives to their life. Independent and unmarried women have the highest rates of emotional stability and the lowest rates of depression. Control over one's decisions and life seems to be the significant factor.

> *I want a man in my life, but not in my house.*
> —COMIC JOY BEHAR, *MORE* MAGAZINE, (OCTOBER 1998)

Interestingly, even though the prevailing attitude is that divorced women are even more desperate to marry than single women approaching forty, the truth is that many divorced women don't wish to remarry. "Why should I remarry?" one woman said to me. "I have a good job, a nice home, friends of both sexes, and a devoted son and daughter. All I would be adding to my life by remarrying would be a man who would try to tell me what to do. It's not worth it." Another explained: "I lived with an unfaithful man for eight years. It nearly killed me. There is no way in hell I will ever again share my living space with a man. Date them? Sure. Marry again? Maybe, as long as he lives across the street!" Women who are financially secure are less likely to remarry. It is a mistake to think that all women are eager to race down the aisle a second time.

The lower rates of remarriage for women compared with divorced men are somewhat startling. Divorced men remarry sooner than women and, on average, marry women ten years younger than themselves. Divorced women—and women with children—are less likely to remarry.

According to Ashton Applewhite's book, *Cutting Loose: Why Women Who End Their Marriages Do So Well* (1997), many divorced women grow and thrive after the end of their marriage and won't easily or readily consider remarriage. After they taste their freedom and independence again, women often decide they like calling all the shots in their life and do not want to come under a man's control again. Contrary to popular belief, many women survive—and thrive—after divorce.

MEN AND WOMEN ARE DIFFERENT

Throughout their lives, men and women have different experiences of marriage—and infidelity. The greater pressures for women to marry, and to stay married at any cost, encourage them to tolerate behavior they find unseemly, like a husband's affair. Many women conclude they are still better off married to a philanderer than they would be if divorced.

Women need to look at marriage as a choice, not as something they must do. Marriage isn't a necessity, and for many women, being single is a haven compared with a bad marriage, such as marriage to an emotionally abusive man or a serial philanderer.

It is perfectly acceptable for women to be work-oriented, and to view home and family as a side choice. It is also okay for a woman to be home-centered, with gainful employment a secondary priority. Each woman must decide for herself what is important for her to achieve during her lifetime, and then set about realizing her dreams. It is each woman's choice—and hers alone—whether she wants to and is able to sustain a marriage to an unfaithful husband. But what all women need to realize is that being a wife is not a secure occupation!

When a woman becomes overly absorbed in her marriage, to the point where she loses her individuality and identity, she is likely to feel she has no alternative but to stay with her husband if he strays. It's better to stick with what she has, she thinks, because she may not be able to find anyone else. Or worse, she may think that all men cheat and so decide to stay with "the devil she knows."

The push for marriage, and the experiences within marriage, are very different for men and women. Even the prettiest, wealthiest, most talented woman will find that societal opportunities favor her husband. Women's experiences in marriage often undermine their ability to make the most of their lives, and many women are convinced they must stay with a man who strays even if they are personally repelled by infidelity. Social, professional, and financial options are more abundant for men in this world; a consequence of this is that many men will stray, and women will stay with them.

However, for the woman who decides to stand up for herself and step out on her own, she can create and master challenges. Ivana Trump is a living, breathing example of a betrayed woman who has blossomed after divorce. Although the glamorous Ivana is wealthier and prettier than most of us could ever hope to be, what has seen the lady through is her determination. She held her head high as she was divorced from her husband, and has made much of life on her own. In *The Best Is Yet to Come: Coping with Divorce and Enjoying Life Again* (1995), Ivana reveals how she coped through her marital woes and divorce.

Some women feel stronger and have more self-esteem *after* their marriages end, according to *Our Turn: The Good News About Women and Divorce* (1993), by Dr. Christopher Hayes, Deborah Anderson, and Melinda Blau. Marriage won't protect a woman from the troubles in the world, nor will it guarantee her a sense of self-confidence; indeed, many women report coming into their own once they decide to move away from a cheating husband.

TAKE NOTE

- Men have more opportunities to stray than women, and are more likely to indulge those opportunities.

- Married women have depression rates twice those of men.

- The majority of women still earn less money than their husbands; financial stability is one advantage for women in marriage—but they pay an emotional cost if totally financially dependent on their man.

- Even today, there is more societal pressure for women to marry than for men.

- Being a full-time wife and mother is not a secure occupation.

- Every woman needs a life outside her marriage.

Chapter 3

The Unfaithful Husband: A Woman's Worst Nightmare

*I*t didn't mean anything. It was just sex.

—*Familiar words from a philandering man*

THE SEX IS THE THING

When men engage in an extramarital affair, it is initially driven by a need for sexual adventure, excitement, variety, novelty, and general pleasure seeking, with no hassles and no strings attached. Over 87 percent of affairs are motivated by the desire for sexual extras, claim the famous sex researchers Masters and Johnson (1994). The "extra" in extramarital means sex that *supplements*, rather than replaces, the marriage.

Most male infidelity can be classified as pleasure-centerd, motivated more by sexual interest than emotional involvement. The majority of female extramarital affairs are more "love-oriented," say psychologists Shirley Glass and Tom Wright, who claim that women pursue extramarital affairs more for emotional reasons, and that sex is merely a part of the equation. While each woman's motivations for having an extramarital affair are unique, generally speaking, women's affairs are more emotionally charged than sexually focused. Quite simply, women want to feel cared for and emotionally connected to a lover, and they usually need to feel this way *before* they have sex.

Affairs Should Come with Warning Labels:
This liaison may be hazardous to your marital health!

It is the rare man who seeks extramarital involvement for reasons other than sex or ego-gratifying attention, at least in the beginning. A new sexual partner is often seen as the ultimate ego boost for men, especially if the woman involved is young and pretty and ready to worship him. However, continual exposure to sex outside marriage with multiple partners, or repeated sex with one partner, often leads to the development of an emotional bond. Familiarity breeds liking; so repeated, positive experiences with a sex partner frequently develop into more and more liaisons, and often, strong emotional ties are forged between the married man and his lover(s).

One of the many very real dangers of extramarital infidelity is the *unexpected*. While a man may convince himself that it's "just for sex," there is no way to guarantee that he won't fall head over heels for his extramarital partner. As careful as he may be, he can still be caught off guard and fall in love. One cannot "love-proof" an affair, any more than one can "affair-proof" a marriage. If a person wants to stray, they will. If a person wants to remain faithful to their spouse, they will, even in the face of temptation. After all, it's when people are tempted that they show their true selves. It's easy to be faithful if you never leave the house and otherwise have no opportunities to stray. But put someone in the middle of numerous opportunities to stray, and they will reveal their true colors. As one forty-year-old divorced man put it: "If you flirt enough, an affair will happen. If you have too many affairs, your marriage will crumble."

This casual attitude toward straying often has very real consequences. "I'm not looking" sexual scenarios can and do flourish into decades-long affairs. As one man told me: "I started having sex outside my marriage because I wanted to spice up an otherwise predictable life. It was like going into a store hungry—and I ended up buying the store."

People complicate their lives by the choices they make. If you throw enough Jell-O at the wall, some of it is bound to stick. So it is with extramarital affairs. "You may find something even if you aren't looking for it, and you will surely find someone else if you go wandering around long enough," one man explained, referring to his three-year affair with his secretary, which began as a one-night fling after a Christmas party.

> *Good sex happens in bad marriages.*
> *Bad sex happens in good marriages.*
> *Great affairs end over bad sex.*
>
> —ANONYMOUS

If all men's affairs were totally sexually motivated, they would surely burn out quickly. "Just sex" is all too often about far more than sex. Whether men realize it or not, they are usually looking for attention, adoration, and unconditional love, as well as sex, but without any hassles or the need to reciprocate.

Indeed, many men who are regularly unfaithful complain about their wives' lack of sexual interest in them. After marriage, and particularly after motherhood, men say, too many women "retire" from real life. They become absorbed with their children, often to the neglect of the marriage. Men report feeling "displaced" and yearn for sexual companionship.

Men often convey their emotions through sex, so while they may be short on whispered intimacies with women, they try to demonstrate their love by making love. This is confusing to women, since men can also have sex with a stranger whom they don't even particularly like.

Guilt Is Good

While some people feel pangs of guilt about lying to their partner, and lying or exclusion of the truth is always involved in infidelity, other people follow a "cheater's code": "Don't tell anyone; don't let anyone see you doing it; don't get caught; and deny it if asked."

A 1995 study by psychologist Roy Baumeister of Case Western Reserve University claims that guilt can be good for you. Feeling some guilt over actions such as infidelity can actually help a person live longer and have a stronger marriage. A reasonable amount of guilt prevents a person from becoming an "interpersonal predator" and hurting other people. The majority of adulterous men, however, lack that guilty feeling. They rationalize and justify their infidelity, so that they feel no responsibility for hurting their wives.

Not only are many men lacking in the guilt department, but some of them are actually proud of their philandering ways. When a man ends an extramarital affair, it is rarely because of guilty feelings. It is more likely that he believed he was going to be "found out," that the sex flame with the lover was burning out, or his wife threatened divorce.

Some men told me they like having affairs because they don't even have to pretend to be emotionally connected with the woman, as they must do with their wives. One man said he hates to show the least bit of interest in romance. All he wants is a good screw—no small talk, no cuddling, just come . . . and then go. He says he doesn't feel any guilt about fooling around outside his marriage. In fact, he feels justified in doing so because, he says, his wife doesn't understand his need for "sex uncomplicated by messy emotional crap." And this man wonders why his wife isn't interested in having sex with him!

For many unfaithful men, guilt simply doesn't register. They tell themselves they are entitled to bed as many women as possible and chalk it up to "sowing their oats." Some men report that they don't even really have to lie to conceal their affairs. They cover their tracks by tacking their visits to their other women on to business trips, dinners, trips to the cleaners or the gym, or working late. Perhaps because they recognize that they have more to lose if they are caught, or because they exhibit a greater capacity for empathy, women involved in affairs are generally overcome by guilt. Many even blame themselves for enjoying their affair.

TYPES OF AFFAIRS

Extramarital sexual involvement takes many forms. Whether an affair is "just" flirting, or a decades-long emotional attachment, there is really no such thing as simple adultery. There are many types of extramarital involvements, but long-term emotional and sexual entanglements between a husband and another woman are particularly difficult for a wife to comprehend and cope with.

Transaction Sex

"Transaction sex" refers to short-term sexual encounters where emotional connection is absent or kept to a minimum. Transaction sex is different from sex for hire because "transaction" here means no money changes hands, but neither does any emotional closeness. The appeal of a transaction affair is that it is time-limited, has little chance of being discovered, usually occurs between strangers, and there is an understanding between the parties that no future contact will eventuate. Examples include:

- one-night stands
- weekend flings
- holiday flings
- seasonal sex

While no one can ever say they will *never* become "involved," the main attraction of a transaction affair, for both men and women, is the "no-strings, no-hassles" promise it holds. "Why not? No one will know" is the general motto of the "zipless fuck," inspired by the Erica Jong novel *Fear of Flying*.

Men and women alike use the transaction affair for sexual adventure, to combat loneliness, to validate their sexual appeal, and often to avenge a cheating partner. One man told me of his weekend fling at a golf tournament. He had no intention of continuing with the woman, whom he described as "angelic." But by the end of the weekend, he was smitten. She was as interested in sex as he was, and she was thinner and more experimental than his wife. His new lover awakened his spirit, he said, and he was continuing to see more of her, even though she lived three hundred miles away. Whenever he traveled out of town on his frequent business trips, he would fly through her city and spend a night or a weekend. Two years later, the affair was still going strong, and he says his wife suspects nothing (or so he thinks). He has no plans to leave his wife, so he figures that eventually his lover will pressure him and the affair will be over.

While many men believe an affair is *just* an affair, in reality the very term "simple affair" is an oxymoron. One man described to me his idea of a simple affair: "To me, a woman should be like a genie in a bottle. My wish is her command, and when I no longer want her, she gets back in the bottle and disappears."

Faithful Affection—or Fatal Attraction?

If you think a one-night stand is safe, watch *Fatal Attraction*—a harrowing tale of what *can* happen when a one-night stand goes wrong. An attractive wife, a successful husband, an adorable child, the picture-perfect marriage— the movie version of domestic bliss. Until the wife goes out of town for the weekend, and the husband has a fling with a single woman he hopes he'll never see again.

The film struck box-office gold when it was released in 1987, and is today considered a classic cautionary tale of extramarital sex. In theaters across the world, women shook their fingers at men, warning them away from potentially rabbit-boiling temptresses. Men would scream, "Kill the bitch!" when Glenn Close's single-woman character, Alex, tried to reveal his dirty little secret to his perfect wife.

One of the most revealing scenes of the movie is when Alex wonders out loud why a married man would be spending time with her if he is so happily married. The "Other Woman" assumes that if a man strays, he's not happy at home. This isn't always the case. Even happily married men stray, because even they have a desire for "extra" sex. It isn't only people in rocky marriages who are unfaithful. However, by being unfaithful, one can create problems in even a strong marriage. Over time, the constant lying and other deceptions take their toll on trust, intimacy, marital sex, and companionship.

Just Passing Through

Men who travel regularly to other cities often have affairs with women in those cities. Sort of like "same time next trip." One man I spoke with told me of his twice-yearly travels. The women he regularly meets for sex are considered friends, although he says they exchange no personal information, only lots of bodily fluids. He never gives his wife his itinerary, despite the fact that he is often away from home for weeks at a time. He calls her regularly while traveling to check in, but feels secure in the knowledge that she can't reach him—and discover his road-trip antics.

Conference Coitus

A 1996 survey by Novotel Hotel Corporation in New York reported that only 11 percent of male business travelers use room service, while three times as many women make use of the service. Men, one can surmise, are more comfortable mingling in the hotel bars and restaurants when traveling alone. Browsing the bars for babes, perhaps? A Roper Starch poll for Hyatt Hotels asked executives what they considered of "great importance" for a business conference to be judged successful. Nine percent answered, "Meeting a romantic interest."

Holiday Sex

The holiday romance is the stuff of fantasy. Perhaps the allure of sand, sea, and sex is why you don't find many couples taking separate vacations to Hawaii or the Bahamas. And who hasn't thought about sex with a stranger in the solitude of a secluded cabin in the snow? Holiday sex makes up millions of fantasies, and many people are acting on their dreams.

The backdrop may be different, and the contact longer, but the unstated understanding is that the affair is to savor sex and then bid each other farewell, with no contact once they return to their "real lives." That may be the hope; the reality is often different. Stalking and other such tragedies are often the result of holiday flings when one party wants more from the relationship than the other person can offer.

Seasonal Sex and the Summer Bachelor

Eighty percent of men cheat in America. The rest cheat in Europe.
— COMEDIAN JACKIE MASON

The Hamptons, that upscale beach area on the easternmost tip of New York's Long Island, is a favorite summer retreat for successful New York professionals. In summertime, many of the men live alone in the city while their wives and children head to lushly landscaped estates near the water. Is such an arrangement a license to cheat? Some men, and a few women, think so. Many men see the summer arrangement as more than just a way to entertain their wives and children. The break benefits them, too, and more than a few take advantage of the extra time available during the week to see a girlfriend or meet other women.

If a man is inclined to cheat, he will cheat whether his wife is in town or out in the country. These affairs, while often ongoing, are still classified by the men as purely sexual in nature. The men have no plans to leave their wives. But, who knows, anything can happen. . . .

Holiday sex rarely extends beyond the lease on the holiday hideaway, but many people take advantage of a new environment to try on a sexier lifestyle. Few men, in particular, are willing to include the summer lover in their life back home. But some men are forced to do so, as many "Other Women" set their sights on winning the man away from his wife. One man, a survivor of a past summer love that resulted in a winter nightmare, told me that, for him, the most feared four words in the English language are: "I'll tell your wife."

Some men believe that if they have sex with another woman away from the town where they reside with their wife, then it isn't cheating! Obviously, many men will justify adultery any way they can. Cheating is cheating, wherever it takes place.

Sex for Hire

The big difference between sex for money and sex for hire is that sex for money usually costs less.

— BRENDAN FRANCIS

A special report in *Marie Claire* magazine, "Why Men Pay for Sex," (March 1997) claims that up to 70 percent of men have paid for sex with a prostitute at least once. One of the main reasons men pay for sex is to have a cut-and-dried deal, and the kind of sex they felt they aren't getting at home. Anal and oral sex were cited as activities men seek with prostitutes, which they say their wives aren't interested in. As one man explained: "It was purely sexual, and that's what a man needs once in a while." Men who pay a prostitute for sex are paying her to go away as well as to make them come.

Beyond seeking out a prostitute for totally uninhibited sex, some men pay for sex in order to ensure a "no-strings" arrangement. They are fearful of sexual intimacy with someone with whom they are emotionally involved. Many men are simply more comfortable exploring their sexual fantasies with a prostitute than with a woman who shares their everyday life.

Prostitutes believe in marriage. It provides them with most of their trade.

— ANONYMOUS

Sex with "professional girlfriends," as prostitutes are often referred to, is easier for some men because it's like taking a woman off the shelf, enjoying her, and then putting her back in her place. No foreplay, and no criticism about the lack of it, is one aspect of sex with prostitutes that men say they enjoy. There are no messy entanglements or emotional scenes.

Women find it difficult to comprehend why men use prostitutes. Since most women equate sex with emotions, they figure the man might as well masturbate instead of using a prostitute who is a total stranger and really serves the same purpose as the man's hand. Except, of course, a prostitute also strokes a man's large but fragile ego as well as his penis.

Most wives are oblivious to their husband's use of prostitutes or escorts. Since few women pay for sex, or hire escorts, it is difficult for them to understand their spouse's propensity to do so. When women travel on business, they often relax in the hotel rather than trolling the town for strip clubs. Or they soak in a hot tub, put on the fluffy hotel robe, and order room service. Some men seem to relish the thought of anonymous sex on the run with a stranger; fewer women find this the best way to spend an evening.

Office Romance

More women are having affairs as the number of women in the workplace increases. There has also been an increase in office romances. When men and women—well groomed and on their best behavior—share interesting work, sparks can turn into infernos for couples who act on their sexual urges.

Extramarital affairs with subordinates, or with the boss, are particularly difficult for married people. Everyone has a lot to lose, especially a secretary having an affair with her married boss. When he is finished with her, he often wants no reminders of the affair around the office—and out she goes. She "knows too much" for him to have her around.

Although more women are in managerial and professional positions these days, the large majority are still clustered in "pink-collar ghetto" jobs—clerical, sales, nursing, teaching. Regardless of their professional status, women have more to lose from an office romance than men do. Even single women suffer more than married men, and married women can potentially ruin their career and their marriage by having an extramarital affair with a man from the office.

The wide majority of office romances tend to end badly for at least one party. One man told me of his wonderful relationship, which started at the office. Still, it had an unhappy ending for one person: his wife.

I'm a forty-year-old lawyer, and first married when I was twenty-three. My first wife had been my girlfriend since age seventeen. We had two children, who are now thirteen and eleven. Shortly after my second daughter was born, a new girl came to work as my secretary. I fell in love with her, and a year later we began a relationship, which was most astounding to me, as I'm the most monogamous person I know. Tragically, my first wife was the last to know. She found out five years after the relationship began, and a year after we had separated.

My secretary and I had been an "open" item for years, although our relationship is now ten years old. For the last three years we have been extremely happily married, and my children live with us half the time.

Adultery On-Line

Can a person be unfaithful without actually having sex? This was the question posed in the recent controversy over a woman accused by her husband of having a cybersex affair. Flirting on the Internet is becoming an ever more popular extracurricular activity for many men and women. The time spent on-line can have a negative impact on a marriage because it diverts valuable time and attention away from the spouse—and into space.

One man tells the story of his involvement with a woman he met in an on-line chat room. He says he became hooked on their talks. "It became as addictive as cocaine," he claims. He temporarily left his wife and family for his cybertramp, only to be dumped by her three months later. Afterward, he learned that she had ruined three other marriages in the same way.

A woman from Washington, D.C., was accused by her husband of having an adulterous on-line relationship. She had been corresponding on the Net with a man for several months, and claims they fell in love on-line. They arranged to meet at a hotel and spend a weekend together, but her husband intercepted their correspondence and the weekend tryst was aborted. The couple are divorcing. Clearly, some men don't even like the notion that their wives could be unfaithful in their hearts.

For most people involved in extramarital affairs, secrecy is of prime importance. On-line flirting is easily discovered. Privacy on-line is virtually nonexistent, and one must be wary of exposing oneself even in the cyber-world. Whether sex is on-line or under the covers, time diverted away from a marital partner saps a marriage of energy, trust, and respect.

Long-Term Affairs

Some couples implicitly adopt two policies regarding infidelity: "Ask me no questions and I'll tell you no lies," and "Don't ask, don't tell." While some people think such a "modern" stance toward marriage is the sign of a strong union, in reality it comes across more as not caring at all what your partner does. If you can't ask your partner who they had lunch with, what they did at work, or where their social function is on Saturday night, why be married in the first place? Privacy is one thing; excessive secrecy in order to conceal infidelity is quite another.

In long-term affairs, some men and women develop a solid emotional attachment to their extramarital partner. These long-term involvements range anywhere from months to many decades. They include emotional ties as well as sexual pleasures. However, the majority of men, though they may be attached to their mistress, still consider her supplemental to their wife and marriage.

Long-term, emotionally based affairs pose the most severe threat to a marriage. Even when the man has no plans to leave his marriage, he is still putting his wife in a very difficult and painful position by forcing a triangle on her. She may or may not know of the affair, but chances are she does; and although she stays in the marriage, she is continually aggravated by the presence of another woman in her husband's life, and in her marriage.

One such long-term involvement was described to me by a very prominent older gentleman called Colin. He has been married for over twenty-five years and has had several mistresses during that time. In addition to these "serial mistresses," he also enjoys the occasional fling, both around town and when away on business.

When his wife is at one of their vacation homes, or away for her charity work, he brings his current mistress of eight years into his marital home and bed. Colin confessed that he feels perfectly justified in doing so, because it's his money that built the home and keeps it running. His wife has never been employed, although she raised four children and is involved in numerous civic causes. Colin also provides his mistress, Suzanne, with an apartment, a car, a generous allowance, and a private phone line for his calls.

He isn't sure whether his wife knows about his double life; she has never confronted him, and he hasn't sensed any changes in her behavior, such as hostility or anger. She treats him very well and he still loves her. He believes, however, that his success should be shared — and he actively seeks out women all the time. He says he simply loves women.

Colin said he makes no promises to Suzanne, although she is approaching her late thirties and, by staying with him, is forgoing her chances of marriage and a family with someone else. He expresses no feelings of responsibility toward her, as he believes she knows the rules and is free to leave at any time. Although Colin is emotionally attached to Suzanne, he said he wouldn't hesitate to cut off the relationship if she became too demanding. He ended each of his other long-term affairs because the women began pressing him to leave his wife. He ends one affair, only to begin another one. "If you have affairs," he maintains, "you must be willing to end them. The family has to come first."

Multiple Affairs

It is common for men who have long-term affairs also to have casual flings with a variety of women. The wife thinks he's faithful, the girlfriend thinks he only sleeps with her, but in reality he is sleeping with them all. Gennifer Flowers once remarked of Bill Clinton: "He cheated on me and Hillary."

If a man cheats on his wife, it is also a fair assumption that he cheats on his "Other Woman." Many "Other Women" convince themselves, wrongly, that their married lover no longer has sex with his wife. Most married men continue having an active sex life with their wife—often as a precaution against raising her suspicion that they may be having an affair. Imagine: a married man cheating on his girlfriends with his wife!

Sexualized Friendships

When men and women are good friends, sex often enters the picture. For people who are attracted to one another, and who share many interests, sexual tension and attraction can be intense. Sexualized friendships are very common between professional men and women, even when one or both are married. The sexual aspect of these friendships is generally short-lived, but the friendship remains strong. Sexualized friendships are generally not threatening to a marriage.

One woman described to me what she called her "affair that had to happen." She had a fabulous male friend to whom she was sexually drawn. She told me she had to have sex with him to get it out of her system. Both she and her friend enjoyed their sexual experience, and it enhanced their working relationship and special friendship bond. Both were married to other people and had no intention of leaving their respective partners, but the sexualizing of the relationship deepened their fondness for one another.

Sexualized friendships are frequent among single coworkers, but now many more married people are also embarking on flings to indulge their sexual attraction. The affair is then filed away as a memory, where hopefully it won't intrude on their respective marriages. Unless of course it is discovered!

Transitional Affairs

A transitory or transitional affair is one in which a man or a woman uses an affair to boost their sexual confidence before they leave their marriage. They are less interested in their sex partner as a romantic partner than as a "tryout" for their new life.

Men in transitional affairs are usually ready to divorce, either after having an affair discovered or after dumping a long-term mistress. The emphasis is on moving forward, and using the sex partner to further their goals. A transitional affair is also one in which a man or woman "tests" another sex partner to determine if they are "missing" anything with their spouse. In this case, the affair is motivated by loneliness, and often convinces a person that "the grass isn't greener on the other side; in fact, it's crab grass."

PERPETUAL AND/OR EMOTIONALLY ABUSIVE PHILANDERERS

Many of the men I interviewed told me that after they had their first extramarital affair, there was no turning back. One man said, "Ninety percent of married men have affairs, and the other ten percent don't know what they're missing."

Some men are not only philanderers, they are also expert liars. Indeed, some are so competent at lying that they say they could convince their wife to doubt her own eyesight: "Who do you believe—me or your lying eyes?"

When a man is a polished liar, watch out—he may be hazardous to your emotional health. If an adulterous man is also emotionally manipulative and verbally abusive, you are in serious trouble.

Unfaithful men and emotionally abusive men have certain negative characteristics in common. Behaviors such as hostility, emotional manipulation, and verbal abuse are evident in a majority of emotionally abusive men. Emotional manipulation, anger, and deception also tend to be exhibited by unfaithful men. Beware of men who behave badly—especially the emotionally abusive man who is also a philanderer. Such a person is particularly hazardous to a woman's emotional and physical well-being.

Characteristics Common to the Wives of Adulterous Men and Abused Women

- The woman suffers low self-esteem
- She believes it is up to her to keep the family together
- She assumes she is responsible for her husband's philandering/abuse

- She suffers depression and physical complaints such as headaches and stomachaches

When a man is repeatedly unfaithful, it wears down a woman's self-confidence. This continual undermining of her spirit makes her question herself. The behaviors a man uses to "successfully" cheat on his wife are the very behaviors that hurt her so much.

Characteristics of the Emotionally Abusive Man

- He withholds attention, affection, and sex
- He criticizes almost everything she does
- He makes negative comments about her looks
- He blames all their problems on her
- He accuses her of being crazy—saying, "It's all in your head"
- He says she expects too much—that she is never satisfied

Abusive behaviors are motivated by a need to control and manipulate, and, often, by the man's need to keep his own emotions and feelings of intimacy at bay. The use of threats to keep a woman in line, feeling vulnerable and unsure of herself, is part and parcel of the man's motives, and is particularly damaging to a wife's self-confidence and self-esteem.

Threats manipulate a woman by focusing on her greatest fears. They are meant to cause her pain and to make he more dependent on her husband. Comments made by an emotionally manipulative husband place his wife in a double bind. She is damned no matter what she does:

- Do what I want or I'll leave.
- Do what I want or I'll take a mistress.
- Do what I want or I'll get a divorce.
- Do what I want or — — — (fill in the blank).

Sources adapted from: Lenore Walker, 1979; Donald Dutton, 1995; Neil Jacobson and John Gottman, 1998.

The emotionally abusive philanderer is also likely to say things like, "It's no wonder I stray, given the way you treat me." The man is projecting, attributing his own abusive behavior to his wife. Living with an emotionally abusive, controlling, unfaithful man is a crazy-making, dangerous situation even for a secure, psychologically well-adjusted woman.

An Issue of Control

Men who cheat on their spouses are generally outwardly charming, but they may become highly critical and cold when alone with their wife. For the great majority of men who pursue extramarital affairs, sex is the motivation. For some emotionally abusive men, however, the driving force is *control*—specifically, control over their wife. These men are generally fearful of intimacy and emotional closeness, so by pursuing relationships outside marriage, they are diffusing the intensity of the marriage. Having "one foot out of the marriage" helps them to maintain control over their feelings and over their spouse. Any threat of emotional closeness makes this type of man more manipulative, aloof, and abusive.

Philandering and controlling men display "gaslighting" behavior. In the classic movie *Gaslight* (1940), a husband drives his wife insane by his criticisms, denials, and manipulative behavior. He convinces her that she is "losing it," and she begins to doubt her own perceptions. So, too, do women who are continually exposed to philandering men who deny their extramarital activities.

The Psychological Double Bind

The hallmark of a woman exposed to an emotionally abusive man is the feeling that she is going around in circles. She is damned if she does, and damned if she doesn't. This type of man literally drives his wife away with his verbal abuse, then tells her he is justified in cheating because of the way *she* treats *him*!

Fiona's Story

Fiona is married to a man who acts out all the worst behaviors of an unfaithful and emotionally abusive man when at home, while appearing charming to everyone else he meets. She is an emotional and psychological wreck, as her husband continually manipulates her feelings, and yet she basically loves him and worries that he is going to leave her. She never feels happy or stable. Most of the time, Fiona's husband yells at her or criticizes her; the rest of the time he refuses to talk to her. She is terrified of his unpredictable mood swings. Some of the comments he has made to Fiona include:

- You aren't going to tell me how to run my life. I'll see as many women as I want to see. My sex life is none of your business.

- If you don't do what I want you to do, I'm going to divorce you and leave you with nothing.

- You're nothing without me.

- Go away for a while. You're violating my privacy. I don't care where you go, just get out of here. I'm sick of looking at you. I'm sick of hearing your voice.

- I can have women over to my house anytime I want. It's my house, not yours.

- If you aren't available when I want you for something, I'll call another woman.

- I don't care if you have male friends, but I'll leave you if you do.

- If you don't want sex when I want it, I'm going to go somewhere else.

- Why don't you get a makeover? You're getting ugly.

- I'm the only option you have. No other man will ever treat you as well as I do.

- I earn the money, I make the rules.

- My work is much more important than yours.

If, like Fiona, you are a woman married to an unfaithful and emotionally abusive man, it is in your best interest to seek professional help. These types of men are highly resistant to change, as they believe everyone else is the problem. In order to regain your sense of self, you may have to leave the relationship. Staying with an unfaithful man who is also emotionally abusive is a different situation entirely from living with a philanderer. Neither is a particularly rosy experience, but the combination of the two forms of abuse undermines a woman's basic sense of self-esteem. A philandering husband is every woman's nightmare. An emotionally abusive and philandering husband is a nightmare beyond belief.

If you ever encounter physical violence in a relationship, or fear for your safety in any way, you must leave immediately and seek professional help!

Tiffany's Story

Throughout her three-year courtship and four-year marriage to Jon, Tiffany has had to contend with an unfaithful and emotionally manipulative man. His behavior is turning her into an emotional mess, and she is trying to get herself together to leave the relationship. She wants to get out and make a fresh start while she is still in her thirties. However, the stronger and more self-confident she becomes, the more Jon cheats on her, which then further erodes her confidence.

Jon is a successful investment banker and Tiffany is a magazine journalist. Both travel frequently on business. Jon meets many women in his job, while Tiffany works mostly with women and gay men. She misses the attention she used to get from men before she married. Now all she gets are insults from her husband. Like so many women when they marry, she traded attention from many men only to be ignored by one man.

Tiffany knows that whenever she heads out of town, even if it's just for one night, Jon brings a woman to their apartment. While she has yet to find concrete evidence at their home, she says she "just knows." She feels that he violates their special space by having sex with someone else in their marital bed.

Not only is Jon unfaithful to Tiffany, but he is also particularly cruel *about it. He frequently tells Tiffany that she doesn't measure up to other women. Even though she is trim, attractive, and dresses well, Tiffany is convinced she can't compete with the women Jon attracts. Her self-confidence seems worn thin.*

Tiffany feels chronically tired and has been in a general malaise for two of her four married years. Jon cheated on her while they were dating and it crushed her. Although they were not in an exclusive relationship at the time, she was faithful to him because she was in love with him and didn't desire anyone else. She suffered a great deal through Jon's affairs, and she can't adjust to him still playing around now that they are married.

It's not just his cheating that upsets her, it is his paying attention to other women while he neglects and belittles her. When they attend social functions together, he ignores her while he works the room, chatting to and complimenting other women. He rarely compliments her, but criticizes her nonstop. Tiffany can't even remember when Jon last told her she looked nice.

What pains Tiffany most is that Jon often denies her sex, pushing her away and telling her she is no longer appealing. On the few occasions lately when Jon initiated sex, he stopped soon after starting, rolled over, and said he'd go and seek out another woman.

Jon can be warm and caring to strangers, but Tiffany says he is cold and withholding of affection where she is concerned. She also complains that he closely monitors every cent she spends. He is controlling and obsessive, and not the least bit affectionate or demonstrative. When she approaches him to give him a hug or to snuggle, he leans away as though she has body odor. Her feelings are always being hurt and she often doesn't want to leave the house or see or talk to friends.

Tiffany has resigned herself to an emotionally empty and lonely marriage—for the short run. She is trying to wean herself from the man she loves and hopes to begin a new life for herself in another city with a new job. She feels she has too much love and passion to waste it on an "emotionally constipated" and unfaithful husband. She doesn't like herself for tolerating Jon's hurtful and humiliating behavior. She wants a more emotionally intimate partner to share her life with.

A caring and stable home life is what most people want. Obtaining it with an unfaithful and emotionally abusive partner is rarely possible.

Tiffany, like many women, is torn between leaving a familiar albeit unsatisfying and unhappy marriage, and the urge to reach out for another man and another relationship that may better meet her needs for affection and fidelity.

Many women are hesitant to leave what is familiar even though they desperately long for something "more," something else. What often nudges women out of their discomfort is the discovery of yet another affair by her mate. Something is usually required to snap a woman out of her "safe" but stifling routine.

Lola's Story

Lola's story is particularly disturbing as it illustrates how nasty a man can be when he wants to cover his tracks. Mark, her husband of ten years, can be a first-class charmer when everything is going his way and he feels in control of the situation. But beware when things aren't to his liking.

Lola is a lawyer in a small town where the couple resides. She also looks after their three-year-old daughter. Mark, a successful management consultant, travels frequently.

Last year when Mark was away on a two-week business trip, Lola received a call from one of Mark's clients. The man said it was urgent he get a message to Mark. Lola took the message and called Mark's hotel, but the line was busy and remained engaged for hours. Finally, she called the hotel desk and asked the clerk to deliver a message to her husband's room.

Within a few minutes Lola received a call from her husband. He screamed into the phone, "What I do is none of your business! I'm not on your leash, so stop acting like a detective. Why didn't you just fax me? Stop trying to spy on me!"

Lola felt numb. Mark had acted this way before, but each time it happened, it shocked her more. She thought she had acted responsibly in trying to get the client's message to him as soon as possible. She vowed not to help him in the future. As she explained, "My husband should be the one person in the world I can call on the phone anytime, anywhere, and have it be okay. I can't deal with such abusive treatment."

Mark is obviously trying to hide his on-the-road flings from Lola, but his lashing out at her only confirms his sense of guilt.

WEALTH AND STATUS ARE NO PROTECTION AGAINST INFIDELITY

In her Pulitzer Prize–winning autobiography, *Personal History* (1997), Katharine Graham, chief executive of the Washington Post Company, recounts how she suffered in her marriage to an emotionally abusive and unfaithful husband. Ms. Graham says that her husband, the late Philip Graham, called her "porky" and constantly belittled her. He took a young mistress and paraded her in public. He told his wife of his numerous other affairs, and then berated her when she became upset. Ms. Graham continued to stand by her husband, despite his philandering and abuse, until he committed suicide, which she writes about in her courageous book.

THE BOTTOM LINE

Infidelity comes in all shapes and sizes, and there is no set way in which a man conducts his extramarital affairs. Some affairs are one-time sexual encounters, others are long-term emotional entanglements. Some men are serial philanderers, moving from one woman to another while remaining married. Some men "fall off the fidelity wagon" and have one affair, for which they are remorseful. The nature of a man's infidelity greatly affects whether a woman stays with a man who strays. The challenge for every woman is to determine for herself what she will and will not tolerate in her marriage.

TAKE NOTE

- If your husband cheats on you, don't blame yourself. Blame him. After all, no one made him do it. Don't let him off the hook easily. Don't make excuses for his behavior.

- No woman deserves to be betrayed.

- Determine if his cheating is a one-time mistake or a pattern of philandering.

- Remember: All extramarital affairs are based on lying. Do you want to be married to a man who deceives you over and over again?

Chapter 4

"It's Just Sex": How Society Condones Men's Infidelities

$\mathcal{L}$ove is one thing. Lust is another.

—*Latin proverb*

$\mathcal{O}$ne lover, that is love. Two lovers, that is passion. Three lovers, that is commerce.

—*French proverb*

COMMON EXCUSES FOR
MEN'S INFIDELITIES

*E*ncouraging, excusing, and condoning a man's extramarital affairs are commonplace behaviors in society today, on the part of men and even some women. As one man explained to me, "Who needs to blame men, when even women excuse them?" Indeed, many people dismiss the act of adultery as trivial or harmless and offer excuses in defense of a philandering man.

These excuses range from blaming the wife, the "Other Woman," the situation—anyone or anything except the man. The popular notion is: "It's just how men are." The problem with this attitude is that it completely ignores the fact that men are adults and therefore should be capable of behaving responsibly and being accountable for their actions. Wives don't drive their husbands to infidelity, as many people surmise. If a man is unfaithful, it's because he wants to be, and because he has chosen the easier wrong—adultery—rather than the harder right—monogamy.

Men's egos are wrapped up in their sexual virility and performance. When a man is not satisfied sexually, he often boosts his ego by blaming his wife. Instead, men should look closely at their bedroom skills and improve their foreplay and perfunctory sexual performance. Their wives will thank them—and demonstrate their thanks in the bedroom.

One very pervasive excuse, particularly in Europe, used to discount men's adultery is, "All men have mistresses." Many people assume that it is normal, after the children are born, for the woman to spend her time caring for the family and home, while the husband works and plays away from home. The wife's "reward" for keeping her mouth shut and ignoring her husband's infidelity is the privilege of being a wife to him and being looked after financially.

Excuses Men use to Justify Their Infidelity

- It's just sex.

- Extramarital sex is like an instant ego-boost machine.

- A pretty, young woman is like an oxygen tank to a middle-aged man's waning sex life.

- Oral sex isn't adultery.

- No married man can possibly make love to only one woman for the rest of his life. If he does, the rest of his life isn't worth living.

- A woman recently called me a "serial womanizer," and she was annoyed that I was flattered by her comment!

- It's one thing to sleep with somebody else; it's quite another thing to actually leave your wife and family.

- All men stray.

- He had an affair—he has a mistress—so what?

Men's excuses tend to justify adultery as "just sex," "just something men do," and "not something to get upset about." Women rarely find another woman's husband's infidelity acceptable, but may offer excuses for it, such as the wife's physical appearance, or blame the Other Woman for luring the man away from his wife. Rarely is an unfaithful husband held fully accountable—by himself, by his wife, or by society.

"It's the Wife's Fault"

Many people believe that if a man cheats on his wife, she must have given him reason to do so. Perhaps he isn't "getting enough" at home? The husband, rather than the wife, becomes the victim. Even mistresses blame the wife for a man's infidelity. Many other women have told me that a man is justified in having affairs "if their wives are frigid, uninterested in sex, fat, or ugly." Blaming the wife for a man's infidelity is common, and nasty.

Sydney Biddle Barrows, known as the "Mayflower Madam" and author of *Just Between Us Girls*, says that men stray because their wives often do little to prevent them from doing so. She says that many men troll outside their marriage because their wives ignore them, overeat, or don't look after their appearance. In other words, the wives *ask* to be cheated on.

Most women inevitably gain weight during pregnancy, and some have trouble losing it afterward. Many men justify their philandering by saying they are turned off by their now-overweight partners. Society is generally sympathetic toward men who say they stray for this reason. Women are other women's harshest critics in many areas of life, especially when sexual attraction is involved. For example: "I'm sorry they divorced. I really am. She did a lot of things to help Newty. But we often wonder, if she would have lost some weight, if it would have helped. She was quite heavy." That from Kit Gingrich, mother of Newt Gingrich, former Speaker of the U.S. House of Representatives, about his first wife.

Effects on the Children

When children learn that their father is involved in an affair, often they blame their mother and excuse their father. "She didn't do enough to make herself attractive to him," they rationalize.

Many parents mistakenly believe they are keeping their infidelity problems a secret from their children. While age is obviously a factor in a child's understanding of infidelity, many children are harmed by living with chronic infidelity. Many women have grown distrustful of men because their fathers had affairs. Some women grow to dislike and disrespect their mothers for tolerating or "causing" the infidelity. And many boys grow up to imitate their father's philandering.

"It's the Fault of the Other Woman"

Several years ago a teenage girl named Amy Fisher approached the home of the man, Joey Buttafuco, with whom she was allegedly having an affair. When his wife Mary Jo came to the door, Amy (who would become known as "the Long Island Lolita") pulled out a gun and, she says, it went off by mistake. Mary Jo survived, but she still has a bullet lodged in her head and suffers partial paralysis on one side of her face. Amy Fisher went to prison, and Joey served a short sentence for pleading guilty to having sex with an underage girl.

The amazing part of this story is that Mary Jo has defended her husband's behavior from day one, and continues to do so. She even dismisses claims that an affair ever took place between her husband and the girl. She blames the "Lolita" for everything.

Many wives blame the Other Woman because it's too threatening for them to blame their husband. They feel they have too much to lose. "How could he say no, the way she threw herself at him?" they wonder to themselves.

"It's the Way Men Are Wired"

Even today, thirty years after the push for feminism, the message that men send out—and that women are socialized to accept—is: "All men stray. Get used to it." In the 1950s, before women had any real professional opportunities for financial independence, they had little choice but to "grin and bear it" and look the other way when their husband strayed. Although more women are pursuing careers and earning good money, many of them still subscribe to the belief that they should stand by their man if he plays around.

The popular gossip columnist at the *New York Post*, Cindy Adams, commenting on Rose Kennedy, mother of the late president John F. Kennedy, in *New York* magazine, said: "I thought Rose was a tough old broad. She knew her husband was cheating and let it go like so many wives should. You want to stay married, that's the way you do it."

While infidelity is a factor in divorce, it seems that women are finding excuses for their husband's dalliances and tolerating a straying mate. Wronged wives are standing by their men in great numbers.

Don't Blame Yourself

It seems incredibly sad that women feel they must apologize to their husbands for wanting them to be faithful. It also underscores the extent to which society defends and condones men's infidelity, and how it encourages women to shoulder the blame.

With men, some women, and society as a whole explicitly encouraging or implicitly condoning infidelity, is it any surprise that many people believe adultery to be an acceptable lifestyle choice? While adultery may be more common in society today, not to mention the White House, that is no comfort to the woman who feels very real pain when she discovers that her husband is unfaithful.

The more society condones and encourages men's infidelity, the more difficult it is for those women who are trying to cope with a straying spouse. They feel they are alone in believing in fidelity. Adultery is *not* part and parcel of every marriage, despite the messages many women receive.

TAKE NOTE

- Extramarital sex is *never* just about sex. It is about planning and deceiving. If it were "just sex," infidelity would not cause so much pain for so many people.

- Ignore the oft-heard sentiment, "All men stray. Get used to it." *All men do not stray*.

- Do not lose your self-confidence if a man tells you that *you* drove him to another woman.

- Regardless of how many women offer themselves to your man, he is an adult and can (and, if married, should) say no.

- Just because the President has an "inappropriate relationship," that doesn't make it acceptable for other men to follow his lead.

Chapter 5

THE TIME
BANDITS:
OTHER
WOMEN

As for sleeping with married men, don't do it. It's a ticket to
pain, and leaves you very bitter.

—*Supermodel Carla Bruni*

*S*ex is always good with a married man as long as you're not
the one married to him.

—*A thirty-four-year-old mistress*

*I*t suggests some kind of service contract—that all I did was
perform oral sex on him and that that's all this relationship was.

—*Monica Lewinsky about Bill Clinton, in the Starr Report*

THE OTHER WOMAN—TIME BANDIT OR TIME BOMB?

A ménage à trois is a crowd. Just ask anyone who has ever been part of a romantic triangle. They are a disaster in the making. When a man engages in extramarital sex, it is usually of extreme importance to him to keep the affair quiet. He will strive to maximize sex, adventure, and pleasure, while minimizing the risk of discovery and any emotional complications.

However, a woman involved with a married man may have different goals from her lover, especially if she is single. Initially, they may have parallel goals—sex, the thrill of a new partner, romantic interludes, conversation. But few married men realize that when they embark on an affair with a single woman, often she will want the affair to end the man's marriage. Despite his best intentions, an affair can put even a perfectly happy marriage on the rocks.

Regardless of the enormous efforts girlfriends and mistresses often make in trying to lure their married man away from his wife, most adulterers do not leave their marriage. As Paul Blanchard reports in his book *Why Men Cheat and What to Do About It* (1995), the odds are definitely with the wife rather than the woman involved with a married man. Blanchard claims that only one man in four leaves his wife when he is cheating. Similarly, Dr. Jan Halper in *Quiet Desperation* says that 85 percent of men who cheat stay in their marriages. Of the men who do divorce during an affair, 97 percent *do not* marry their lover. Of the 4,100 men she surveyed, only 3 percent eventually married their illicit lover.

Some psychologists argue that an affair is a symptom of problems in a marriage. This is not necessarily true. I have spoken to many happily married men who say they love their wives and don't want to hurt or leave them, but also want a bit on the side. An unhappy marriage is not necessarily a precursor to an affair, nor is a happy marriage a guarantee against adultery.

Problems can be created even in a perfect marriage when one or both parties begin an extramarital affair. Affairs take time and energy, and when these valuable commodities are channeled away from the spouse, there is not much left to give to the marriage. An affair robs a marriage of time and intimacy. Affairs regularly require deception and evasiveness, which undermine the closeness and trust in any relationship. Lies eat away at the foundation of a relationship as termites erode the foundations of a house.

"Stolen" Hours

There are only so many hours in a day. Time and financial resources are limited, so if both are expended on a girlfriend instead of a wife, trouble is sure to follow. Even in marriages where finances aren't a problem, when money and attention are focused away from the primary relationship, it is very disturbing to a wife. When a woman learns that her husband is lavishing nice lunches, dinners, clothes, jewelry, and holidays on other women, she is rightfully furious. After all, it is also *her* money being spent on the affair.

Even more than the money, the attention lavished on a third party really angers wives. When a man is involved in an extramarital affair, he spends a lot of the time he would otherwise spend with his wife and family on the other woman.

A woman feels that if her husband has any spare time, he should spend it with her. After all, companionship is part of the reason for marriage. When a man spends time with another woman instead, wives feel slighted. In a marriage where problems do exist, *more* time should be devoted to the marriage to help get it back on track. Instead, men often spend *less* time on the marriage and more on an affair. One can never fix a problem by adding another complication, such as an extramarital affair.

CODE OF SILENCE?

Every married man's worst nightmare is having a girlfriend
who will kiss and tell!

When a man begins an extramarital affair, he is usually concerned about keeping it a secret from his wife. While most philandering husbands don't explicitly tell their lover or extramarital sex partner to keep quiet, most assume she will. This is a dangerous assumption! Although adulterous relationships are, at their very core, based on deceit, not all women want to comply with a code of silence about the relationship. Some men end their extramarital dalliances because they sense their lover is being indiscreet and telling others of their affair.

A woman involved with a married man, whether she herself is single or married, often becomes emotionally tied to him, and wants his wife and others to know of the affair.

DISCREET INDISCRETIONS: AFFAIRS WITH MARRIED WOMEN

If a married man feels he *must* have an affair, it is generally safer to do so with a married woman. As one man told me, "Only have an affair with someone who has as much to lose as you do. She'll keep quiet." Most married women have as much to lose as married men, so they are the safer bet for an affair. They are less likely than single women to want to disrupt a man's marriage. And, like many men, they probably don't want to leave their marriage. Many are just looking for an emotional and sexual supplement to their home life, rather than a new husband.

Is Half a Loaf Better Than No Loaf at All?

Some single women are willing to settle for a few crumbs now and again from a married man. Many women involved with married men report that they like the arrangement because they can pursue their own interests, without having to look after the "domestic" side of a man. Leave the drudgery, like the washing of the socks and jocks, to the wife, thank you very much. But despite their best efforts, many "new" other women end up like the Other Woman decades ago, getting much less from the relationship than their married lover does.

While few single women set out to snag an already married man, some do. I spoke with several women who make a sport of seducing other women's husbands. And while some are content to stay put for years in an unequal, limbo-land affair, others are deeply disturbed by doing so. Still, they do it, and often for decades!

One woman who had a forty-year extramarital affair with her lover and recently wrote about it, is Lillian Ross, the noted journalist. Ms. Ross claims in *Here But Not Here: My Life with William Shawn and the New Yorker* that "After forty years, our love-making had the same passion, the same energy . . . as it had in the beginning." Though Ms. Ross writes that her affair allowed her to concentrate on her career, it is evident to me throughout her tribute to her long-term affair, that there was a longing for it to be "more." After all, most women who become involved with married men do so in the hopes of the illicit liaison becoming much more permanent, where the mistress will no longer be an open or closed secret, and will bask in acceptance.

Ms. Ross's story stirred controversy. It seems that people did not think highly of her writing about being a long-term mistress, or of doing so while her lover's wife was still alive. Given the amazingly favorable approval ratings of Hillary Clinton for standing by Bill in the wake of "Monicagate," people everywhere are sending the message that the loyal wife is to be much admired, while the mistresses and temptresses are to be scorned. Not many people can think highly of a woman who will intentionally cause pain in someone else's marriage. Is it any surprise, then, that mistresses generally live an unhappy existence?

He Keeps Me Hanging On

It is difficult for many people to discuss extramarital sex and mistresses in an honest, straightforward fashion. As a result, it is impossible to assess the number of single women who are involved with married men. It is safe to assume, however, that the number is large, and that many, many single women, at some time in their lives, have slept with a married man. According to a variety of sources, a good estimate is that one in three women have dated a married man. Some of those relationships were short-lived; some lasted for decades. A very few made it to marriage.

Sometimes It's Great . . . Sometimes It's Not

With all the turmoil an extramarital affair can bring, what keeps a married man returning to his Other Woman? And what makes a single woman keep returning to her married lover?

Apart from love, there are two very simple psychological principles at work that keep many women tied to unsatisfying relationships. These principles are *positive reinforcement* and *intermittent reinforcement*, both of which are described at length by the renowned psychologist Professor Albert Bandura in his classic book, *Principles of Behavior Modification* (1969).

The positive reinforcement principle means that we receive a reward for our behavior. For a woman in a relationship, the reward can be seeing her lover, talking to him, making love to him. If an activity makes her happy, she is likely to feel encouraged to invest more of herself in that activity in order to receive even more good feelings. The more a woman sees her lover and enjoys his company, the more frequently she will want to see him in the future. Her desire for more contact will follow. This is what leads her to start making "demands" on him.

Intermittent reinforcement theory holds that sometimes we win and sometimes we lose. In a relationship, intermittent reinforcement keeps both men and women putting more and more energy into that relationship because doing so rewards them—sometimes. *Sometimes* is the key here. When a relationship is *all bad*, people bolt. When it's *all good*, they get bored. But when it is *sometimes up, sometimes down*, they get hooked because they think the "good" must be just around the corner and they keep chasing after it.

A single woman stays with a married man, despite frequent lonely times and no promise of a future together, because *sometimes* things are great. A philandering man stays with a lover, despite the fear of discovery of the affair, because of *some* of the benefits he receives from doing so.

Intermittent reinforcement is so powerful it can keep people locked in unproductive patterns for years because they know from past experience that, at some point, a reward—such as feeling good—will be forthcoming. They don't know *when* it will come, so they hang on longer and longer, waiting. This is how otherwise intelligent women can stay for years with a married man who keeps promising to leave his wife but never does. The promise that he *will do it at some point* is still out there, and along the way they are getting goodies to keep them going.

In reality, only 15 percent of men will leave their wives, according to research by Dr. Jan Halper cited earlier, and even fewer will marry the woman they were involved with at the time they left. Still, many women wait around in false hope for a married man to leave his wife. And some women wait for decades, only to end up alone anyway.

Married . . . with Mistress

A mistress shouldn't strain the brain. She should strain the zipper.
— Anonymous

Many philandering men are happy to have another woman around for sex, pleasure, and companionship. What they don't want is hassles. Many have told me that "time bandits" are a respite from real life and from the demands of their wives and marriages.

As long as a mistress doesn't threaten the marriage, or impose too much pressure, an affair is likely to continue—sometimes for decades, and even through a man's multiple marriages! One man I spoke with had had the same "girlfriend" through three marriages and countless flings. Does his mistress enjoy banging her head against a brick wall? I wonder. He had the chance to marry her three times, and chose other women.

If you marry your mistress, you create a job vacancy.
— Businessman Sir James Goldsmith

The stories of married men returning to their wives, or of never leaving them to begin with, are much more abundant than the Other Woman success stories.

Most single women report extreme unhappiness in their affairs with married men. After the novelty and the euphoria wear off, they are often left feeling lonely and empty, even if the affair continues. Always taking second place to another woman and another relationship eats away at their self-confidence, much as it does when a wife learns of her husband's Other Woman. The only person who seems to benefit from a romantic triangle is the man. He has two women, a cozy home, and an erotic lust nest. Why would he want to make a choice to give one up unless he is backed into a corner?

Some of the "other women" I interviewed expressed regret at having devoted years of their lives to men who seem unconcerned about their welfare. One mistress reported that she stopped seeing married men after several painful experiences and one triggering event. "I stopped dating married men because I woke up and I got tired of waking up alone," she says. I have interviewed and received letters from many such women. They may steal something special from a married man's wife, but they rarely walk away with the man himself.

Is "Mistress" Synonymous with "Misery"?

There are few happy endings for women — whether married or single — who are involved with married men. Nikki's experience is all too common, and should serve as a wakeup call to women who are wasting their valuable time on men who will never be more than a fleeting sex partner.

Nikki's Story

A twice-divorced career woman, with one child from her first marriage, Nikki has been involved with a married business executive for the last few years. She sees him once or twice a week, and they travel together whenever they can.

He sometimes takes her to business-related social occasions, instead of his wife. Nikki says that some of his colleagues appear uncomfortable with this and don't know how to react to her. She's sure they are wondering if his wife knows about her and the affair. Nikki assumes the wife does know and is offended and upset by the situation. Still, Nikki hopes that one day her lover will leave his wife for her. She is beginning to become impatient, but she tries not to think about it too much because it only upsets her.

Nikki has accompanied her lover on out-of-town business trips many times, but she has to remain in the hotel on those occasions and is unable to accompany him to evening functions. She is starting to feel that the affair is futile. She loves him very much and believes they could have a happy life together. But her lover seems to be comfortable with the arrangement as it is and is in no hurry to change it.

Nikki knows that her lover has had other long-term girlfriends in the past, and that when they got too serious, he broke off with them. While he tells her his wife is boring, she is concerned because he seems to respect her and to feel a sense of responsibility toward her. Nikki also suspects that he has flings around town and when she doesn't accompany him on out-of-town trips.

Nikki has lately begun to question if the relationship is worth it. Even though she is a strikingly attractive and well-dressed fiftyish woman, she says her self-confidence is fading. She tells me she is worn out from all the deception and the lack of promises about the future. She doesn't know if she will stick with the affair. If she does, she says, she will also look for other men to date. She has focused her energy on her lover, and while her career is going well, she wants more from a relationship than her lover is willing to offer.

Though the probability that a man (or a woman) will divorce as the number of affairs they have increases, the majority of men (and women) don't divorce their spouse to be with a third party. The man usually moves from one affair and fling to another while remaining married. Even when a man *does* divorce his wife, he seldom marries his lover. Instead, he starts a new relationship with a fresh face. The double standard of looks, aging, and social status affects who cheats, who stays, and who leaves. Married women are at a disadvantage in the dating and professional spheres, so they naturally face greater difficulty in deciding whether to stay with a man who strays.

Any third party can be a real threat to a marriage, whether or not the philandering husband acknowledges that possibility. At the very least, another person makes life difficult for everyone involved. Three *is* a crowd.

Women who have sex with other women's husbands should be aware that if a man lies to his wife, he will certainly lie to his lover. Extramarital affairs are based on deceit. A solid marital relationship cannot be successfully built or maintained on such shaky ground.

TAKE NOTE

- If a man lies to his wife, he lies to his mistress.
- A man who strays usually cheats on his mistress with his wife.
- A man who strays usually cheats on his wife and his girlfriend.
- "Other women" give up valuable time in pursuit of another woman's man.
- Wives have many advantages over mistresses—they have home and hearth on their side. And a marriage license.
- Most men do not leave their wives for their girlfriends!

Chapter 6

Secrets and Lies: How Women Discover Their Husbands' Infidelities

He lied. She spied. The marriage died.

—*Dateline NBC*

Say it with flowers, and say it with mink, but never, ever, put it in ink.

—*Jimmy Durante*

"I DON'T WANT TO KNOW"

Not to know is bad. Not to wish to know is worse.

— NIGERIAN PROVERB

𝔐any women feel that if their husband must have affairs, they would rather not know about them. They don't want to contemplate the idea that their husband is having sex with another woman. If they acknowledge it is happening, they may feel they have to do something about it. As long as they can pretend it isn't happening, they can keep up the charade of their perfect marriage. Some women even tell their husbands to do what they want, as long as they do it out of sight, don't take up with a woman in their social set, and are discreet about it.

The problem with this head-in-the-sand coping technique is that whenever there is a third party involved, everything spins out of control. To paraphrase Diana, Princess of Wales, the marriage gets a bit crowded. No longer are there two people involved in protecting each other's feelings. Now a third party has an agenda, which is often to break up the marriage.

The driving force behind the "I don't want to know" stance is the desire to collude with a husband to cover up his affair(s). If a woman doesn't "know" about her husband's philanderings, she can then pretend everything is fine in her marriage. By colluding to cover up an affair, she doesn't have to decide on a course of action. If she chooses to confront a philandering spouse, she may have to decide whether to stay or leave, and for many women, this is just too anxiety-provoking. Instead, they bury their heads in the sand, using denial as a way of coping while hoping the situation will just disappear.

A betrayal by a spouse causes pain. The coverups actually double the pain, because then a woman is lying to herself as well as being lied to and cheated on by her husband. It is no surprise that many women tend to ignore the question of infidelity altogether. It can simply be too threatening for them to ponder. They figure they will leave well enough alone. For many women, the less they know about their husband's behavior with other women, the better. However, what they don't know can definitely hurt them. As Helen Gurley Brown says in her book *The Late Show* (1993): "I think having your man involved with another woman physically makes you feel about as bad as you can feel and you *always* know unless you have been living in a little hut, or have no girlfriends."

Women's Infidelity Radar

When a woman suspects that her husband is cheating on her, she is usually correct. Women are very astute at interpreting others' behavior, and they can detect even slight and subtle changes in a man's demeanor that scream, *"Affair!"* He may start being overly critical of her, or even accuse *her* of having an affair. There are always clues; but whether or not a woman chooses to take notice is another matter. Many women told me they suspect something is amiss in their marriages, but they are fearful of provoking a confrontation, or of being accused of being crazy or imagining things. Many couples have an unspoken agreement not to "speak of the unspeakable."

Far too many women want to ignore the clues and believe the lies their husbands tell them, because the truth is scary. At some point, however, women are usually forced to deal with what they have tried to avoid. With three people in a marriage, the truth becomes hard to hide and problems eventually arise. *One way or another, sooner or later, the wife always finds out.*

When a woman learns for sure that her husband is lying to her and cheating on her, she usually feels devastated. Perhaps for the first time, she is forced to contemplate the unthinkable about her husband and another woman. Many women's confidence is leveled by the realization that their husband may be involved with another woman.

THE TRUTH HURTS . . .
BUT SO DO SECRETS AND LIES

Extramarital sex *always* involves lies and deception. But at some point, the truth will come out. And the truth comes in many forms: audiotapes, videotapes, letters, faxes, diaries, gifts, receipts, newspaper headlines, and e-mails.

There is some truth in the saying, "The wife is always the last to know."

The reason is usually not that the wife hasn't picked up the warning signals, which may be obvious even to a neutral observer, but that she has *chosen to ignore them*.

It is extremely rare for men to admit to being unfaithful, even when they get caught. One man told me that even if his wife walked in on him having sex with his girlfriend, he would be able to talk his way out of it. One woman commented of her husband: "Women used to call him up at night and say, 'I'm in my black nightie, the champagne's on ice, come by.' He told me about it because he was hoping I'd understand."

Eventually, a man or woman almost always does find out that their partner is cheating. Stray receipts break trust, banish love, and often destroy marriages and careers. It is wise to follow one's instincts: If you suspect your spouse is straying, he probably is. *Trust but verify* is a useful motto to follow— or even *Mistrust and verify*! Trust him but keep your eyes open!

Clues That a Man Is Straying

Overall any major change of routine is a general tip-off that something may be going on. We are all creatures of habit, so a dramatic change in routine, habit, or in pursuing new adventures should raise a red flag for women:

- He begins exercising, especially jogging (he may be heading to another woman's house).

- He stops having sex with you, initiates more sex, or begins new sex behaviors.

- He starts watching what he eats or goes on a diet.

- He buys new clothes; switches from boxers to jocks, or even to nothing at all; changes from cotton to silk.

- He gets nervous when the phone rings. When he answers it, he speaks softly.

- He works late unusually often, and on weekends.

- He finds reasons to stay away overnight.

- If he travels for business, he won't share his itinerary, flight, or hotel information. He yells at you for asking where he will be and when he will return. He says he can't be reached.

- He goes off alone for periods during the weekend, giving some lame excuse.

- He gets nasty or defensive when you ask when he'll be home or where he's going.

- He begins misplacing credit card receipts, phone bills, etc.

- He gets his own phone line.

- He heads for the shower, or brushes his teeth, the minute he enters the house.

- He is unusually secretive about his schedule and the people he sees. He snaps at you when you show an interest, viewing your normal interest as an invasion of his privacy.

- When you phone him at work he won't take your calls, or he cuts you off. When you call him at work in the evening or on the weekend, he doesn't answer.

- He isn't where he says he's going to be.

- He stops taking you to job-related social events. If he does, his co-workers act differently toward you.

- He gives you jewelry or flowers, when he hasn't done so before. These are guilt-relieving presents.

- His moods are erratic. Living with him is like being on a roller coaster; you never know when he'll explode at you.

- He starts criticizing your looks.

- He starts reading books about sex.

- You receive strange phone calls, such as: "I think you should know about your husband."

- If he has worn a wedding band, he stops doing so.

- When you are out together, he seems more flirtatious than usual with other women. He notices women more.

- He starts doing his own laundry.

- He is overly protective of his wallet and briefcase.

- He no longer wants you to accompany him on out-of-town trips.

- He begins talking in his sleep and is generally more restless than usual.

- He starts making positive comments about one particular woman.

- He starts carrying condoms in his travel bag.

- He clams up and shuts down completely when you ask him anything about himself.

- He feels like a brick wall when you try to hug him.

- He stops being affectionate.

- He stays so far from you in bed at night that he almost falls out the other side.

- He begins sleeping in a spare bedroom, citing "sleep disturbances."

- He is unusually short-tempered and irritable.

- He seems distant from you and preoccupied most of the time.

- He tells you he needs his privacy and suggests you go away for a while.

- He is indifferent to you or ignores you completely.

- He is even less communicative than usual.

- He is unusually cold and distant.

- He spends Sundays and holidays in the office. (Remember the Oval Office!)

Actions Speak Louder Than Words

All the denials in the world won't erase what detectives call "physical evidence." Many "other women" want their lover's wife to find out about the affair, hoping it will break up the marriage. While a married man may believe his lover wants to keep "our little secret," he should not underestimate his girlfriend's desire to bring their relationship out in the open. And all it takes is a phone call, a letter — or a dropped earring if the husband is disrespectful enough toward his wife to have sex with someone else in the marital home.

Here are some of the items married women told me they have found in their marital bed or home, and the clues other women have intentionally left behind:

- bracelets and watches, especially engraved ones
- lace underpants stuck inside the pillowslip
- lipstick
- hairclips on the night table (the oldest trick in the book)
- a spray of perfume in the wife's closet
- the wife's underwear drawer or cosmetics rearranged
- semen stained clothing/dress
- condoms under the pillow
- lipstick stains on a handtowel
- food rearranged in the refrigerator
- a photo of the husband with the Other Woman
- photos of the house and marital bedroom sent in the mail to the wife
- spermicidal gel tube left in bathroom garbage can

Nora Ephron, the writer and director of the popular movies *When Harry Met Sally*, *Sleepless in Seattle*, and *You've Got Mail*, is also the author of a novel called *Heartburn* (1983) that was later made into a movie. The book and film are a thinly veiled tell-all about Ephron's marriage to former *Washington Post* Watergate journalist Carl Bernstein.

The story is a classic portrayal of a wife discovering her husband's infidelity. Meryl Streep plays Rachel, a magazine food writer, who marries Mark, a newspaper columnist, played by Jack Nicholson. While Rachel is pregnant with their second child, she discovers her husband is having an affair, *an emotional affair, not just a sexual one,* with a local socialite and wife of a diplomat, called Thelma Rice.

The realization that her husband is having an affair strikes Rachel while she is at the hairdresser. As her hair is being cut, her stylist is gossiping with another stylist about how she just learned her boyfriend was cheating on her. The words are like a switch for Rachel, and the light bulb in her head clicks on immediately. She jumps out of her chair and rushes home, where she finds the key to Mark's locked desk drawers and searches frantically through his receipts. She finds evidence in the form of hotel bills and flower receipts. As Ephron puts it: "There's never a good time to find out your husband is cheating on you—but pregnant must be the worst time!" Rachel confronts her husband with the evidence of his philandering. He is speechless and leaves the house immediately.

The reactions and emotions conveyed by the husband and wife in *Heartburn* are typical of many millions of couples confronting adultery.

When the Private Becomes Public

Two can keep a secret only if one is dead.

—JOAN COLLINS

Sex Lives and Friends with Audiotape

Many cases of infidelity are disclosed in videotapes, audiotapes, and letters, by speed cameras, newspaper photographers, airport security cameras, and television cameras, and, increasingly, on the Internet. Telephone redial buttons are a particularly common way for a woman to learn of her man's philandering.

Linda Tripp is probably the most notable current nightmare example of a person letting the entire world know about an extramarital affair. Monica was indiscreet in discussing an illicit liaison between herself and Bill Clinton, but Ms. Tripp was even more indiscreet by continuing to discuss the affair with Monica and by violating trust between friends in taping the conversations, and then sharing them with others.

Photographs and Love Letters

When an Italian magazine ran photographs of Princess Stephanie of Monaco's husband Daniel Ducruet romping naked with a beauty queen, it brought their marriage to an abrupt end. Was he set up? No one knows for sure. Whatever the case, he got caught on film, red-cheeked, with his pants down!

There's the case of a woman who is divorcing her husband after his photo appeared in a national newspaper with his arms around an attractive blonde. The two were hugging and kissing while walking in a public park on a beautiful day, and were snapped by a roving photographer who didn't realize they were in the midst of an extramarital liaison.

A similar incident occurred at a sporting event, when a television camera picked up a couple engaged in a passionate kiss. Their image was beamed to the large screen in the stadium, and to home viewers on the network carrying the game. The man's wife was at home loyally taping the event for him and saw his image on the screen. As one chronic philanderer told me, "When you are screwing on the side, and your wife finds out, which she inevitably will, you will know what it is to be totally screwed."

Not only mere mortals get tripped up by evidence. Wesley Hagood's book *Presidential Sex* reports that when President Franklin D. Roosevelt was ill with pneumonia, his wife Eleanor sorted his mail. While doing so, she was devastated to find love letters written to Franklin by her own secretary, Lucy. She reportedly confronted her husband, and he agreed to end the affair. However, he and Lucy allegedly continued their involvement for another thirty years, until his death in 1945.

The boss-secretary-wife triangle is a notoriously common nightmare. This is particularly difficult for a wife to handle because her husband sees the woman every day, and possibly every night, too. One woman learned about her husband's affair with his secretary when she called his office and heard from one of her husband's disapproving employees that the pair had taken off for a weekend of skiing when he was supposed to be going out of town to give a speech.

Extramarital affairs don't exist in a vacuum. Many people are willing to blow the whistle on a man and woman involved in an affair—just think of Linda Tripp! Where sex is concerned, there is no such thing as a secret. People love to gossip. *Everyone* has their own agenda, and many people want illicit lovers to be caught. "Friends don't audiotape friends" is a sentiment espoused but frequently violated. Letters, photos, audiotapes, and videotapes are telltale clues of extramarital dalliances that may find their way to an unsuspecting wife or husband. Where affairs are concerned, trust no one but yourself.

The Charles-Camilla-Diana Show

Learning about your husband's infidelity via a videotape is bad enough, but when that tape is viewed by millions of viewers around the globe, the humiliation moves to an even higher level.

On June 29, 1994, a British television show featured journalist Jonathan Dimbleby interviewing Prince Charles. During the interview Charles admitted that he was unfaithful to her only when the marriage had irretrievably broken down, in 1986. Diana was quoted as saying, "Part of me wanted him to say he had committed adultery, but the other half wanted him to deny it." The couple did not divorce until 1996—a full ten years later. Living with an unfaithful spouse is tough for most women to do for a day, let alone years.

Though Diana grabbed headlines in London's newspapers the next day with a glamorous photo of her in a sensational "Take that!" dress, she must have been devastated by her husband's confession. Even the most beautiful woman in the world can be emotionally undone by her husband's admission of adultery. Three proved to be too much of a crowd for that marriage.

Hearing It Through the Grapevine

Friends and enemies alike wonder whether they should disclose infidelity to a philanderer's spouse. Sometimes the motivation to do so is altruistic; other times it's downright nasty. Whichever the case, many women hear of their husband's affair through "the grapevine."

True friends may agonize over whether they should tell a friend they are being betrayed. Some people believe it is none of their business and decide to stay out of it. Others think how they would feel if their husband was carrying on all over town and nobody told them.

Sadly, women often shoot the messenger, meaning they lash out at the people who disclose their husband's infidelity, leaving well-meaning friends in the dust and attacking them for their "rudeness." In time, though, most women are grateful that a friend has cared enough to tell them about their philandering spouse. Even though they were hurt and angry at the time, the knowledge jolted them into action and helped them to reclaim their lives.

The F-Test

Some women who suspect their husband of cheating refuse to buy his "trust me" denials. If you want to know if the love of your life is getting cozy with someone else, help is available to you. Lately there has been a proliferation of private investigative agencies across the country offering services that allow you to check up on your partner. These services use a "decoy" female to approach your man and see how he reacts. Clients, the majority of whom are women, are given a chance to put their partner to the fidelity test, or F-test.

The F-test consists of an attractive woman posing as a decoy and flirting with the male target to test his willingness to engage in a sexual encounter. As the owner of one decoy agency commented, "It's alarming how quickly many men become willing to throw away their relationship for the promise of a no-strings-attached night of pleasure." One woman decoy claims that business and professional men are the most inclined to have affairs and to betray the trust in a relationship. She is quoted in *Elle* magazine as saying, "A lot of them think it's their right to have a loyal wife and a mistress."

On November 21, 1996, *Dateline NBC* presented a show called "Love, Lies and Videotape," which explained the fidelity test and how women decoys are used to catch married men who stray. Decoy and investigation services are becoming increasingly accepted as people realize that "other women"—and affairs—are the downfall of many marriages. As one woman said, "The decoy is the best friend any woman could have."

The owner of a decoy service said that in his experience, nine out of ten married men deny being married when they meet decoys. "I don't feel bad for the men. I feel bad for their wives, because they start thinking they're crazy." Many women who have used decoy services feel they have gotten their money's worth. Even for services costing $750 and up, women say they are buying piece of mind. Not every woman will decide to leave a man who is caught cheating or who flunks the fidelity test; but most believe they are much better off not being left in the dark about their husbands' extramarital activities.

Spying on Your Spouse

Women who have a "gut feeling"—but no proof—that their husband is straying have several options when it comes to confirming their suspicions.

One woman, Emma, who suspected her husband of having his girlfriend over to their home whenever she had an evening or weekend business meeting or dinner, decided to use a baby monitor to listen in on her husband. She told her husband she was going to dinner and a movie with a friend and would be back at midnight. That would give him five hours alone in the house.

Emma placed the transmitter part of the monitor under her pillow and took the receiver with her. She parked her car around the corner and walked to her backyard, where she sat quietly under a tree beneath the master bedroom. She got more than she expected. Not only could she hear very clearly from the open window that her husband was having sex, but she heard it over the monitor as well.

As devastated as Emma was, she was relieved to have her suspicions confirmed. Her husband had been lying to her and was even causing her to doubt her own perceptions. She felt vindicated. The baby monitor had saved her sanity.

Regularly going through her husband's wallet and briefcase gave Wendy peace of mind—when she didn't find evidence of a liaison. After her husband had had several affairs and then pledged "to behave," Wendy would regularly go through his wallet while her husband was in the shower. After an out-of-town trip, she would riffle through his briefcase. When she didn't find "clues to a tryst," as she called them, she would be elated. When she found condoms on more than one occasion, she went into a spiral of depression and vowed never to snoop again.

Since Wendy had decided to stay with her husband on the understanding that he had ceased his philandering, she wanted "proof" that he was living up to his word. Understandably, her trust was shattered, and she was trying to rebuild it by verifying his word. Once she found telltale evidence that caused her yet again to doubt him, Wendy stopped searching her husband's personal belongings. She had decided to stay married and she realized that she was going to have to ignore evidence of affairs. The only way to do this was to accept what her husband told her and cease snooping. For Wendy, knowing—but not really knowing—was the way she chose to cope with her marriage and her husband's occasional unfaithfulness.

Learning that the man you love is having sex with another woman is never an easy situation. The truth hurts, but it can also heal. Not knowing about your husband's affair will almost always hurt you more in the long run.

Secrets and lies are not the way to nurture a vital, loving, caring, close, and thriving marriage. Once a woman learns about her husband's affair, she will face the next steps in her journey as the mate of a philanderer. At some stage, every woman married to an unfaithful man will ask herself two questions: *Why* should I stay with a man who strays? *How* will I stay with a man who strays?

TAKE NOTE

- It is much better to know that your husband is having an affair than it is to pretend it is not happening. Information is power. Denial and other self-delusions, in the end, only delay the inevitable.

- More information—and sooner rather than later—is best.

- Forewarned is forearmed. Finding out details of your husband's dalliances will help you prepare your stance.

- Stray receipts and telephone redials are common ways women learn of affairs.

- If you have a suspicion your man is straying—he probably is.

- Don't hesitate to check up on your man if you think he is having an affair. You must protect yourself emotionally, physically, financially and psychologically from his infidelity.

Part Two

STAYING TRUE TO ONESELF WHILE STAYING WITH A STRAYING SPOUSE

Chapter 7

WHY WOMEN STAY WITH MEN WHO STRAY

I'm not sitting here because I'm some little woman standing by my man, like Tammy Wynette. I'm here because I love him and I respect him and I honor what he's been through and what we've been through together.

—*Hillary Clinton on* 60 Minutes, *January 27, 1992*

I'd rather not be married to someone who doesn't love me enough to be faithful.

—*Alice Starr in* Ladies' Home Journal, *March 1999*

SAINT OR SUCKER?

The first question people generally ask themselves when they learn of an extramarital affair is: "Does his wife know?" Their second question is often: "*Why* is she staying with him?"

A betrayed woman faces a firestorm of criticism—no matter how she reacts. She is scorned by men and women alike for staying and tolerating the adultery. "Hasn't she any self-respect?" they wonder aloud. Often she is criticized, too, for not being able to keep her man from straying or even for "driving him to it." On the other hand, if a woman leaves her philandering husband, she likely endures criticism for *not* standing loyally by her man and for abandoning him at a difficult time.

It seems that however a woman copes with a philandering husband, she will be a lightning rod for controversy. It is little wonder, then, that women themselves question what course of action they should take when they learn of their husband's extramarital dalliances. While most of the women I interviewed hadn't wanted to know if their husband was unfaithful, all of them eventually found out. Even then, most of them wanted to pretend the infidelity hadn't taken place. Almost all the women who participated in my research initially sought refuge in denial. When they were finally forced to confront their husband's philandering, they inevitably asked themselves: *Should I stay with him, or should I leave?* It is a most painful question to ponder, because no one wants to leave the man they love—and least of all to hand him over to another woman—without putting up a good fight.

When women finally acknowledge to themselves that their man is indeed having an affair, they usually feel like they've been "hit by a brick," "run over by a truck," or, as Elizabeth Hurley described it, "shot." Here is how one woman, Victoria, put it:

When the light finally went on and I realized why Ken was acting so distant and hardly ever touched me anymore, I knew. I felt like I was totally alone. I was jealous of whoever it was he was sleeping with and showering attention on. I vowed to find her and confront her. She was going to pay for interfering in my marriage. My heart sank. I moved from tears to terror and back again. My trust was shattered, and I felt like I was being swept out to sea. My love scattered into a million tiny pieces. When I snooped and found out the details of Ken's affair, and that it was his secretary he was sleeping with, I was sadder still. To think that he went off to her every morning after sharing a bed with me. Every time he leaves for work, or even goes out of the house, I know he must be going to see her. I doubt his every word. Even though I haven't yet approached him about his affair, his infidelity has already changed everything for me. Some days I hate him, and other times I still adore him. Before I talk to him, I want my feelings to calm down to some sense of rationality.

Most of all, I want him to stop seeing her, but I'm afraid if I confront him, he'll drop me instead of her. I want to rebuild our marriage without a third party. I believed we had a loving and solid marriage. How could he do this to me?

Victoria was at once shocked and shamed by her husband's infidelity. But, like millions of women, she didn't want the marriage to end. She just wanted the other woman out of the triangle so that she and her husband could get their marriage back on track.

Many women react similarly to Victoria. They initially blame the other woman for their husband's affair, despite its taking two to tango, saying that if the woman had stayed away from him, the affair wouldn't have happened. Or they blame themselves or otherwise excuse their husband's bad behavior. Blaming their husband is, initially, too anxiety-provoking.

Although most married women say they want their husband to end his affair, increasing numbers of men are either refusing to do so or are "taking them underground" by being extra sneaky and discreet. One woman I interviewed confided that when she begged her husband to stop sleeping with one of his coworkers, he just ordered her to stay out of his sex life:

It's as though he's two people—the nice family man, and the oversexed, suave playboy at the office. It disgusts me. I'm so disillusioned and lonely that I don't know what to do. I'm annoyed with him, but I'm furious with her. Why can't she find a man of her own? I wish she would get fired. So many women in the workforce today go after married men—they tempt the men too much. I wish she would get tripped up and charged with sexual harassment. Have women no respect for another woman's marriage? Just wait until she gets married. I hope every pretty, twentysomething girl sets their sights on her man.

DEGREES OF INFIDELITY

While the notion of "a little infidelity" is an outrageous thought for most women to even contemplate, many do, in fact, react differently to a husband's unfaithfulness depending on his degree of involvement with the other woman.

Many women don't consider a one-night fling with a stranger in a distant city as being as hurtful to them as would be an ongoing, emotional relationship with a woman who is "right under their nose," such as someone in their own social set. Though none of the women I spoke with willingly approved of *any* sort of extramarital sexual activity, if forced to deal with the situation, they said it would be much more difficult to cope with a husband's perpetual philandering than with a casual, out-of-town or one-time fling.

In France, and to a lesser extent among the British upper classes, having a mistress is common. The wife often recognizes the situation and discreetly overlooks it, while resting assured that her husband won't leave her. She looks after the family and turns her head to her husband's dalliances. She may even have ultra-discreet affairs herself. However, I recently asked a French businessman who travels frequently to America if his wife knew about and condoned his affairs. He said she had no idea that he indulged in extramarital activities, and if she ever found out, she would leave him. He said that she reminded him of this often, and he believed if she ever *did* discover his mistresses, she would, in fact, leave the marriage. Still, he doesn't curb his philandering.

WHY DO WOMEN STAY WITH MEN WHO STRAY?

Since most women don't want to share their beloved with another woman, why, then, do they stay with a man they know is having sex with someone else? And why do they stay when he is emotionally involved with another woman?

A woman stays married to an unfaithful husband for essentially the same reasons she married him in the first place. Women stay with men who stray for *personal*, *social*, and *financial* reasons. Quite simply, women want to be married and have a family, and many see their entire adult identity as merged into the role of wife and mother. Whatever many women strive for or achieve careerwise, they still relish their roles as wife and mother. While a woman doesn't want her husband sleeping around, she often stays when he *does* stray because she reasons that a bad marriage is better than no marriage at all. Millions of women settle for "crumbs" instead of insisting on the "entire loaf," even when the price is staying with a philandering spouse.

A few years ago I attended a seminar on relationships given by a self-proclaimed "love doctor." A woman in the audience asked a question of the so-called expert: "My husband keeps having affairs. What can I do? It's driving me crazy and I'm losing my self-esteem." The love doctor replied, "Dump him. Next question?"

The woman who had posed the question was left stunned and bewildered. She was looking for some support for her plight, and constructive advice on how to solve her problem; instead, she was left feeling embarrassed that she had opened up on such a painful topic—as well as cheated of the several hundred dollars she had paid to attend the seminar. She needed validation that it was okay to feel bad about an unfaithful husband. She also needed encouragement to evaluate her options, as well as practical advice on how to prepare for the ending of her marriage. She got none of it. Her plea for support and help was dismissed outright.

As this example shows, it is very easy to tell a woman to dump her philandering husband. It is much, much harder for a woman actually to carry out the actions necessary to prepare herself emotionally to leave him.

Most women want to get married and stay married. They just want the extramarital dalliances to cease. They don't want to disentangle their entire lives. They love their husband and want to stay married.

As I said, women stay with a straying husband for personal, social, and financial reasons. But, at some point, many women ask themselves: *"How could I have stayed? And how could I have stayed so long?"*

Personal Reasons

According to several polls, only three out of every ten women say they would leave their marriage if their husband was unfaithful. The longer women were married, the more likely they were to stay married, even when faced with a philandering husband. The women in the survey gave as their reasons for staying: they feared loss of love more than they objected to their husband having sex with another woman, and they loved their husband.

The results of this survey underscore the importance women place on love, and more importantly, the *loss* of love. Women felt that giving up a marriage meant loss of love, whereas a straying husband didn't necessarily mean they were losing their mate's love.

Personal Reasons Why Women Stay With a Straying Husband

- They love their husband.
- They love their children.
- They love their family life.
- They enjoy their lifestyle.
- They don't want to hand their husband over to another woman.
- All men cheat, so why divorce?
- They won't ever find anyone else they could love, and who would love them in return.
- The personal arrangement suits the wife and her husband. He pur-

sues his career, and she enjoys the benefits of his success. ("He cheats, I shop" type of bargain.)

The intensely personal reasons why a woman stays with a philandering man revolve around the deep feelings she has for her man and for her marriage. A woman doesn't want to give up on a marriage that means the world to her, just because some other woman has temporarily lured away her husband. A wife may feel somewhat superior and able to dismiss the Other Woman: "She may have sex with him, but my name is on the mortgage." Or: "She gets occasional sex with him, but I have all of him."

A refrain I heard over and over from women who have stayed with a philandering husband was, "I stay because I love him." Great; love is wonderful. But have these women asked themselves this vital question: *Does a man show love to his wife by cheating on her and deceiving her?*

One sixty-year-old woman told me she felt strongly about her marriage vows: "I made a commitment to this marriage, and I never intend to break it. What he does is his responsibility, but I want to make my marriage work at all costs." Devotion to "love," and to the institution of marriage, is a powerful and often inexplicable factor in many women's decision to stay with a straying husband. Even the Princess of Wales told BBC journalist Martin Bashir in a November 1995 television interview that she didn't want a divorce from Prince Charles. In the interview, which was beamed around the globe, Diana said: "I desperately wanted my marriage to work. I desperately loved my husband . . ."

Another overriding personal reason women give for staying with a man who strays is: "For the sake of the children." Most women simply don't want to break up their family. Of course, many use the children as an excuse for all sorts of things, and staying with an unfaithful man is one of them. While divorce is difficult for all involved, there is no real evidence that children are better off in a home with fighting parents, and a lying, deceitful, philandering father, than they would be living with one parent. One unhappily married woman I spoke with said:

I have pitied my mother for how she stood by and let my father walk all over her. She was probably staying with him for us, but she would have been better off if she had kicked him out. I don't trust men because of the way my father lied to my mother, and this gives me trouble every day in my marriage. But I have trouble dealing with women, too, because my mother acted like such a wimp.

A woman who stays with a man who strays does so at great personal and emotional costs to herself. Just because a woman decides to tolerate infidelity in order to keep her marriage intact, it doesn't guarantee that her husband will not leave *her*.

Several women I spoke with told of being dumped for another woman after they had stuck by a philandering husband for years. Not only had these women gone against their own instincts by putting up with behavior they abhorred, but in the end, they were cast aside after showing love and devotion to their mate. These women suffered emotional abuse, humiliation, lack of emotional—and often sexual—closeness with their husbands, and risked contracting sexually transmitted diseases for years, with the sole purpose of staying married. Yet their efforts were in vain. Now, in their fifties and sixties, many of the women are alone, with little prospect of finding a job or a new man. And many of them are devastated that they gave away the best years of their lives to men who cheated on them. They blame themselves for not waking up and taking action sooner.

If a woman decides to wait for her husband to give up an affair, she is, in fact, enabling, condoning, and tolerating his infidelity. If she is to move out of this "wait-and-see" purgatory, she must decide what *she* wants, and then take action. No one forces a woman to stay with a man who strays. No matter how compelling a woman's personal reasons for staying may be, she may end up wasting years of her life on someone who will eventually leave her.

Social Reasons

It is no big secret that there aren't equal social opportunities for women in this world. A woman's adult role is still assumed to be connected in some way to a man's life. Many women I spoke with—even those in their thirties—firmly believe that they are nothing without a man. More women than we realize define their adult identity by their marital status. There may be fewer marriages these days, but it seems most women still aspire to what they see as the "higher plateau" of marriage. Every single woman I spoke with told me she wanted to be "chosen"—meaning married; and the married women said they wanted to stay the "chosen one"—at almost any cost, including sometimes putting up with their husband seeing another woman.

Social Reasons Why Women Stay with a Straying Husband

- Unequal opportunities for divorced women.
- Loss of status following divorce.
- Loss of lifestyle following divorce.
- Poor prospects for meeting someone new.
- Fear of becoming socially invisible.
- Divorced women seen as "damaged goods."
- Women of a certain social stature "need" a husband.
- Humiliating to give in to another woman.
- Societal pressure to endure husband's infidelity and silently "stand by her man."

Women list many social factors in their decision to stay with a straying mate. These include the stigma of divorce. While more couples are divorcing these days, many people still feel branded with a big "D" on their forehead. Divorced people, including men, are often looked down upon for not being able to make their marriage work. As one man told me, "It's one thing to fool around; it's another thing to leave your wife." Obviously, some women feel the same way.

One woman's comment to me was reiterated many times in the course of researching this book:

All men cheat. At least I have a nice lifestyle. Why would I want to turn him in for another man, who will also cheat on me and who probably could never provide me with what I have now? I would have to be crazy to turn him over to his bed partners. I'm his number one, no matter how many women he has flings with. He'd never leave his family. We mean too much to him. And I certainly am not going to ruin my life by kicking him out — for what? Another man who could never measure up to him?

Many women spoke of the nightmare of having to face the social scene if they divorced their husband. Here is Megan's reaction:

All things considered, I don't think a man who has out-of-towners is all that bad. As long as he keeps it away from me. The thought of being a fifty-year-old woman alone on the dating scene is too much for me to handle. I guess it's the lesser of two evils. I have a decent life with a man I adore, even though at times I feel like cutting off his testicles. I could never love a man as much as I love Harry. We have some kind of special attachment to each other, in spite of his on-and-off philanderings over our twenty-year marriage. Let's face it, twenty years is a big investment in a person. I'm not going to send it down the drain.

I hear horror stories all the time of divorced women my age trying to meet new men. It sickens me. I couldn't bear it. Most men are real losers, real sex addicts. I count my blessings. Things could be much worse. I feel sorry for women who are alone, and I surely don't want to be like them. I avoid those women, because I'm so fearful of the kind of lives they have. They seem so very desperate for love and affection. I guess they are bitter. Hell, I'm bitter too, but at least I'm married. At least my husband comes home to me most nights.

I really hate that he cheats on me. But I hate lots of things and I have to live with them anyway. For me, it really is the lesser of two evils.

Megan's comments are representative of many of the women I spoke with. They thank God for what they have, rather than hoping in vain for their husband to quit having affairs. Women don't want to rock the boat, lest they lose the marriage altogether. For them, their status and lifestyle — their entire life — is wrapped up in being Mrs. So-and-So.

Such motivations are strong, particularly when people read the dire statistics about women over forty trying to meet eligible men. The slim pickings on the social scene for divorced women with children, or for women over fifty, convince many to stick by their man regardless of how appalled they are by his philandering behavior. The truth is, the pickings on the dating scene for divorced women over forty-five, especially if they aren't particularly attractive and/or have children, *are* slim. These women are less likely to remarry, some out of choice, but mostly because of the dearth of suitable men.

An abundance of research—including Susan Faludi's landmark *BackLash: The Undeclared War Against American Women* (1991) and *The Janus Report on Sexual Behavior*—points out the tremendous difficulty for women over fifty who are looking for men to date and marry. One problem is the old double standard of looks and age. Men tend to marry women younger than themselves: a fifty-year-old man will be sought after by women aged twenty-five all the way up the age ladder. A fifty-year-old woman, by contrast, will have difficulty finding even a man her own age to date. She may have to look for a sixty-year-old; but since men tend to die younger than women, there is a shortage of men in the older age groups. For every hundred women in the sixty-plus age bracket, there are probably forty men.

Given the dire circumstances in the dating and sexual arena that await middle-aged women who leave a marriage, it is no surprise that many of them choose to stay married to men who stray. Even if they are insulted and humiliated by their husband's infidelity, many see it as a better alternative than being divorced and alone. As Anna explained:

I have some leverage over the hordes of pretty young women who throw themselves at my husband only because of our long, basically happy history together. If I were to have to compete with them on the singles scene, though, I would come in dead last. Let's face it, a woman over fifty with stretch marks isn't as appealing to a man as a nubile and adoring thirty-year-old—unless he shares a mortgage and stands to lose half his wealth! I would have to be nuts to let go of what I have. Yes, I wish my man would keep his dick in his pants and out from under strange women's skirts. But I'm thankful he stays with me when he really does have so many opportunities to go elsewhere. In some strange way, I feel lucky that I'm the woman married to him.

Another woman put it this way:

The minute anyone hears that a marriage is in trouble, the woman might as well have leprosy. Everyone will avoid her and stick like Velcro to the man. Nobody wants an unattached woman around. It reminds other women that they may suffer a similar fate, and it also makes women uneasy that you may be going after their husband.

Social opportunities and social conditioning are powerful reasons why women stay with men who stray. Women seldom see what they have to gain from divorcing a straying man, but they are very aware of what they would lose by doing so.

Some women don't believe they deserve any better treatment than a man who lies to them and deceives them, which is what infidelity really means. Many women have such low self-esteem they can't see past their immediate situation and cannot believe they could improve their lives, and themselves, by leaving a straying spouse. Women often tolerate a lot of bad behavior from a husband, all in the name of staying married. As Maris, a thirty-five-year-old executive, confessed: "If my husband would apologize to me for his affair, and tell me he still loves me more than her, then I would stay with him, even if he keeps seeing her."

Social reasons for standing by a man can kick in even before marriage, as they did for Danielle, a thirty-five-year-old fashion writer. The night before her wedding, James shoved a prenuptial agreement under her nose, saying he would refuse to marry her if she didn't sign it. The document included a clause saying that he couldn't promise he would be faithful, and that if he left her for another woman, she would receive no financial settlement. Distraught, but in love, Danielle signed the agreement and has regretted it ever since. Five years into her marriage, she is lonely and constantly worrying about James and the women he interacts with. She is certain she will lose him, and also will end up with nothing for the time and love she has devoted to him. She is thinking about leaving him now before he abandons her. She figures she is still young enough and attractive enough to meet a man who will respect her feelings and want to love her, and her alone.

Over and over, I heard women say they would feel adrift without a man in their life—especially, and justifiably, after a long period of marriage. One woman said, "I need my husband as an anchor." Another said, "John is the oxygen that gives me life. I would be lost without him. His philandering is a small price to pay." The social structure of relationships and society encourages women to marry, and to stay married, in spite of a philandering spouse. While women dislike a cheating husband, they dislike the thought of divorce even more. Such a situation forces women into an uncomfortable predicament. Social opportunities favor men, and are particularly lacking for women of a certain age.

Most divorces these days are initiated by women; yet many women stay married and tolerate infidelity. Some women prefer the A-word—adultery—to the D-word—divorce. Though they would all like the M-word—monogamy—most of all.

Financial Reasons

Unequal social opportunities are one strong reason why women stay with men who stray, but financial concerns are an even stronger reason women cling to a faltering marriage. Since the majority of women earn less money than their husbands, marriage is a financial lifeboat for most. When a man strays, women fear they will be abandoned, and lose their lifestyle along with their marriage. For many women, a dissolved marriage means financial disaster.

Financial Reasons Why Women Stay with a Straying Husband

- Out of financial necessity.
- Women's financial standing often decreases after divorce.
- Unequal career opportunities for women.
- Gave up career for marriage years ago.

A study carried out over a decade ago by Dr. Lenore Weitzman, outlined in her book *The Divorce Revolution* (1985), claimed that, after divorce, a woman's financial standing goes down approximately 72 percent while a man's increases about 42 percent. While her book was controversial, it is clear a discrepancy exists between many ex-wives and their husbands' financial status; just compare where they live, what they drive, and where they vacation!

A woman's post-divorce financial situation often worsens, while a man's improves because many women are full-time housewives, and others are part-time workers. According to the 1996 Census Bureau reports, even women employed full time in professional careers earn less money than men. In a divorce, a husband walks away with the greater earning potential, leaving the wife to pick up the pieces.

Most women are aware of their precarious financial standing and all too aware that, without their husband, they are, as one woman described it, "one man away from poverty." Or, for some women, one man away from middle class.

Financial concerns are not only a worry for working-class women; even women in high-income families are concerned about their financial stability if they should divorce. It is no secret that there are very unequal career opportunities for women. How many women do you see heading companies, or in high-level government posts? How many women are in the Forbes 400? Not many. The ugly truth is, even when women are employed, most of the female population rely on their husband and their marriage for financial stability.

When men occupy most of the high-paying jobs, women face blocked career opportunities. Financial survival becomes a real factor for women married to men who philander, because if the husband decides to leave the wife, the household will be rocked in more ways than one.

Men benefit in a variety of financial ways in which women don't, in part because more women than men work part time or not at all. Women's childbearing and childrearing decisions often mean that they work part time, thus earning less than full-time workers. Women, even if they do work, are still the primary caregivers, and this is as true today as it was twenty years ago. It is unlikely to change, and a woman's role as a mother is one reason she fares so poorly economically.

Looking around America today, it is evident that some women, even if they are employed, are still financially dependent on a man. So when a man strays, and a woman must contemplate whether or not she is going to stay with him, her financial situation is one of the first things she thinks about. Many women I spoke with wanted to keep their marriage together because of love and financial necessity. While the women said they loved their husband, they also realized that leaving him would mean leaving their lifestyle. Married women are loath to give up their lifestyle and let another woman waltz into their place. Here is how one woman sees it:

Look, sex, is sex. Christopher is not even remotely good in bed. We have sex, but mostly I tolerate that aspect of life with him anyway. What, maybe twenty minutes three times a week? Why would I give up the good parts of him because of sex? How crazy. If he gets sex elsewhere, so what? As long as he still loves me and we share an entire life together, I won't leave him because he has nooners.

Frequently it is status and money, as well as love, that keeps many women staying with a strayer. As one prominent lawyer's wife told me, "As soon as you're not the wife of Mr. Big Shot anymore, you are persona non grata."

Generally speaking, the more financially independent a woman is, the less likely she is to tolerate a man who strays. If a woman can walk from a marriage without feeling the financial squeeze, then she is more likely to divorce. However, personal and social reasons may be more important than financial considerations in a woman's decision to stay. Such is the case with Serena, an up-and-coming architect. She earns more money than her husband—in fact, she supports him. He is an unemployed musician, and he cheats on her constantly. Still, she "adores" him, and while his dalliances bother her, she has no plans to leave him, even though she clearly is in a financial position to do so. In Serena's case, her personal feelings override other considerations in staying with a philanderer.

The more money a man can offer a woman, the less likely she is to give up the relationship, provided love is also in the picture. Financial worries are a fact of life for most women, and the dilemma is this: should I stay with a straying spouse and have a decent lifestyle, or should I divorce him even though I will end up alone and with less money? For the majority of women, the answer is a no-brainer: *Stay!* Love is a powerful motivator for tolerating a straying husband. So is financial necessity. But one must wonder what emotional cost a woman pays for staying.

Divorce is generally financially devastating for any couple. For a middle-aged woman, it can be downright traumatic — emotionally, socially, and particularly financially. Most women would prefer a monogamous marriage. However, life is rarely as we want it, so each woman must make her own decision about staying with an unfaithful husband. One thing is for sure: if she decides to stay, a rough road awaits her. She must figure out *how* she can tolerate living with her husband's sexual, and perhaps emotional, involvement with another woman.

TAKE NOTE

- Women stand by a philandering man for a variety of personal, social, and financial reasons.

- A woman who stays with a man who strays is not a doormat. She is doing what she believes is best for her individual situation.

- The bond between two married people can't often be interpreted by observers of the marriage. The people in the marriage must determine the ground rules for their marriage.

- *Why* does she stay? Because she wants to. *Why* does he stray? Because he wants to.

- Even financially independent women stay with men who stray.

- Love may or may not conquer all, but it is a glue keeping many women in marriage.

Chapter 8

How Women Stay with Men Who Stray

We know everything there is to know about each other, and we understand and accept and love each other.

—*Hillary Clinton to Matt Lauer on* The Today Show, *January 27, 1998*

Hillary Clinton is a litigator. She gets up every morning and fights for her case. Bill Clinton is her case.

—*David Maraniss to Tom Brokaw on MSNBC Television, September 12, 1998*

STANDING BY YOUR MAN—
EASIER SAID THAN DONE

*O*nce a woman finds out her husband is being unfaithful, she faces a set of challenges: Will she stand by him and the marriage, or will she leave? If she decides to stay, she must then figure out how she will live each and every day with a man she knows is sexually, and possibly emotionally, involved with another woman.

Being married to a man who is involved with another woman is a heavy burden for any woman to carry. Women interviewed for this book said they wondered how they would possibly be able to handle the double life their husband led—married to one woman, yet romancing another. Trying to make a marriage work as part of a crowd is a difficult, if not impossible, task to accomplish. As Chelsea, a forty-one-year-old woman, described it:

I can't possibly allow myself to think of him with that woman. If I do, I become so jealous I can't function. I have to blot out all thoughts of my husband—both good and bad ones—or I can't go about my everyday life. Just thinking of him draws my rage. I don't want to share him with anyone. That's not what I want at all. But if I don't go along with him, I'm afraid I'll lose him altogether. I'm afraid I'll lose the one man I have ever loved deeply. It makes me physically ill to think of him doing the same things sexually with her that he shares with me. I'm confused about whether I should continue sleeping with him. I don't want to, because I'm annoyed with him for cheating on me. I worry, though, that if I don't have sex with him, he'll surely leave me for her. When we do have sex, I try to make it the best I can. I guess I'm trying to show him he doesn't have to look elsewhere for sex.

This is the worst situation I could ever imagine. Maybe divorce is better than this constant checking up on him, wondering when he is lying to me. He is hurting me and our marriage so much, perhaps it will be best to give him up and end my suffering. Sharing him is killing me, but I don't want to send him off to her. He's my husband and I don't want to give him up to a slut who is trying to steal him from me and ruin our life together. How can he do this to me?

Chelsea's experience was echoed time and time again in the course of my interviews. Women's experiences clearly show the huge emotional — and possibly physical — costs a woman pays for standing by a philandering husband.

Women use a variety of coping strategies to retain their sense of confidence while remaining married to a straying husband. None of those I spoke with approved of or encouraged their husbands' extramarital affairs. In fact, many of them had begged their spouses to give up cheating. Not every woman confronts her husband about his affairs; but those who do often find that their attempts to convince their husband to stop seeing another woman fall on deaf ears. These women realize they then have a choice between staying married and trying to tolerate the philandering, and leaving the marriage. Many women choose to stay with their unfaithful husband and find some way to live within the dreaded triangle.

STRATEGIES FOR COPING

Denial: Hear No Evil, See No Evil. . . .

Coping strategies women use to stay with a man who strays include *denial, self-delusion,* and *collusion* with the philanderer. These defense mechanisms help a woman pretend the situation isn't really happening. By denying the existence of another woman in her husband's life, she is attempting to obliterate the pain her husband's behavior causes her. As Kim explained:

I won't go anywhere where I might run into his whore. We live in a small town, and he works with Kelly [the other woman]. I refuse to go to his office functions, so our social life is suffering. I fear that when I stay home and he goes to functions without me, I'm pushing him to her, but it's just too difficult for me to see her and know she shares a part of the man I love. Plus, the office knows about the affair, so I want to avoid those people, too. It's pure torture for me to go about my business in town. One day I was at the cinema with our nine-year-old daughter, and she ended up a few rows behind us with her girlfriend. The theater was very empty, so I felt her eyes burning into me the entire two hours. I don't know why I felt bad, because, after all, I'm his wife. She's the tramp sticking her nose in our life and going after a married man. still, I couldn't—and still can't—shake the knowledge that she is a wedge coming between my husband and me. I desperately want my husband to be faithful. We have a lovely daughter and an otherwise calm and charmed life. I don't know why he needs to see her. She's not even attractive!

I don't want to lose the part of him I have, so I'm forced to share him with another woman. A disgusting woman at that. It makes me sick every day. How I'll live with this situation long term I don't know. It's already nearly two years. I'm so depressed. Each day is a real struggle. I feel like taking to my bed and never leaving it.

Kim has chosen to try to ignore a situation that is unbearable. But as much as a woman tries to ignore the Other Woman and her husband's affair, it's often difficult not to notice and be angered by the triangle.

Denial is a way of trying to ignore a situation we find too painful to deal with. However, not wanting to deal with a problem won't make it go away. When emotions are suppressed, psychosomatic reactions often occur, such as migraine headaches, stomach and gastrointestinal upsets, eating and sleep disturbances, and so on. The body knows when the mind is upset.

When she can no longer deny the fact that her husband is seeing another woman, perhaps after catching them together, a woman often deludes herself about the causes of the problem. She may rationalize that "the Other Woman pushed him into it," or "it's only temporary."

Another way women cope with a straying husband is by colluding with him. When a woman colludes with her philandering husband, she keeps quiet and pretends not to know what's going on, even though it is painfully obvious that she knows about his cheating. By being passive, she allows him to do what he wants out of a fear that if she confronts him about his affair, her marriage will end.

Many women simply don't want to rock the boat, and usually a marriage encounters difficulties only after a woman acknowledges to her husband that she knows of his philandering. It then becomes a make-or-break issue, as the secret is out in the open. When colluding, or "enabling," stops, it's time to act and to do something about the affair—and the marriage. Women dread getting to this point, so they keep quiet and allow their husband to go on with his affair believing his wife is "in the dark."

Confront and Conquer

Another way women try to handle an infidelity triangle is by confronting the "Other Woman." This can prove tricky, for the Other Woman inevitably runs to her lover about the confrontation. Often, the married man takes the side of his lover, further enraging and devastating his wife. One woman described how she waited for her husband's mistress outside her office one day and followed her down the street, shouting: "You're just like all the rest! He does this all the time, and he still stays with me. You'll end up just like his other girls!" When her husband heard about the encounter, he moved out of their bedroom into the guestroom. However, the other woman soon ended the affair, saying her lover's wife was making her life a misery.

Women can be driven to distraction by their husband's affairs and do things they wouldn't normally do. One woman followed her husband's lover for two weeks. Another got drunk at her husband's office Christmas party and threatened the young coworker he was having an affair with, saying: "If you don't stop seeing my husband, you'll never work in this town again!"

Women are quick to blame other women for trying to poach their husband. Many I spoke with said their husband would never make the overtures to begin an affair, but would respond if a woman approached him. Wives blame other women for setting their sights on a married man, claiming that such women have no respect for marriage, or for other women. According to Andrew Morton's 1997 book, *Diana*, Princess Diana confronted her husband's lover, Camilla Parker Bowles, saying: "I would just like you to know that I know exactly what is going on between you and Charles . . . don't treat me like an idiot." While the confrontation didn't spark a breakup of the affair, it made Diana feel better. "The next morning when I woke up I felt a tremendous shift. I'd done something, said what I felt. Still the old jealousy and anger swilling around, but it wasn't so deadly."

Many women feel relieved once they confront their husband and/or the Other Woman. Being able to express their anger, rage, hostility, and jealousy frees them emotionally and enables them to deal with the situation more effectively and realistically. When a woman confronts her husband's lover, she is often trying to let the other woman know who is the boss. In a way, she is asserting the power that derives from her unique status as the wife. Sometimes this is enough to get the other woman to back off. However, it can also go the other way, with the other woman declaring all-out war and doubling her efforts to break up the marriage and have the man for herself.

The "woman-to-woman" confrontation can get very ugly, as many men who have been caught in the middle confirm. Others relish the thrill — and ego boost — of having their wife and their lover fight over them. These men are likely to use their leverage to taunt both women.

Some women I talked with described taking direct action to compete with their husband's lover for his affection. They endured plastic surgery, went on crash diets, and spent thousands of dollars on skimpy lingerie in an attempt to keep their man. However, many said they ended up feeling even more depressed and humiliated by these attempts to compete with another woman for their husband's attention.

Sometimes their efforts backfired, as was the case with thirty-five-year-old Sarah. One night when Sarah overheard her husband on the phone, she sensed he was talking to another woman. For months, she had suspected something was amiss. Oliver had been working later, and there had been numerous hang-up calls at home in the middle of the night. Sarah describes her devastating experience:

I realized he was having an affair, so I stopped having sex with him for a few weeks. I thought he would stop the affair and return to me after I told him I knew about his activities. He was stunned when I confronted him, but he neither denied nor confirmed the affair.

I began to feel guilty for not sleeping with him, and I really missed cuddling with him at night. I decided I was going to woo him big time, even more than I usually did. I had a complete makeover at a day spa and met him at the door that night wearing sexy new lingerie. I wanted to do everything I thought his new lover must have been doing for him.

When he saw me at the door, he just pushed me aside and laughed at me. I felt totally humiliated. I felt like such a fool that I haven't slept in the same bed with him for months now. I fell into that trap of thinking I was responsible for his seeing other women. But I'm not — he is. I tried to compete with his lover and I feel I lost. We're still married, but he doesn't seem to care at all about me or my feelings. I have had to continue sleeping alone, because it's the only way I can deal with the situation. To be around him and realize he doesn't want to be close to me is more than I can deal with at the moment. I don't know what's going to happen. I don't want to lose him, but I can't go on this way much longer.

You Cheat, Therefore I Shop. . . .

For many women, the only way they can cope with their husband's infidelity is to look their best at all times, and to shop as much as they want! Women I spoke with described feeling that since *he* was spending their money on *her*, they were entitled to buy nice things whenever they wanted to. Shopping became a way of consoling themselves, as well as a way of boosting their self-confidence by looking as attractive as possible. Sandrine buys a new pair of Manolo Blahnik shoes every time she thinks her husband has bedded a new woman. She despises his behavior, but takes some pleasure in her chosen form of treatment: shopping.

There is certainly an element of revenge in retail therapy, but when a woman's self-confidence collapses, as it almost always does once she discovers her husband is cheating on her, she will seek to restore her good feelings about herself in any way she can. For most women, that means making themselves look good. By upgrading her wardrobe and improving her appearance with a makeover, or even cosmetic surgery, a woman almost always feels better about herself and regains the strength to deal more effectively with her life — and her philandering husband. Despite the emotional turmoil that comes with learning of a husband's affair, the last thing a woman wants is for other people to comment on how she has let herself go, as if that were explanation enough for her husband's behavior.

Looking good—looking better than the Other Woman, in particular—plays a large role in rebuilding a woman's confidence when her husband has a lover. Attractiveness is a major weapon women use against other women in the war to win a man—or to win a man back from another woman. Just look at Hillary Clinton on *Vogue*'s December, 1998 cover!

Finding Comfort in Food, Alcohol, or Antidepressants

While shopping helps many women to replenish their self-esteem in the wake of their husband's affairs, a surprisingly large number turn to food or alcohol to comfort themselves. It has been said that "food is the good girl's sex," and there is some truth to this. Some women, when they feel emotionally empty, turn to food to "fill them up." Princess Diana told Martin Bashir that her bulimia "was rampant" when she was trying to deal with the fact of her husband's relationship with Camilla Parker Bowles.

Overeating, and the eating disorders bulimia and anorexia, are not uncommon in women dealing with infidelity. Women, sex, and food have long had a mysterious connection, and several women I spoke with described how food satisfied them, nourished them, and gave them comfort during times of stress. Chocolate and ice cream seemed to have a particularly soothing effect.

A number of women also admitted that they began to drink heavily when their marital problems with infidelity started. One woman said:

I had never been much of a drinker, but when I found out my husband was sleeping with another woman, I turned to booze. At first, small amounts would numb my pain. But before I knew it I was drinking a bottle of wine after dinner, and not even getting a buzz. After about eight months of this, I was really worried about myself. I would take the bottle and climb into bed and watch TV, trying not to notice the time and the fact that my husband wasn't home. Finally, I went away alone for a few days, and since I've been home I haven't taken a drink. I took a good look at a woman I know who is a heavy drinker. Her skin is wrinkled prematurely, her face bloated, and her eyes glassy. And she's overweight—she looks like a beach ball. She drinks because her husband cheats on her, too. I don't want to be like her.

I was afraid of what I was becoming. I love my husband, but I'm not going to ruin my life because he deceives me. No one is worth destroying my life for. I still feel lonely, and I'm tired of being alone while he goes out with his lover. I have to take better care of myself. I won't drink again. I look at it as a fluke—something I never did before—and won't get into again.

Venting

Another way some women cope with staying with a straying husband is by venting their outrage indirectly. For example, one woman told me that she occasionally urinates on her husband's toothbrush! She said that this venting behavior helped give her a sense of power over her spouse and enabled her to deal with a situation where, ultimately, she felt helpless. She was doing something that wouldn't really hurt her husband, but it helped her feel like she was getting back at him for betraying and hurting her. Another woman told of mixing cat food in the casserole she served to her husband. He didn't notice anything amiss, and she felt immense satisfaction at having tricked him.

The lengths to which some women will go in order to cope with a philandering husband illustrate the extreme distress women feel when their husband cheats on them and they see no alternative but to stay and tolerate the situation.

An Affair of One's Own

When you see your husband in the arms of another woman, there's only one thing to do. Seduce another man.

—ADVERTISEMENT FOR MELROSE PLACE

THE REVENGE AFFAIR

"I'll be true as long as you, and not a single minute after" is a sentiment echoed by many women married to men who stray. A common way women reassure themselves of their physical and sexual desirability after a husband's betrayal is to have an affair of their own. Revenge affairs, at least in the short term, can provide women with the attention and ego boost they need following a betrayal. However, some revenge affairs backfire, especially if a woman becomes too emotionally involved with a new partner who doesn't return her degree of affection. Under these circumstances, the woman feels guilty and used.

If a woman is particularly fond of and attracted to the man with whom she has the affair, and he dumps her, she suffers a double rejection. Since many women are driven to revenge affairs as a way to recapture emotional stability, as well as to get back at their straying husband, they will eventually feel disappointed with the affair.

Many revenge affairs are intended to "settle the score" with a straying husband. However, many men don't respond as women hope they will. Women hope that by having an affair of their own, they will make their husband jealous, so that he will give up his own lover and return to his wife. This does happen, though not very frequently. More often, men end up leaving their wives. It is harder for a man to stay when a woman strays. Unfair as it is, the sexual double standard for extramarital affairs is alive and well.

One fifty-year-old woman, Skye, told me that after her husband began an affair, she went out to clubs looking for men to pick up. "I desperately needed to feel wanted," she explained. After three brief and discreet flings, she knew she "still had it," as she put it, but she grew weary of the constant search for validation of her attractiveness and stopped seeing other men. Once she had confirmed to herself that she was attractive enough to attract other men, she no longer felt as desperate and despairing over her husband's affair. She wasn't interested in replacing her husband, whom she still loved. She decided to stay married to him and to try to overlook his philandering and build an identity apart from him.

Some women believe that "the best defense is a good offense." Indeed, several women told me that the only way they could stay married to a philanderer was to have affairs of their own. For these women, extramarital affairs made them feel powerful, and less dependent on their husband for approval, attention, and affection. Anna's situation illustrates why some people stay married even though both partners have other lovers:

My husband has always cheated on me and he always will. I accept that, although I don't like it and I'll never really get used to it. But if I want to be married to him, I have to accept that part of him. I used to get livid before, but since I've taken to flirting and having my own affairs, I'm better able to tolerate my husband because I no longer expect affection from him and don't get upset with him for his wanderings. By receiving attention from several men, I now get more attention and "goodies" than I ever did from my husband. While I ache to have my husband all to myself, I know that won't happen. I'm happy, though, because other men treat me well and like me. Having affection from different men gives me the attention I need, and I don't pressure my husband as much anymore.

My husband comes from an emotionally frigid home, so I can't expect him to display something he's never seen. His affairs aren't grand passions, because he's incapable of that with anyone. At least I'm his wife, and I'm grateful for that. He's a good man, just not a demonstrative one. It seems odd that he's such a flagrant philanderer even though he's not physically affectionate. I guess his lovers just want some quick sex with a handsome and successful man.

I know he's "faithful to me in his heart," and I've grown to realize that that's all he can offer me, and that it's pretty special.

Women's revenge affairs have long been in vogue. In his book *Jack and Jackie: Portrait of an American Marriage* (1996), Christopher Andersen alleges that Jackie Kennedy had a fling with the actor William Holden to get back at her philandering husband, President Kennedy. The book also claims that Jackie was aware of John's womanizing, but she turned her aristocratic head the other way, as so many women do.

THE SUPPORTIVE AFFAIR

Every good wife should commit a few infidelities to keep her husband in countenance.

— GEORGE BERNARD SHAW

If some women are driven to have affairs as a way of getting back at their husband for having a lover, many others begin their own affairs out of a desire for emotional closeness following the discovery of their husband's affair. They are motivated by the lack of emotional connectedness with their husband, rather than by a need for unbridled casual sex.

Women's affairs are often begun out of a general dissatisfaction with their husband's philandering, as well as their disappointment with their marriage. At some point in almost every marriage, women wonder why they are "putting all their eggs in one basket" and not getting enough return on their investment.

I heard many stories of women involved with emotionally illiterate men who cannot express their emotions, either verbally or physically, and yet somehow manage to have affairs with other women. When a woman feels she isn't getting enough love, romance, or sex from her husband, she is justifiably upset. She feels even worse if her husband is providing another woman with the affection he is denying her.

Women often told me gut-wrenching stories of marriages devoid of sexual and emotional connections. Many married women feel lonely, depressed, vulnerable, and disillusioned as a result of their husbands' affairs. Some of these women, like thirty-six-year-old Cornelia, turn to other men for what they perceive is lacking in their marriage:

I'm so tired of begging my husband for affection. He recoils and backs away from me whenever I touch him. I couldn't stand his cold rejections any longer, so I began an affair with a married man I know through work. I'm happier now because I don't feel like I'm "running on empty" in the sexual touching department.

I know this isn't a permanent solution, but it feels nice to be wanted again. I guess I'll have to continue my twice-weekly massages and have affairs for the rest of my life if I want to be touched and to feel the warmth of a man's hands on my body.

Cornelia's experience illustrates a feeling that is familiar to many women: when women turn to extramarital affairs, what they are often seeking is an affirmation of their sexual desirability, and a sense of being wanted, cherished, valued. Most can never get too much appreciation, attention, and physical displays of affection. It's little wonder that many women say they want more foreplay than their mate generally offers.

Women long for a happy marriage, and a deep emotional connection with their husband. Sex, while important, is almost secondary to the near-universal desire for emotional nourishment. Women want their emotions touched, as well as their breasts. They say that affairs build and rebuild their self-esteem; provide them with emotional closeness absent from their marriage; and make them feel younger, sexier, prettier — and appreciated. Many women also say that affairs help them to establish or reestablish a sense of independence from their husband and their marriage, as well as a transition out of a marriage they have decided to end.

It is often said that women give sex to get love and men give love to get sex. While this may be a slight exaggeration, it is clear that although men and women both desire sex and attention, they go about meeting their needs in different ways. These different ways often lead men into the arms of other women in pursuit of sexual variety, and women into the arms of other men looking for attention.

Women can trip themselves up emotionally when they think they want sex for the sake of sex. If a woman is attracted to a man, and then has sex with him, she will usually grow more fond of him after she becomes sexually involved. For most women, emotional attraction precedes sexual activity. So, once a woman becomes intimate with a man, everything changes for her.

Women who cope with their husband having an affair by having an affair of their own can create an array of problems for themselves. So far as women are concerned, *sex creates bonds where none existed before*, so a "harmless" affair too often becomes a real emotional involvement. Women are generally not as adept as men at compartmentalizing different parts of their life, so extramarital affairs become a big deal. The vast majority of married women have to feel an emotional pull toward a man before they will have sex with him.

If a married woman becomes emotionally dependent on a man other than her husband, she may feel uplifted in the short term; usually, though, she will end up being hurt, because she is still married to a philanderer. One woman explained that her five-year marriage had started out "as soothing as a warm bath," but is now "drying [her] up," and her "self-confidence and identity are rapidly going down the drain." In desperation, she began an affair with a man she met on a business trip to a town she visits frequently. For a while the affair felt like the early stages of her marriage. "It was never about sex," she explained. "It was about wanting to be talked to, listened to, touched, and hugged." Today, she wants to end the affair, but says it's difficult to do so. She has grown dependent on the "extras" the affair brings to her life, even though she doesn't particularly *like the man any longer.*

Very few of the women I interviewed said they were motivated by the sex involved in their extramarital affairs. Rather, the affairs were a way of sustaining a view of themselves as sexually desirable and attractive while learning to cope with a philandering husband, as the following two stories illustrate.

> *Sex is hardly ever just about sex.*
>
> — SHIRLEY MACLAINE

Gabriella's Story

Gabriella a stunning thirty-four-year-old television producer, has been married for six years to a successful — and much older — banker. Recently, Gabriella learned that her husband was having an affair, and she has reacted by taking a lover of her own.

The only time my husband touches me is when he wants sex, and when we do have sex, it's over quickly. He's not interested in the many sensual things

I enjoy, such as taking baths and showers together, and using lotions, food, and sex toys in lovemaking. He's a "plain vanilla" man when it comes to sex. He really is quite boring. I'm in no way kinky, but I like sensual and erotic things. I'm growing more and more dissatisfied with his coldness and his lack of sexual skills. This especially angers me since he must be doing this stuff with his new lover.

When I try to talk to him about improving our sex life, he blames me and threatens to leave me. He is emotionally manipulative and very controlling. I have become close to a man I met at a work-related party. Soon after we met, we became lovers. He's married too, and has a young child. Neither of us plans to leave our marriage. I enjoy the times I spend with him, but I wish I could get the same admiration at home.

I really agonized over my decision to begin this affair, but I realized I'm still way too young to give up on passion. It feels good to be wanted. I have a nice body, and I want desperately to share it with a man who cares about me and desires me. If my husband won't touch me, and he makes love to other women, I have to get my needs met somehow.

I work hard to keep up my appearance because I love to look nice, and I also like having a man compliment me. My husband never says anything nice about how I look or the things I do for him. He criticizes me constantly about my looks, my figure, my clothes—everything. I know I'm attractive and well groomed, so his nasty comments are intended to hurt and belittle me. He dumps on my career plans and says things like, "I'll believe it when I see it," and, "You'll never make it." He constantly manages to undermine my confidence.

By the time I connected with my lover, I was certain I would grow old without ever having a satisfying sexual experience again. My lover gives me hope. My husband gives me misery. I get totally despondent when I think of my husband kissing another woman. Whenever I try to kiss him, he holds his hand up like a STOP sign!

I believe in monogamy. I tried everything I could to get my husband to be more affectionate and attentive toward me. He would usually just verbally abuse me and push me away. I remember several times when I dressed in sexy lingerie for him and he just laughed at me. I've really lost interest in him. I've grown tired of always making overtures to him that are *turned down. I'm tired of being insulted, criticized, and pushed away, while he goes off to see a lover. I still love him, but I wonder how much longer I can go on [being] married to a man who makes me feel like shit. He's driving me away, yet I still hope he'll end his affair and rekindle our sex life and marriage.*

I'm enjoying sex now with my lover. He takes his time and goes out of his way to please me. It's not just the sex with him that makes me feel good. It's the way he treats me. He respects me, likes me, and seems genuinely to care about me. Still, I wonder how he can be so good to me while at the same time he's lying to his wife, but I'm doing the same thing to my husband. But he did it to me first!

It feels wonderful to be wanted by my lover. He makes me feel like I matter and that I'm special. He is a dream friend and a great bedmate. My career is going better now, too, because I'm content with my lover. I finally have some of the emotional stability I've longed for. For me, sex and emotions are inseparable, so while I'm relishing my new lover, I'm worried about how I'll feel when we break up and all I'll have is my marriage. I don't see how I'll be able to survive another thirty years or more married to a man who is an iceblock. I feel so lonely when I'm at home. I'm only my positive, happy self these days when I'm at work or with my lover.

I don't know what's worse for me, a divorce or having an affair. For now, I don't want to think about it. I just want to enjoy my life to the fullest. I don't want to look back years from now and think I missed out on good loving from an attentive man.

Gabriella's experience is common. She is married to a man who is not particularly demonstrative, and who cheats on her. There is not much that's positive going on in the marriage, and the prospects of its lasting aren't great. Gabriella must determine why she is tolerating her husband's bad behavior. She is already questioning how she can live long term with a man who insults and ignores her and yet showers other women with attention. In this situation, Gabriella's affair is only a crutch to help her regain her self-confidence and tolerate her husband's infidelity. But prolonging a bad situation isn't an adequate solution for her in the long term.

A theme I heard many times when interviewing married women was men's inattentiveness. When combined with a man's extramarital affairs, it can tip many women over the edge and encourage them to seek a revenge affair, a supportive affair, or to end their marriage.

Sarah's Story

Sarah's husband, Ross, is obsessed with watching sports on television, and when he isn't home in front of the set with a six-pack of beer, he is out watching a game somewhere. Sports are especially irritating to Sarah because Ross has affairs with women who are sports fans. He is totally obsessed with sex and sports, and so Sarah has turned to another man for companionship, attention, and sex.

In my marriage, sports on television replaced me years ago. How does one compete with a television set? My husband has a lover and his TV set, so he doesn't seem to need me. I have become the "Other Woman" to another married man. My husband and I lived together for several years before we married, and our relationship during that time was pretty good. But if I wanted to go to any social events, I had to go alone. He wanted no part of it. Maybe I should have seen earlier how things were, but there's that saying, "Love is blind."

On our wedding night—which was only a party at our apartment after a civil wedding—Ross stayed up very late watching sports on TV. However, our relationship was reasonable then, and our daughter was born three years after we were married. I've been employed since my daughter was a year old. I finally persuaded my husband to let me have another child, and we had a son.

After several years my husband moved into an apartment attached to our home. I do all the cooking, cleaning, washing, and ironing for him, in addition to my job and looking after the children. I take the kids to all their activities. My husband never goes to anything with us as a family. He only socializes with sporting types, and doesn't want me to go along with him. He has had numerous affairs over the years with women sports groupies.

After being married for twenty years, I started a new job. My boss started making advances to me, and having been neglected by my husband for so long, I jumped at the chance and we ended up lovers.

My lover's wife has had cancer for the last several years, and though she's still an attractive woman, she no longer desires a sexual relationship with him. Neither my lover nor I want to end our marriages, but we both have needs that aren't being met at home. In the last several months I have had to change jobs in order to earn more money for the family, so I'm no longer an employee of my lover. We still get together as often as possible.

As for my husband Ross, I don't even know where I am on his priority list. He told me early in our relationship that if I ever had a lover, not to tell him. He has always denied his affairs, but I just know he has them. At this stage it bothers me less, perhaps because I'm so used to it or because I'm too emotionally numb to get upset, or because I, too, have a lover. For over a quarter of a century, Ross was the only man in my life; but after a while, loneliness became too much for me.

I'm now over fifty, and I'm working to keep my family going. I feel like I've given everything in my life to my husband, and for what? My affair is for me.

Sarah, like so many women, plunged into an affair as a way of soothing herself after years spent in an emotionally stifling marriage. Even when a woman dearly loves her husband, tolerates his adultery, and wants the marriage to last, she can eventually become so lonely that she will seek out an affair.

THE TIES THAT BIND

Women try to cope with a philandering husband by denial, confrontation, overeating, drinking, shopping, working, pursuing hobbies, devoting themselves to their children, and sometimes by having affairs of their own. Through all of this, most stay devoted to their marriage. What is the glue that keeps so many women stuck to difficult marriages? The same psychological principle that keeps "'other women" tied to married men: *intermittent reinforcement.*

Intermittent reinforcement keeps a wife holding out for expressions of her husband's affection and attention—and for his hoped-for return to her.

She figures that if she stays long enough, the tide will turn and her husband will once again be faithful to her. As Faith explains:

I stay married because of the contentment I used to feel each morning waking up in John's arms. It's been ages since we've cuddled in bed, because he usually stays way over on his side of our large bed these days, but I know we'll get back to our snuggling.

Faith is remembering the good aspects of her marriage, and is hanging in there because she believes those happy days will return.

Another powerful psychological principle running through all the coping strategies discussed in this chapter is *post-decision justification*. After a woman has made a commitment to marriage, she will usually hang in there even in the face of adultery. Having made the decision to commit herself to her husband, she will continue to find reasons to support her decision. Because she is determined to stay with her straying husband, she may revert to denial that there is any infidelity at all, even in the face of damning physical evidence.

Whatever coping strategies a woman uses to help her stay with a straying husband, she must realize that life continues while her husband is having an affair. It is imperative that she get a life of her own, and make the most of it.

TAKE NOTE

- Women use a variety of techniques to cope with a straying husband. The negative ones are alcohol, drugs, and overeating. Turning to these substances creates a new set of problems, and doesn't solve an adultery one.

- Women often find that trying to tolerate what is nearly impossible to tolerate makes them moody and depressed.

- If you find yourself acting totally out of character, or if you start overdrinking, overeating, overspending, or indulging in drugs, you must reassess your decision to stay with your straying man.

- Every woman must have a life of her own apart from her man and her marriage.

- If the only way for your marriage to work is for you to tolerate your husband's infidelity, you must ask yourself if you really want to be in such a marriage.

Chapter 9

STORIES OF WOMEN WHO STAY WITH MEN WHO STRAY

The heart will break, but brokenly live on.

—*Lord Byron*

He cheats, therefore I shop. But after a while, no amount of CHANEL, Armani, or Prada soothes the loneliness and emptiness left by my husband's philandering.

—*Long-suffering wife of an executive*

STAYING ISN'T EASY—BUT NEITHER IS LEAVING

When a woman learns that her husband is cheating on her, she feels sad, angry, and jealous. Her heart feels as if it has shattered into a million tiny pieces, and her trust for her husband is in tatters. When a woman expects fidelity and honesty in a relationship, she is betrayed twice, for she is confronted with a husband who is being unfaithful and who is also lying to her to cover up his philandering. This double whammy really hits hard, shredding her self-confidence. One woman described her feelings as "being in an emotional cul-de-sac." She felt she was going around in circles and getting nowhere.

Wealth and celebrity do not shield a woman from the pain infidelity inflicts. After Hugh Grant was caught "in an act of lewd behavior" with a prostitute, his girlfriend, Elizabeth Hurley, was visibly shaken by the experience. Quoted in the *Los Angeles Times* after the incident, she said: "I am still bewildered and saddened by recent events and have not been in a fit state to make any decisions about the future."

Many women feel devastated and destroyed by infidelity. They believe that the end of their love—and their marriage—is just around the corner. While this may be the case for some women, many men who have affairs have no intention of leaving their marriage. They simply want a wife, a happy home, and a sexy, young girlfriend, while keeping their double life in two neat and tidy separate compartments, hoping the two never intersect. For a variety of personal, social, and financial reasons, as we have seen, many women decide to stay married and try to tolerate just such a situation. Wealth or social status is no barrier to betrayal.

The many women I interviewed, and the women who wrote to me for this book telling me stories of their husbands' affairs and their attempts to cope with them, show similar patterns of infidelity. But since no marriage is of the "one size fits all" variety, each affair is unique. Women told me of unfaithful husbands who stray throughout their marriage. I heard about men whose mistresses have become like second families. I learned how some men flit from dalliance to dalliance and tell their wife each dirty detail. I heard about men who have no intention of leaving their marriage yet flaunt their long-term affairs. And, sadly, I heard often how women suffered through adultery, only to be divorced against their will. I learned of very few cases of women leaving philandering husbands; but the women who did leave told me of their renewed confidence and contentment following divorce.

Of the women interviewed for this book, the ones most likely to stay with a straying husband were over fifty, had marriages of long standing—generally over fifteen years—had children, lacked educational credentials and employment experience, and possessed few financial resources apart from their husband. Given the societal double standards of looks, age, marriage, and infidelity, the commitment women make to their marriage seems to strengthen with time. Regardless of the love they say they feel for their husband, women's investment in marriage increases as their other opportunities decrease.

A strong devotion to marriage is admirable, but it is also not always in a woman's best interest. An unbelievable number of women learn the hard way that their devotion to their husband and marriage goes unrewarded. As they watch their husband waltz away with a younger woman, they wonder why they placed so much faith in a philandering man.

The stories that follow are the harrowing tales of women's experiences with unfaithful husbands. Few of the stories have happy endings, and many have yet to approach any sort of resolution—the women living in limbo with men who cannot or will not decide between wife and lover. Saddest of all are the stories of long-suffering women—those who decided to stand by their man and their marriage, regardless of the philandering—who were left by their husbands after long marriages. The stories told here are representative of the many that I heard from women who participated in the research for this book.

SHE STAYED, AND GOT DUMPED ANYWAY

A popular woman had to navigate her way through an infidelity minefield during her thirty-eight-year marriage. She often received anonymous letters from women who felt they had a claim on her husband. She also received numerous letters over the years, some of them anonymous, and most hurtful, that criticized her for not leaving her marriage.

Of all the stories I heard about betrayed women and philandering men, few were as upsetting as Holly's. Holly and her husband had enjoyed many memorable years together—thirty-eight to be exact—and despite real difficulties, she did not want to walk away from the man she loved. Neither did she wish to abandon the marriage and family to which she had devoted her entire adult life. She believed leaving the marriage would equal failure—her failure. So she stayed. She stayed through the innuendoes, the winks, the nudges and stares, and the vicious gossip. She stayed married because she loved her husband. She said she was his life partner and that was sacrosanct. Unfortunately, not all men think *their* life partner or marriage is sacrosanct.

No happy twilight years together awaited Holly and Keith. In spite of Holly's devotion to her husband, her marriage, and her family, she got dumped. Her situation, though heartbreaking, is, sadly, increasingly common. A man leaves his wife just at the time they are about to enjoy *their* time together. After a hectic existence—of her raising children, his developing his career—and just as they are about to embark on their new life together in retirement, the man bolts for a younger, more independent woman.

Just when Holly and Keith were about to move into their newly built dream home, Holly was dumped for a younger woman. She ended up alone in a small house, while the new wife moved into the mansion and assumed Holly's life!

Holly's experience illustrates that even if a woman stays with a man who strays, there is still no guarantee that the couple will stay married "till death do us part." Even when a woman decides to stay with her man who strays, there is no guarantee that *he* will stay with her. Even a woman who does her best to look the other way or to tolerate a painful situation can still end up without her husband. What a terrible waste of her valuable time and her devotion.

Holly said she stayed in her marriage, even after considering a separation, because "I retained a fundamental commitment to our partnership in marriage." She believed that Keith stayed for personal and career reasons, while she stayed—as many women do—because of home and financial considerations. She understood that it was important for her to have a life of her own. "I realized that the more I could do outside the home, the more it added to the quality of our lives." But sadly, Holly's quality of life with her husband did not improve.

Now divorced, Holly is involved in many charitable causes, and enjoys her children and grandchildren. Still, she often wonders why she so willingly gave away years of her life to someone who is not now even in her life.

HE COULDN'T SEE ANY FUTURE FOR THEM

$\mathcal{K}$elly and Phillip's marriage lasted twenty-five years before he left her for a younger woman. He had had a number of affairs, but Kelly was shocked into acknowledging his behavior only after he told her he was leaving her. She had stayed while he strayed, and although she claims she was unaware of his philandering throughout their marriage, she says things often "weren't quite right." However, she never pushed him, never asked questions or went through his pockets or drawers looking for clues. "I guess I didn't want to believe he could be cheating on me," she said.

Kelly's story is a cautionary tale to women that they should wake up and smell the philandering in the air.

I am fifty-one years old, and my former husband is fifty-two. We were married for twenty-five years when he left me. We have three grown sons, all over age twenty. I was employed part time in the early years of our marriage, and I supported Phillip when he was studying to become a lawyer.

When I found out Phillip was leaving me for another woman, I sat curled up on my sofa for what seemed like three months. I went on antidepressants and felt like I had gone to hell and back.

Even though lots of my friends have been through exactly the same thing, I didn't think it would ever happen to me. Until the day Phillip walked out, I didn't know what was happening. Only when I started connecting the pieces did I see he had been cheating for a long time. I knew things were wrong, but I didn't know why.

Not until a few weeks before he left did I see that his excuses were becoming more feeble. "Working late" became a habit. He had other excuses too, and they became too regular to ignore. He was picking on my appearance and criticizing me for no reason.

I put everything down to his stress at work. Gradually he brought more work home at night and began cutting himself off from the family. He was really distancing himself. He took up new activities. He was determined to learn how to ski, and on one holiday he took three lessons in one day. He grew more indifferent toward me. He bought new clothes, especially new ties and silk jocks.

I received "guilt" presents every now and then. He began drinking a glass of wine, then it turned into a bottle, then a beer before the bottle, and then bottle after bottle. He stopped seeing our dear old friends, and he grew more concerned about his image in his office.

So much was going on and I was just coping day to day. I can look back now with 20/20 vision and see what was happening. I just didn't see it then, or want to see it.

Whenever I would initiate sex, he was too tired, too stressed, or just not interested. I would say to him, "What's the matter? Is there anyone else?" he always said no.

He bought new things, like a television and a VCR, and he put them in his study. The night before he left, he ignored me and watched television alone. The next morning he packed up all his expensive booze. He said he wanted to make a new start.

I remember now that about a month before he left, he said something that concerned me. He said, "What do you see us doing in five years?" He couldn't see any future for us. He said we didn't have long-term goals together, and that there were no longer challenges in the marriage.

He left me on a Saturday. The following morning he rang and said, "I'm missing you. I need time to sort myself out. I need to know who I am." He never said there was someone else, but he said: "I don't think you could cope with the lifestyle."

Soon afterward he stopped paying the bills. After the electricity was turned off for nonpayment, I took him to court for money for food and bills.

We had always lived well, but he did all the finances. I had no say; he wouldn't let me. He kept the papers hidden in old briefcases.

I've aged ten years in the last two. I've tried to get him back, but I've worn myself out. I have a lot to lose financially. I have no job prospects. Who is going to hire me? I'm over fifty and have no qualifications. Divorce makes paupers out of women.

What could I do? I had to let him go. He only cared about himself. We had a fabulous lifestyle, a large waterfront home, a boat, nice cars. I even had to borrow money until we worked out a temporary financial arrangement.

He left me for a thirty-one-year-old woman. They are now living the life I envisioned us having. She is reaping the benefits of my hard work. When he left, I felt I had no reason to live. Then one day, after several months, something happened, and I picked myself up. Not all of my friends were supportive. One woman said to me, "If it happened to you, it can happen to me."

It has been hard finding a social life. I could never marry a gardener; I have to have a man with some status. Even though I now have a companion, I still go through moments over Phillip. He was everything to me. It was meant to be. It was love. That's why it's so hard to get rid of.

Phillip and I have been divorced for five years now, and he won't speak to me. I think it's his guilt. I also think he's jealous of my new life. He said to me once, "I didn't think you'd do as well as you have."

I don't know whether I want to get married again. After the breakup I lost twelve pounds in two months, I didn't sleep, and I didn't eat. I don't ever want to go through something like that again.

I have bought new clothes and moved to a smaller home, which I have decorated just the way I like it. I'm relaxed and content now. I actually feel better than I've ever felt in my life. I'm really happy. I have become very content living alone. My marriage was wonderful for twenty-five years, but at the end we were living separate lives. Now I have my life, and a fun companion. I have good health, and all my needs are being met.

I have self-confidence and a positive attitude. Despite all that's happened, I'm still lucky, and I think that's what life is really all about. At the time it was horrendous, but I lived through it. I've cried all night, and drunk myself into a stupor—but for what? I was the only one who suffered.

These younger women are very clear-cut about what they want, and will go after a married man no matter what. Phillip married Natalie, and now she has all the things I worked for with him. It's frightening that we can put so much faith in another person—in a man. And then he just goes away.

Like Holly, Kelly believed in her husband and was committed to her marriage. Still, she lost her longtime spouse to another woman. The hints and clues went on for some time; but Kelly didn't pick up on them, whether out of innocence and trust in Phillip, or out of denial.

Had Kelly been given the option of staying with Phillip and tolerating his affairs, one can only wonder if she would have stayed. The decision to end the marriage was Phillip's, and given the no-fault divorce policy, Kelly had no choice but to comply. Whether she would have been happier still married to a philanderer than she is divorced, one can only speculate.

Despite the pain of discovering Phillip's philandering and contending with a divorce, Kelly was able to regain her self-esteem and build a new life that she enjoys. Although she clearly would still prefer to be married to Phillip, she is no longer interested in marrying just to have a man around. She has discovered the joy of independence, and has grown enormously since her marriage ended.

SHE TRIED, THEN SHE LEFT

There are many more women who stay with men who stray than women who leave such men. But some spurned women eventually *do* leave and begin a new life. Barbara Cochran Berry is just such a woman. Even she is amazed she had the courage to do it. As Barbara wrote in her book *Life after Johnnie Cochran: Why I Left the Sweetest-Talking, Most Successful Black Lawyer in Los Angeles* (1995), she had been raised with the belief that when a woman married and had children—she stayed with her family no matter what.

Barbara did *not* live happily ever after with Cochran, who later became the lead defense attorney in the O. J. Simpson criminal murder trial. In her book she describes her seventeen-year marriage to a man she refers to as a "nightmare to live with," and who had a child with his longtime white mistress, Patty.

Barbara describes the pressure she received from her family and friends to look the other way at her husband's philandering, since he was supporting her financially. She tried to do so for many years in order to keep her marriage together, but she was never able to accept the infidelity.

When she finally tired of suspecting her husband was cheating on her, she hired a private investigator and learned that her husband had a mistress—and a child. Learning the truth was the most humiliating thing that had ever happened to her, she says. But in the end, it strengthened her enormously. The effort of trying to keep the marriage together wasn't worth it, she decided. She had lost admiration and respect for him, but, more importantly, also for herself; she left the marriage in order to regain her self-esteem.

Barbara says in her book that it is hard to believe she stayed so long with her cheating husband, even after learning about the child. Once out of the marriage, she realized just how much of herself she had given up by colluding with her husband in sustaining their unhappy union.

Sweetheart Deals

There are some couples for whom infidelity is an implicit agreement. While a woman may not really condone or be enthused about her husband's infidelity, she nevertheless colludes with him in his affairs. She draws benefits from staying married—such as lifestyle and status; in return, the husband can do what he pleases and with whom he pleases. These sorts of arrangements are extremely rare and are mostly found in high-income families, where men can afford two lifestyles.

None of the women or men I interviewed who participated in this type of "arrangement" would call their situation an open marriage. Instead, they described their circumstances as one where the man dallied from time to time, and often for a long time with one woman. However, the husband always stressed that he valued his wife and family, and that he had no intention of abandoning them. In these "sweetheart deals," both husband and wife benefit from the marriage and are therefore motivated to keep it intact, even if the husband has a long-term lover. The wives I spoke with also strayed on occasion, usually out of loneliness and boredom rather than a search for a supplemental sexual partner.

Some of these arrangements last for many years; most of the women believe they must accept and deal with the situation and be thankful for what they have, rather than focus on the negatives of life with a cheating husband. The case of Rose, a fiftysomething woman married to David, a major mogul who has a thirtysomething mistress, Brittany, is a good example. This triangle occasionally expands to include other women, as David also cheats on girlfriend Brittany, as well as on his wife, by having frequent one-night stands and mini-weekend flings.

While the outward functioning of the Rose-David-Brittany triangle is a stable one, Rose doesn't really like the deal, and Brittany knows her time with David is limited. He has a longtime habit of mentoring women, sleeping with them, then dropping them after a few years. The only beneficiary of this complicated arrangement seems to be David. For much of their twenty-plus years of marriage, David has lived apart from Rose, though he has no intention of divorcing her. If they divorced, he would have to split his substantial fortune with her. The status quo provides him with a secure home base in his marriage and family, while also giving him the freedom to run wild without having to be accountable to his wife.

Rose admitted to being continually pained by David's need for other women. She says it gives her a great sense of relief and satisfaction that he also cheats on his mistress. She knows that David has constant access to young, attractive, talented women, and he makes the most of his powerful position to indulge his sexual cravings. Rose tells herself she is lucky to be married to David, because she wouldn't want to be "just one of his girls." She lives alone in a beautiful waterfront home, tends to her garden, travels frequently, lunches with her many friends, and is a major socialite. She enjoys those aspects of her life; and even though she would receive a tidy financial settlement from a divorce, Rose doesn't want to give up her life with David just because he has "serial mistresses," as she refers to his dalliances.

Since David lives and works elsewhere, and only comes home several times a year, Rose says she has the best of both worlds. She has her freedom, and David has his. Yet she also has a husband to whom she has been married for over twenty years, and their two grown children.

Rose's main worry is that one day David will leave her for one of the many women he has been involved with in lengthy relationships over the years. She also gets upset when she visits where David lives and works. He has fixed up his current girlfriend in an apartment near him and takes her to all his corporate social functions. When Rose is in town, he takes her, and she feels eyes burrowing into her at such events. She tries to hold her head high and rise above David's behavior, but she can't help but feel humiliated when so many people know about his girlfriends.

For many years, Rose said, she was a wreck—drinking and crying to people about her husband's behavior. She had finally tired of people ignoring her, deferring to David, and condoning his affairs. The fact that he has all the power in their relationship has made her bitter. "Everyone who knows us seems to condone what David does. At the same time, they look down on me and say how bitter I am. *Of course* I'm bitter, who wouldn't be?"

Rose tells her story:

Finally, I became resigned to his behavior. It took me nearly eighteen years to get to the point where it didn't hurt me deeply anymore. I think I was just too exhausted and couldn't waste any more energy trying to get him to stop something he was never going to give up. I have essentially given up on him and have become resigned to his philandering. I feel much better— relatively speaking, anyway. I'm now doing more things alone and have focused on my own interests. I have a wonderful garden on which I shower all my love. I give myself permission to buy whatever I want for it, because I've earned it throughout my marriage.

Our sex life happens about twice a year, during holidays. It seems that's all David wants of me. David and I don't live totally separate lives. We still visit and speak regularly. His position is now away from where we own our family home, so his work gives us an excuse to be apart.

I do wonder what will happen to his young girlfriend. I believe he will stay with me, and yet here is this woman spending her precious childbearing years on a man who will never be hers. I don't envy her. At least I'm legally his wife and, in the eyes of the law, his financial partner. I'm okay now and will be okay even if he does walk out. I know I'm luckier than most women. I'm married to the man I love, and he is one of the most successful men around.

I do genuinely care about David, but I just can't feel passion anymore for a man who must have other women. I will never understand the ego boost it brings him. Maybe it's because he's not particularly handsome, so the attention makes him feel important. Most of the women only pay attention to him because of his career. He is in a position to do a lot for ambitious young women. He introduces them to a great social life; I guess many women act like high-class call girls with him. There is definitely an exchange of goods and services going on.

For now, anyway, I'm content. Some days, though, I worry that I'm giving away too much to David. I'm over fifty, so I won't have many men after me, and that's just one more reason to hang on to the man I have. David has his faults, but I know what they are, and we are really comfortable together. Perhaps I'm lucky—I have a lovely home and life, and get to enjoy it without an annoying husband around all the time. Some people might even say my life is enviable. I guess it is, but I'm so lonely. It's not about sex, it's about feeling special on a deeper level with the man I love—and miss, and don't want to lose.

I doubt I will ever leave David, because when he is around we are okay together. I do worry, though, that one day we will have grown so apart from being geographically and emotionally separate that he won't even bother to come home again.

It hurts me that my husband has to have relationships with other women. The middle of the night is when I miss David the most. That's the time we should be together. Not just our bodies—but our spirit. If I can't get that back during his upcoming visit, I'll wonder what I'm waiting for by staying married. Then I realize that marriage is the only lifestyle I've known. I don't really remember any other way of living. I live alone most of the year now, but I'm deeply attached to David and our marriage. It's not like I'm really alone in the world, the way I would be if we divorced.

When people say, "sex is just sex," I partly agree. It's not all it's cracked up to be, but it sure causes problems. I don't get too teary anymore over the matter. I think I'm cried out. But, God, my heart still sinks. I guess I'm not strong enough to stomach David's ongoing infidelity. There must be a better way to have a marriage.

Rose's wealth and status give her options not available to many women with unfaithful husbands. She could leave her husband without suffering any financial or social dislocation. However, like so many women, she loves her husband deeply and doesn't want their marriage to end. Even though Rose sees David only a few times a year, their marriage is an anchor in both their lives. Their family means a great deal to both of them. David acts as if his other sexual activities have nothing to do with his wife and family. This is difficult for Rose — indeed, for most women — to comprehend.

It is obvious that Rose wishes David would not have girlfriends, but she would rather be married to him than give up the marriage because of David's sexual escapades. In a strange way, Rose feels superior to all of David's "girls," as she is the one who, she tells herself, really matters in his life.

When Rose initially learned of David's philandering in the early years of their marriage, she suffered from severe depression and developed a drinking problem. She has since gotten her life back in order. She still disapproves of his womanizing, but she has come to terms with the fact that she cannot change him. He does what he wants to do, regardless of whether it hurts or displeases her.

The big question mark for Rose — and for any woman living in such a situation — is: what if her husband really falls for one of his lovers and decides to leave her? This thought consumes Rose, and yet she has no way of knowing the answer. The probability that it could happen some day is very real, as men who chronically philander often do eventually fall for another woman and leave their wife. It happens often enough to give mistresses encouragement and wives migraines. Rose has evaluated her circumstances very carefully and accepts that staying married to David is the best way for her to get her needs met. While her situation would certainly not suit many women, for Rose, it's her life.

It is also the kind of life endured by many women who are married to extremely successful men. Successful men are much more likely to be unfaithful, and they have the discretionary time and income to hide their cheating. If the infidelity is out in the open, the man may overpower his wife with intimidation and control.

Another woman I spoke with had to contend with a situation similar to Rose's. Tania, a socialite, is married to a successful attorney, Morgan. Morgan travels extensively and always takes his mistress, Collette, with him. Collette is known to Morgan's colleagues as his regular traveling companion. Tania always feels uncomfortable when mixing with Morgan's colleagues and their wives, because she correctly senses that they know all about Collette. But Tania reluctantly accepts Morgan's philandering because she believes in devotion in marriage.

Tania is involved in many charities and basically lives a separate life from Morgan. It bothers Tania that Morgan pays for Collette's apartment in the city and prefers to take her on his travels rather than his wife. Tania feels left out and ignored; yet she sees no way out of her situation. After twenty-one years of marriage, she says she has only been close to Morgan and has shunned the attentions of other men. In spite of Morgan's flagrant philandering, Tania has always been loyal to him.

Tania sits back and takes Morgan's unseemly treatment of her because she wants to stay married to him. She feels her repayment for tolerating his philandering is a nice lifestyle and a promise from Morgan that they will never divorce. Still, Tania is concerned that he may break his promise.

Both Rose and Tania are living in limbo, reluctantly tolerating philandering husbands, yet half-expecting at any time to be divorced. Living in limbo in the name of love is a common theme for women who stay with men who stray. These women put up good fronts and seem to be fully functioning in life. However, they are profoundly unhappy with their circumstances and express feelings of loneliness and emptiness as a direct result of living with men who devote so much time to other women.

Rose, Tania, and the many other women I heard from who are standing by their men need to take a good, hard look at what they are giving up in the name of love. Love is fabulous, but a man who chronically cheats on his wife is *not* showing loving behavior toward her.

Standing by your man and marriage is admirable. But you must stand by yourself first and foremost.

ONE TOWN, TWO FAMILIES

If a town isn't big enough for one man and his two lovers, then how can it possibly be big enough for a man and his two families? No town is big enough to conceal the secret of a chronically philandering man with two families. Max, sixty-two, has developed a successful business. He has been married to Jessica, with whom he has two children, for twenty-four years. He also has two children from his first wife, who died of cancer. Max cheated throughout his first marriage and continues the pattern with Jessica. He even cheats on his longtime mistress, Alexa, with whom he also has a child.

Max, Jessica, and Alexa all live in the same small town, and have done so since they were born there. Jessica worked in public relations prior to her marriage and is considered to have a very proper social upbringing. Alexa, on the other hand, is from a blue-collar family. Max, also from a blue-collar background, has become financially successful through his business and is one of the wealthiest men in town. Still, he considers Jessica necessary for his social acceptance.

Max started his affair with Alexa when his first wife, a woman of means, was battling cancer. When she found out about the affair, she cut Max out of her will and left all her money to her children. After his wife's death, Alexa felt certain Max would finally marry her. Instead, he met and married Jessica, the more elegant and socially acceptable of the two. However, Max continued his affair with Alexa, and fathered a child with her.

The paths of the two women in Max's life didn't cross until Alexa's daughter, now a teenager, had an accident at school. Alexa wasn't available to attend to the emergency and Max, who was named as the father in the school records, was called instead. The closet was opened and the skeleton fell out. A seemingly innocent event revealed a long-guarded secret.

When Jessica found out about Alexa—and Max's second family—she also learned that Max's family, including his mother, had long known about and accepted Alexa as a part of Max's life. Jessica was shattered. She met with a divorce lawyer and threw Max out. When Max realized how much a divorce would cost him, he told Jessica he would end the affair with Alexa and never see her again.

Jessica continued to live in their mansion alone; Max lived with Alexa in her more modest home, even while promising that he would leave her. He soon tired of the arrangement, however, and convinced Jessica to let him move back in with her. He made an effort to stop seeing Alexa but it didn't last long. Soon he was back spending some nights with Alexa, though he continued to try and woo Jessica by taking her to lunch and showering her with gifts.

All the while, Max continued to have flings when away on his regular interstate and overseas trips. Unbeknown to either Jessica or Alexa, he had another longtime girlfriend he saw regularly on his business trips to a city a few hours away.

None of the parties in the triangle seem willing to make up their mind to end this uncomfortable arrangement, so it continues, even though it is fairly evident it serves mainly Max's interests.

Following an extended holiday alone in Europe, Jessica decided to stay married to Max and try to work on "curing him of his philandering." Amazingly, Alexa is still hanging on, hoping that one day Max will marry her. Jessica told me she still loves her husband and is enjoying his renewed courting of her. She still has sex with him. In her mind, Alexa is an annoying pain in the rib that won't go away, but Jessica is determined to live her life regardless. She has resigned herself to Max's other life; but, incredibly, she blames Alexa. If Alexa would only disappear, Jessica believes, then her marriage to Max could get back on track.

While Jessica is not really happy with her marital arrangement, she has decided she is going to make the most of the situation. If she can't have all of her husband, she says, she will have all the clothes and luxuries she wants. To her, that is some compensation for a broken heart, and insurance against a broken marriage. Jessica once told Max: "Keep my closet full of designer clothes and my cabinets stocked with the finest champagne, and I won't hassle you about Alexa"!

If a woman allows a man to have it both ways—as Jessica and Alexa are doing—then he is likely to continue his betrayal. Unless a decision is made to end the situation, the wife—and the "Other Woman"—will remain in limbo instead of free to pursue other avenues in life.

When a man wants to leave a woman and marry another, he *will* eventually do so. I once knew a man who cheated on his wife for eight years.

For six of those years the wife condoned his behavior, though they no longer had sex together. Finally he left her and married another, younger woman. The wife was now fifty-two, with few prospects of meeting someone else. If she had taken control and divorced her husband sooner, she would have had a better chance of improving her life. Instead, she was dumped past what society sets as most women's use-by date.

The longer women stay in an unsatisfactory marriage, the more they have to lose should the couple eventually split. Like it or not, a woman's value decreases with age and a man's increases.

Jessica comes from a more socially prominent social background than Max. She has interests and money of her own, as well as social standing. So why does she stay with Max? She says, "Because I love him." Here is a woman with the means to walk away from a philandering spouse. She has the money and status to escape relatively unscathed personally, socially, and financially, yet she stays with a man who continually lies to her. It is difficult to understand Jessica's decision to stand by Max, but she has her reasons for doing what she does. Whether or not her decision is in her best interests is debatable.

Women stay with men who stray for all sorts of highly personal reasons. One main reason is their lack of self-confidence in their own ability to build a happy life apart from their philandering husband. What keeps a couple bound together under a cloud of infidelity is truly a mystery. For many women, a better life—one free of philandering and deceit—can be possible if they would take back the power they have handed over to their husband.

"I'LL ALWAYS HAVE A LIFE OF HELL, BUT EVERY TIME I SEE HIM, I WEAKEN"

I was amazed, when researching this book, by the amount of time and energy women were willing to invest in their philandering husband when there was no sign that his cheating would end. Women may be initiating many divorces these days, but many are still standing by a cheating husband in the hope that their love will change him — that he will eventually, finally give up philandering.

One gut-wrenching story I heard came from Hannah, a fifty-four-year-old woman who is currently "in limbo" with her husband of thirty-five years, Taylor. For the last several years Taylor has been having an affair with a coworker, Brooke. Even though Taylor has moved out of their home, Hannah has been hanging in there with him, hoping he will decide she is still the one for him. However, the situation is becoming intolerable for her. She wants her life in limbo to change, one way or the other, but she is unable or unwilling to take the steps either to reconcile herself to Taylor's affair or to end the marriage. None of the three people involved in the triangle is making any moves to change the situation. Even though Hannah *says* she doesn't like the arrangement, she is doing nothing to alter it. One can only assume, then, that she is extremely ambivalent about wanting Taylor out of her life completely.

Hannah doesn't like sharing her husband with Brooke or any other woman; yet she tolerates his philandering anyway. Hannah reasons that the only way to have Taylor in her life is on his terms, which, for her, means standing by him throughout his extramarital liaisons and hoping in vain that he will eventually give up the other women. Here is how Hannah describes her life:

I have never really been employed during my marriage, but the last few years I have worked in real estate sales. It's a way for me to meet people and also to earn some money.

Taylor moved out a year ago, which was about eighteen months after he started his affair with Brooke, a woman he works with. He has known her for many years and knew that she had had affairs with others in the firm, including the boss.

The first twenty years of our marriage were great, except about seventeen years into the marriage when Taylor had an affair with one of the girls in his office. I found out because he used to work late every Friday night, and one night he came in at 1:00 A.M., and our son, who was twelve at the time, said to him: "No one works from seven A.M. until one A.M.."

Taylor and I married young, and I was his first girlfriend. He felt he had led a very sheltered life, and he wanted to make up for lost time. I confronted him about it, and he denied having an affair. He kept denying it until I finally got him to admit it, because I thought I was losing my mind. During this time I still had sex with him, because I wanted to show him I was better in bed than his girl from work. He stopped the affair and we resumed as before.

Then, a year later, I found out he was cheating again. This time I kicked him out. After three days, he came crawling back. I told him I would try to forget, but that I couldn't ever forgive him. I probably treated him a lot less affectionately than I did previously in our marriage, but I was upset with him. His affairs killed off a lot of the respect, love, and affection I felt for him. I just couldn't get the deep feelings back for him after he lied to me and broke my trust.

Perhaps he started sleeping around with many women then because I treated him offhandedly. Looking back, maybe he treated me so horribly because he wanted me to be the one to walk out on him. He blamed me for his fooling around!

With this most recent affair with Brooke, I found out one day when I put my arms around him to welcome him home from a business trip. He stiffened up, and I "just knew." He had been traveling on business with Brooke, so I suspected her. My suspicions were confirmed when Brooke started calling our home at all hours asking to speak to Taylor. She was making stupid excuses to call Taylor, and I could see what she was trying to do. She was trying to let me know she was in his life. She had no respect for me or our marriage.

I was really devastated when I put two and two together and worked out they were having an affair. I lost a lot of weight and wasn't sleeping or eating properly. My parents were no help at all. They told me to "just be nice." "Stay with it—stay with it," they kept saying.

Taylor moved in with Brooke and I started going to local bars to pick up men. I wanted to get revenge on Taylor, and I desperately needed to boost my ego. I needed to know I wasn't too old or too ugly to attract a man. After three or four one-night flings, I felt better about myself. I knew I could get a man, but I soon realized I didn't want one. I just needed to feel

*better about my desirability to someone else. After the flings, I would go out
to flirt and get attention, but I stopped sleeping around. That was a relief,
because I've never been the free-sex type of woman.*

*I met many men who were looking for a wife. If I divorce Taylor I will
have enough money, so I won't need a man to take care of me, and I
certainly don't want to spend my time looking after another man's "socks
and jocks."*

*I was really surprised by the number of impotent men over fifty I found
out there. My own husband began having erection trouble shortly before he
became involved with Brooke. He has since told me, "With her, I can get an
erection twenty-four hours a day. Every time I look at her, I want to take
her to bed."*

*Taylor told me recently that he doesn't want a divorce. I have to admit,
I didn't either. But in the last two weeks, I've changed toward him. I feel
real hatred for him. He was out of town on business and I called him at his
hotel. He wasn't in his room, and the operator asked me if I wanted to
leave a message for Mr. and Mrs. So-and-so. He had checked Brooke in
using my name. I'm so upset over this that I don't even want to talk to him
or see him. I feel much colder toward him. It was bad enough that he
moved in with her and still wants to see me, but now he's passing her off as
his wife. That's more than I can handle.*

*Taylor is devoted to our two grown children. He wants to be close to his
family, and he wants me as his best friend, but he also wants to have sex
with Brooke. Can you believe he had the nerve to say to me, "Brooke irons
my shirts better than you do"! What kind of man makes statements like that
to his wife? Let her do all his ironing from now on.*

*He has also recently taken to telling me I am fatter than Brooke, and
older—as if there is really anything I can do about my age. Besides, I'm
still younger than he is.*

*Taylor used to be my best friend, and we were so compatible. But he
recently said to me, "After thirty-five years of marriage, sex just can't be the
way it was for us before."*

*His first affair really killed my passion for him. For almost three years
after that I wasn't very responsive toward him. I couldn't help it, it wasn't
on purpose. It's just that I found it hard to relate to him physically after he
hurt me so much by betraying the trust I had in him. Maybe I should have*

left him then, because our relationship—both the sex part and the friendship—hasn't been the same since. Something inside me died for him after that first affair. Afterward, it was no longer like making love, it was straight sex, which I don't find satisfying or enjoyable. I have continued to sleep with him even though he's quite disinterested in me. He has even said to me, "I can't raise it for you."

Since he has moved in with Brooke, our two children haven't called him. Our daughter says, "He's gone. End of story." Neither she nor her brother want anything to do with him because of the way he has treated me.

Taylor keeps telling me, "I'm coming back after I get her out of my system." I'm not desperate, and I'm coming to peace with myself. But he confuses me when he says things like that. I have to think if I want him back now. I don't know if I do. Checking into that hotel as Mr. and Mrs. really irked me. He lied again. His lies really get me down. It makes me wonder what I can believe. If he lies about that, can I believe him when he says he'll come home? Or when he says he doesn't want a divorce?

Taylor is trying to keep me on the side in case the thing with Brooke doesn't work out. I'm really down right now about Taylor. I'm still numb from that hotel incident. Taylor is such a smart man except when it comes to his dick. And it's his dick that is a priority these days. God gave man a dick and a brain, but he forgot to tell them how to use them at the same time!

There is no way Taylor can avoid being around Brooke. They are both at the top of the pyramid at work and they travel together all the time. He can't very well get rid of her, especially since the boss likes her and probably feels too scared to sack her since they have slept together as well. The boss is married, and a scandal would be all over the media. Taylor says he must get Brooke out of his system, but I'm tired of waiting for him to do so.

Maybe I should leave, but Taylor now tells me lots of things. He is trying to be my best friend, he says. I really think he is trying to make me hate him so much that he'll force me to be the one to end the marriage. He's being a coward, and I think he's trying to push me to make the changes he's too wimpy or guilty to make.

It's really getting ridiculous. Taylor comes over three or four times a week for lunch, and it's like he's cheating on his girlfriend with his family! I think she is pressuring him to marry her, and perhaps he comes to see me to get away from her. He isn't taking action in any direction to resolve this situation. He can't seem to let her go—or me. I can't understand why he keeps coming over to see me so often if he wants me out of his life. It confuses and angers me. Still, the longer I can stay with him, the more financial leverage I will have in the event of a divorce. Taylor earns more money each year, so the longer I wait, the more I'll get in a divorce.

When he used to come over at night we got along okay. We'd cuddle and snuggle, but he doesn't respond sexually to me at all anymore. It has been six months since he had an erection with me. At first, after he moved in with Brooke, he was still having sex with me. I hated that, but I didn't want to give up holding my husband, or to push him into her arms.

I cry after every time he leaves me to go back to Brooke. He told me he has to honor his commitment to living with her! What about his marital commitment to me? I know I should let my love go, but something inside me keeps saying, "Just give him another chance." But I don't know how many more chances I can give him. I try to go on a short holiday every month to soothe myself, but even that doesn't help anymore.

I realize Taylor is a very weak man and that I'm probably being too good to him. He wants me to be on hold for him. He refuses to take his things out of our home because he says he's coming back. I'm waiting for him to make a decision about our future. Brooke is waiting for him to make a decision about their future. But no one is making a decision. No one is closing any doors.

Each day I care less and less for Taylor, but we are still good companions and I have a nice lifestyle. We are like brother and sister, and I don't see that changing. Too much has happened. I just don't care anymore. One day I want him back and the next day I don't.

His wife and mistress get scraps, while he gets us both. I guess I have to put my foot down and say, "No—enough." But instead I go back and forth, wanting it to change, and then accepting it as it is. I don't know what's worse: losing him, or living like this, waiting for something to happen.

Maybe now I'll do something because I've cooled toward him since the hotel incident. I have given Taylor ultimatums, but they don't work because

I cave in. I'll always have a life of hell while he continues with her. But every time I see him, I weaken.

Hannah's story is, unfortunately, common. She is stuck in the quicksand with a philandering husband who will neither leave her nor recommit to their marriage. Hannah is in an extremely difficult situation, for she will always find excuses to stay with Taylor, while at the same time finding reasons to leave. Her thoughts, and his misleading actions, will keep her struggling for years — *unless she takes action and leaves her marriage.* Hannah describes how hard it is for her to contemplate walking away from Taylor, but by allowing him to "have his cake and eat it too," Hannah is telling her husband she will allow herself to be mistreated. Hannah's rationale is that if she continues to love and be available to Taylor, he will one day return to her. Perhaps the hotel incident was the jolt she needed in order to wake up and realize she is compromising too much of herself by waiting around for Taylor to return to her. Breaking free from Taylor's emotional grasp will be Hannah's first step in moving forward with her life.

Hannah is fighting like crazy for the man she loved but who she isn't sure she even likes any more. She is living in the past when she needs to focus on the present. Hannah is the only member of the triangle who can retrieve the power she has given away. Only *she* can make the necessary changes to alter her situation. If she waits for Taylor to make a decision, she can never be sure he will. She has put her life on hold while she awaits her husband's decision. She needs to get a grip on her own life and make her own decision, because only then will she be sure that her best interests are being considered.

ON THE BRINK

Forty-four-year-old Dawn is deeply devoted to her husband and her marriage. She has been married to Andrew for eight years and has never cheated on him. As an advertising manager for an influential magazine, Dawn travels frequently for business and is a regular at social events around town. She was a much-sought-after date in her single days, and continues to be popular.

She told me that her priorities for her life were a caring and trusted companion and an interesting job.

Dawn said her main requirement for a husband was that he be her best friend, and always be loyal to her. She had been burned by high-profile, womanizing men in the past and could never imagine being married to such a man. After she met Andrew, she believed he was her soulmate. Much to her chagrin, he cheated on her with two different women during their courtship. Both times, Dawn found out. She describes her marriage:

Andrew just started acting differently. I called him on his behavior, and he denied it several times with both women. Even after I made a fool of myself by confronting the other women, he still lied to me about his involvements. Sure, we weren't yet married, but he had led me to believe we were in an exclusive relationship headed toward marriage.

The biggest mistakes I ever made were to take him back after those incidents. I think they were "signs" that I should have left him then and there. Instead, we began our relationship afresh, and eventually married. I made it clear to Andrew that there was no way I would stay with a husband who cheated on me. I thought he got the message, but obviously he didn't. Or else he thought I wouldn't find out; or if I did, he would be able to sweet-talk me out of leaving, as he had done when we were dating.

The first few years after we married, things were really nice, with Andrew being more attentive to me than ever. I felt I had made a wise decision to stay with him and to marry him. I set out to make my marriage special. I have never liked children. I always thought they would detract from my career and relationships. I knew years ago that if I ever married, I would never be talked into having kids.

Andrew was perfect for me because he, too, dislikes children. Great, I thought, we can each focus on our careers and still have a wonderful life together as lovers and best friends. And our marriage was like that for a while.

Now, though, Andrew has affairs with younger women, even though he is eight years older than I am, and let's face it, I'm not old. I even look younger than my years, and because of my career in fashion and media, I really keep in shape and I'm up on the latest styles and trends. Still, Andrew has some pathological need to befriend secretaries and other women who may need him in some way. His modus operandi is to take them to lunch, then dinner, then to bed. He's Mr. Nice Guy to them all. Who can blame them for falling for him? Of course, the women never stop to consider that maybe Mr. Terrific isn't really so great if he is lying to his wife and cheating on her.

Andrew broke my heart in the past, and now that he has done it again it is even worse, because the wounds from before have reopened. Besides, I feel so left out when Andrew takes other women to dinner and then ignores me at home. He can shower attention and affection on other women, but not on his own wife. In spite of my great job and friends, I feel terribly empty because of the way the man I love is treating me.

Andrew doesn't even go out of his way to hide his cheating anymore. Of course he denies everything if I ask him and tells me I'm imagining it all. I feel so distressed because this is the man I trusted and counted on more than anyone I have ever known. How can he treat me this way?

I have numerous opportunities to become involved with very appealing men, but I've always chosen not to because I fundamentally believe that extramarital affairs are wrong. It means a lot to me to be loyal in my marriage and trustworthy across the board. Even if Andrew would never find out if I slept with another man, I would know I had, and I wouldn't feel right about it. I often wish I could have affairs, just to show Andrew that I'm attractive to someone, that some man will pay attention to me, but I know he wouldn't even care. He and his entire family are totally devoid of any ability to show warmth.

I can't even figure out now why Andrew and I ever married. He never touches me, and I can't remember the last time we had sex. And I have a very good memory. He is always putting down the way I look, whereas he used to compliment me. He is always distancing himself from me. When he picks up the phone to someone else, I hear how his voice becomes enthusiastic—but to me, it's like: "Oh, it's only you."

Andrew keeps me hanging on by being nice every once in a while. He ignored me for months lately, then the other day he asked if I wanted to go away for an overnight stay. Of course I did—I thought it would be a wonderful chance to rekindle our sex life. Wrong. He brought work with him, and I ended up touring on my own. The setting made me feel even more lonely than I had been at home.

He misleads other women and lets them think his marriage is in trouble. I heard him once on the phone saying, "I don't want to say too much about my marriage." I guess he figured if he didn't mention me, then his girlfriend would think he was seriously interested in her. It hurts me so much that he downplays our marriage. If he really feels that way, why are we married?

I'm now thinking about ending my marriage. What is really pushing me to the brink of leaving is being ignored by Andrew, while at the same time knowing he's taking other women out. I married him because I wanted a true partner in life, and now I see I don't have that. I don't want to be attacked from inside my marriage; that happens enough from the outside world. I don't want it from the man I love.

I don't feel as close to Andrew when I know he is lying to me, and the last thing I want to do is touch him when he is so blatantly deceiving me. What's it all leading to? What's the point of being with him, and cutting out my other options, if I'm not getting what I truly want out of my marriage?

Some days I think staying married to Andrew is better than leaving, and other days I think the worst thing is to stay in a marriage full of lies. The thought of spending the next half of my life being lied to, and not having my needs for closeness and affection met, are taking me to the brink. I don't want to feel lonely in this marriage for the rest of my life.

At the moment I feel totally cold toward Andrew. I might as well be alone in bed at night, because I feel like I'm sharing it with a total stranger— a stranger I don't even want to know.

Everyone in my work circle cheats, but I have a very strong sense of loyalty and of right and wrong. I can't explain exactly why, but I don't think it's a nice thing to cheat on one's partner, married or not. Everyone needs one person who won't dump on them or betray them, and I offer that to Andrew. I just wish I was receiving the same gift in return.

It's one thing if a husband cheats and then regrets it, and tries to apologize to his wife and is loyal ever after. But not only does Andrew not apologize for hurting me, but he essentially says: "What's your problem? I'll do what I want. You'll never tell me what to do." With an attitude like that, I don't see any happy ending for my marriage. I don't want to be married to a man who is so nasty to me.

I'm so angry at Andrew right now, but mostly I'm deeply disappointed in him for not giving his all to me and our marriage. I feel cheated out of the chance to make my marriage work, because both partners have to want the same things, and it's obvious we don't.

I could stay for fifty years and we still won't agree on infidelity. He basically thinks it's okay, that he can lead other women on and not have it affect me. But it does affect me, because I don't approve of it. Being cheated on makes me feel like dirt.

I have always had a realistic view of the world—and of marriage. I never expected marriage to be bump-free, but I don't see why Andrew goes looking for trouble with other women. The way some men treat women makes me wonder why more women aren't gay.

All I want is a happy and contented home life with a devoted husband. That's not asking too much, but I can't seem to have it with Andrew. I no longer see the point in being married if I can't talk to my husband and get honest responses in return. I can't even ask Andrew about his day at work, or he thinks I'm spying on him. If I ask him about lunch, or his projects, he yells and says I'm violating his privacy. Excuse me! I'm just interested in sharing his experiences. To me, that's what marriage is about.

I have my own money and my own friends, so there's no point in staying married to a husband who won't provide me with the one thing I want out of marriage—a loyal and affectionate partnership. I want more from my life than a man who deceives me in the one way that hurts me the most.

Dawn is living in quasi-limbo, but it's interesting to note that she is much more confident about what she wants in life, and is more determined to get it, than many of the other women I interviewed for this book. Throughout the interviews, it was striking to notice that the older women—those over-fifty—were much more likely to cling on to lifeless marriages than to try and reinvent their own lives. Women like Dawn, young women who have careers and their own money, are more likely to leave a philandering husband. While they may still love their husband, they believe in reciprocal loyalty in marriage, and in the absence of it, are likely to bolt and search for it elsewhere.

It is the rare woman—and man—who condones sex with other partners.

Open marriages, as immortalised in the 1970s-era film *The Ice Storm*, just don't work. They create sexual jealousy and fuel fears of abandonment; most importantly, they are the antithesis of what a caring relationship is all about.

TORN BETWEEN TWO LOVERS

There are certainly some couples who try to accommodate the husband's need to wander, but the number who do so successfully remains small. One woman who "allows" her husband to have other women says she likes to meet his lovers to determine whether the woman will be a threat to the marriage. If she senses the lover is after more than sex, then she vetoes the woman. This supposed "open arrangement" is not really so open at all, because the wife is still saying she doesn't want another woman to come between her and her husband. The woman is trying to go along with her husband's desire for other lovers only because she is afraid he will dump her if she doesn't. She would prefer a faithful husband. In her own way, meeting and "interviewing" her husband's lovers to ascertain their intentions is her way of controlling her husband's philandering.

What this woman, and others in her situation, fail to take into account is the "You Just Never Know" phenomenon. Whenever a man strays, there is *always* the possibility that he will fall hard for the other woman and leave his wife. And the more a man womanizes, the greater his chances of truly falling for one of his lovers.

No matter how much a woman tries to control the situation, extramarital affairs are always risky business for all concerned. It is for the wife to decide for herself whether an adulterous husband will lead her into marital limbo, or whether she will use his infidelity as a springboard to a better way of life. A woman who refuses to stay with a man who strays may ultimately be happier and more confident than one who stays. Each woman must make her decision based on her own individual situation.

TAKE NOTE

- Just because you stand by your man today doesn't guarantee that he won't leave you tomorrow.

- Even though you stay with your straying husband, you will vacillate back and forth—"Should I stay, should I leave?"—many times each day.

- Staying with a man who strays is not an easy thing for many women to do.

- Make each day count for yourself.

- By staying with your lying and cheating husband, you may be missing out on a better way of life—a life, perhaps, with a man who will respect you and be faithful to you. A life in which you are not consumed by worry over where your husband is, what he is doing, and who he is doing it with.

Chapter 10

SHOULD YOU STAY WITH A MAN WHO STRAYS?

$\mathcal{D}$on't forget to love yourself.

—*Soren Kierkegaard*

$\mathcal{T}$here is so little difference between husbands that you might
as well keep the first.

—*Adela Rogers St. John*

$\mathcal{T}$he only two people who count in any marriage are the two
that are in it.

—*Hillary Clinton to Matt Lauer on* The Today Show, *January 27, 1998*

TO STAY OR GO? OR STRAY?

A philandering spouse goes behind your back and leaves you in the dark about his behavior. Think very carefully if this is how you wish to live. You *do* have a choice.

Infidelity is pervasive, but that doesn't mean it's the right thing to do, at least not if you want a thriving, happy, and lasting marriage. Nevertheless, adultery abounds, and it may even be happening to you. Perhaps nothing is as important to your overall well-being as your decision whether you will stand by your cheating husband. If your husband is cheating on you, you must think carefully about how you will cope with the situation. There is no such thing as "simple" infidelity, and there is no easy answer to the question you must ask yourself: *Should I stay with my philandering husband?*

There is always room for one mistake. But twice is a pattern. You must ask yourself if your man is really going to give up philandering, or if he will only be more discreet and deceptive in trying to keep his adultery from you.

Based on the interviews for this book, it is clear that not all adultery is created equal. Whether a man is engaging in a series of one-night flings, paying occasional visits to a prostitute, or is involved in a sexually and emotionally intimate long-term relationship will influence a woman's decision to stay or leave. Most women view *any* infidelity as an insult, but many nevertheless stand by their man and try to tolerate the infidelity. Some women find a onetime casual fling less threatening, and more forgivable, than a long-term affair.

No one knows for sure how many men are compulsive womanizers, or who are sex addicts; but for women married to such men, the challenge to cope with their behavior can be daunting, and considerably more difficult than dealing with a "garden-variety" philanderer. A real relationship—one that entails deep emotional as well as sexual involvent between the husband and another woman—generally causes women the most concern, is the most difficult to tolerate, and is what often propels women to leave a marriage.

All extramarital sex is a threat to your emotional well-being, your physical health, and your marriage. Contrary to what many men say, infidelity is *not* something all men engage in.

DOES YOUR HUSBAND REALIZE THE PAIN HIS INFIDELITY CAUSES YOU?

*I*n evaluating your situation, pay particular attention to your husband's ability to recognize that his adultery is a problem for you. If you talk to your husband about his affair, does he laugh off your comments, yell at you, change the subject, dismiss your concern and say he'll stray anyway, or tell you it's all in your head? The way your husband reacts to your attempts to discuss his infidelity will say a lot about his respect for you.

Does your husband tell you to grow up and accept his dalliances? Or does he apologize, tell you he wants to change his behavior, and ask you to help him? A man's ability to talk with you about his affair is a big step toward ironing out infidelity difficulties.

Change is difficult for anyone, especially for a man who doesn't want to change or to give up other women. Even if your husband actively seeks to make changes in his behavior, it's a hard thing to do. And it is nearly impossible to change the behavior of another person unless they desperately want to change themselves. If your husband doesn't want to be faithful to you, there isn't much you can do to change his mind.

Remember: Leopards don't change their spots; apples don't become oranges. If you are waiting around hoping that one day your husband will decide that he doesn't want to be unfaithful to you any longer, think again. Many men told me that once they had cheated on their wife, there was no turning back. Sadly, it seems, once unfaithful, always unfaithful. Are you willing to live with this? Can you *really* accept it? Can you survive—or, more importantly, thrive—in a marriage that exists in name only? Do you even want to try? The choice is yours. You don't have to tolerate behavior you find distasteful.

Of the many women I spoke with who are trying desperately to live a productive and happy life with a serial adulterer, most described a situation akin to an emotional cul-de-sac. They keep going around and around in circles, yet nothing changes, and they end up feeling depressed and sad. Many women who stay with a straying spouse live in a constant state of emotional turmoil.

KNOW YOURSELF AND YOUR PRIORITIES

I know women who move out the first time the guy does something wrong, which is crazy. You have to decide what you want and who you want.

—SUPERMODEL JERRY HALL

You must determine what *really* matters to you, and then decide how to go about getting what you want from your marriage. You may not always get what it is you seek, but you have a good chance of avoiding what you really *don't* want. Life is a series of trade-offs in our personal and professional lives. You need to determine what will make you happy in your marriage and your life as a whole. Decide what you need from your husband in order to be happy in your marriage, and then determine if he will ever be capable of satisfying your desires.

Why do you want to stay with your straying husband? List all the reasons why you should stay, then list all the reasons why you should leave. If you want to stay, how will your marital situation have to change in order for you to be content with it? In answering these questions, consider the following factors, which influence many women's decisions to tolerate a husband's philandering:

What Is Important to You in Your Marriage?

- *Money?* Do you need the financial stability and security of marriage?

- *Sexual exclusivity?* Do you want a monogamous marriage?

- *Friendship?* Do you want your husband to be your best friend?

- *Career success?* Are your professional opportunities worth compromising to stay with a straying husband?

- A *happy family/children?* Are you staying with a straying husband because you believe it is best for your family?

Write down all the important things about marriage in general, and your marriage in particular, that matter to you. List your spouse's good points and bad. What aspects of your marriage do you want to live with? What *can't* you live with? On what issues are you willing to compromise? Do you have a list of non-negotiable wishes? If so, what are they? Are you being realistic? You must ask yourself these questions and think about your answers. They will help guide you in determining whether you should stay with a man who strays.

One woman interviewed for this book, Nicole, forty-eight years old, decided to leave her straying husband and begin a new life for herself. For well over eighteen months Nicole suspected that her husband, Scott, was cheating on her. He began working every weekend, traveling even more frequently than usual, and was abrupt with her whenever she wanted to spend time with him. He withdrew sexually from her, and Nicole was miserable about his behavioral changes. Every two or three months she would try to speak with him about what was on his mind. She knew he was preoccupied, and she wanted to be involved in his world. Scott constantly rebuffed her. Finally, she began asking him pointblank if he was involved with someone else. Scott denied it—for over a year.

After all the attempts Nicole made to try to show Scott she loved him and missed their closeness, Scott broke the bad news to her: his girlfriend was eight months pregnant! Nicole was shattered, not only because of the betrayal and the pregnancy, but because she had asked Scott so many times if he was seeing someone else, and he lied to her repeatedly.

Scott told Nicole he wanted time to think about what he was going to do about his situation—whether he was going to leave the marriage for his lover (a coworker at his law firm) and child-to-be, or stay married and still play a role in his new child's life. Nicole made the decision for him. She ordered him out of the house that very day.

Nicole never regretted her decision to end her marriage. She had been through months of turmoil when she suspected Scott of having an affair, and grew angrier and angrier with him for not being honest with her. When he finally leveled with her—and it was worse than she imagined—she decided she was better off without a lying, cheating husband.

Nicole has been on her own for two years now. Since her divorce she has moved to a new city, sent her only daughter off to college, begun a new job, made new friends, and started seeing a man she met through a local exercise walking club. She says she could not imagine what a miserable life she would be living if she had stayed with Scott. She did not want to share the life of a child her once beloved husband fathered with another woman, and she has never seen the young boy, who is now the half brother to her daughter. (Scott married his former coworker, a lawyer.)

Evaluating her life how, Nicole says she would never want to be back in her former existence. Even though she loved Scott until the end of the marriage, and still feels occasional pangs for the good times they shared, she in no way regrets standing up for herself and leaving a situation she did not want to be a part of. So, at the age of forty-eight, Nicole is living life on her own terms — and enjoying the new chapter she has begun for herself.

STAY OR LEAVE?

Should I Stay With a Man Who Strays?

WISH LIST

• Rank in order of importance the things that mean most to you in a relationship.

Example: *Sexual fidelity*

REALITY LIST

• Now list, in descending order, what you actually have in your relationship.

Your wish list and reality list will give you a clear picture of what you want out of your marriage and what you perceive it is lacking. It is important to recognize that you have formed a personal "bargain with your betrayer." You accept the good things your husband brings to your life; but in exchange, you also accept the negatives.

We all make a number of trade-offs in our daily lives and in our relationships. The key is to know what you are willing to give for what you receive in return. For many women, being Mrs. Anybody — a wife — is worth putting up with a man's philandering. Other women won't put up with a cheating husband for all the money in the world. *You* must make your own decision, because it's your life to live.

Staying with a Man Who Strays May Be Hazardous to Your Health

It would have killed me staying with Mick.
—Marianne Faithful, onetime paramour of Mick Jagger

Some trade-offs are bigger than others, of course, and trying to survive and thrive in a marriage with a long-term unfaithful husband can try the patience of even an exceedingly tolerant and loving woman. Not only do you put yourself at risk for sexually transmitted diseases your straying husband may pass on to you, but by staying with a straying partner you may also put yourself at risk for other health hazards, such as depression, alcoholism, and obesity.

Lack of control over situations has been found to predispose a person to a higher risk of heart disease. Lack of control over one's living situation — and living with an adulterous husband certainly creates a tension-filled environment — has also been demonstrated to increase depression.

When a woman finds herself in an untenable situation over and over again, and sees few options for leaving the situation, what is called "learned helplessness" sets in, and she becomes increasingly depressed about her predicament. Living with long-term infidelity may create an environment in which the woman sees no way out — she sees no options for leaving her philandering husband or for getting him to quit his affairs. She sees a depressing situation if she leaves and a depressing one if she stays. This situation can lead to a downward spiral in her emotional and physical health. The long-term effects on well-being of tolerating a philandering husband are not yet fully known, but many married women I spoke with said they turned to alcohol and food to help them cope with feelings of worthlessness brought on by their husband's affairs. Unfortunately, such abuses can create even more problems for a woman.

Anger and hostility have been shown to be detrimental to one's health. Bottled rage is implicated in heart disease, high blood pressure, depression, suicide, and an increased risk of certain cancers. *Betrayed women are angry as hell,* but many women are taught it isn't feminine to display anger, so they suppress it. In doing so, other dysfunctions — such as heavy drinking and excessive eating — may set in. Depression, too, can be traced to anger. It is widely held that depression is anger turned inward. When a woman feels that she cannot openly confront a problem she is facing, she often represses her feelings. Of course, they spill over later into a variety of other problems, from sleep disturbances to headaches and stomachaches.

Many of the women interviewed for this book were in a constant state of anxiety and depression, which seem to be side effects of staying with a man who strays. When a person lies to you, deceives you, is evasive with you, it leads to anguish and tension, neither of which is conducive to a calm and peaceful life. For some women, "the stomach knows." Some of the people I spoke with who are tolerating their husband's dalliances suffer chronic stomach discomfort. Sometimes the body tells us things our mind is trying to ignore. Listen carefully to your body; it will let you know when you have had enough.

An adulterous marriage can also have a negative impact on a woman's psychological functioning. Infidelity is a form of emotional abuse, as repeated betrayals and deception eat away at a woman's self-confidence and basic sense of herself.

SHOULD YOU BREAK UP YOUR PARTNERSHIP BECAUSE YOUR PARTNER CHEATED ON YOU?

A marriage is, first and foremost, a legal arrangement. Husband and wife are business partners in the marriage. Would you stay with a business partner if they repeatedly defrauded and cheated you? That is exactly what a husband does when he is unfaithful. He is lying and deceiving not only his business partner but also the woman he professes to love. And for whom he vowed to forsake all others. Do you want to stay in a partnership with such a man?

What's in it for You?—Do You Want a Marriage in Name Only?

Ask yourself what you will gain by staying with a man who continually cheats you out of love and trust. How long will it be before you are emotionally bankrupt?

In business you divest yourself of a colleague, and in marriage you divorce a partner. Divorce has a bad smell to it, despite its seeming popularity. However, is a divorce really worse than a marriage in name only? Each day you remain in a marriage with a man who is cheating on you is another day you are depriving yourself of the chance to be in a happier situation. Each day you remain Mrs. Put-Up-with-His-Deceit, you are robbing yourself of precious time to live your life openly and honestly.

Yet many of the women I spoke with were waiting to see if their husband would end his affair(s). They didn't want to take any independent action for fear of forcing their husband's hand and driving him to ask for a divorce. The majority of women interviewed said they were trying to cope as best they could while "allowing" their husband to continue seeing other women, hoping that he would tire of the philandering. As one woman told me, "I'm waiting it out until he comes to his senses and the affair runs its course."

Some women stay with their man because they believe he has given up the Other Woman and sworn off affairs for good. Many times women are rewarded thereafter with a faithful husband. Unfortunately, some men feel that once they have had an affair, there is no way they will go without another one in the future. These men tell their wives they vow to be faithful; in reality, they become extremely deceptive, and their philandering "goes underground."

Even for a man who genuinely wants to "kick affairs," doing so can be difficult, especially if he maintain friends and is still in a workplace that previously figured in his affairs. Even though he is motivated to be faithful, environmental factors—such as women continually throwing themselves at him—can make his philandering continue.

Regardless of whether a woman offers herself to him, a man can always say no—even when it is difficult to do so. A man should not be opening his zipper for every woman he desires, any more than a woman can unzip her wallet for every dress she wants.

> *"I'm trying not to do this. I'm trying to be good."*
> —WHAT MONICA LEWINSKY CLAIMS PRESIDENT BILL CLINTON
> TOLD HER FOR WHY THEY COULD NOT CONTINUE THEIR
> SEXUAL RELATIONSHIP. THE STARR REPORT TO THE
> U.S. HOUSE OF REPRESENTATIVES, SEPTEMBER 11, 1998.

If your spouse is cheating on you, do you really have a marriage anyway? When a man has sex with a woman other than his wife, he is not only depriving his wife of fidelity; he is also keeping her in the dark about behaviors that directly affect her. Since most adultery isn't sanctioned by the other partner, infidelity operates in a shroud of secrets and lies. The wife is then robbed of her trust in her marriage partner.

Do you want to give up your valuable and vital years to a man who seems to value you so little that he lies to you? Adultery always involves deception—sometimes outright lies, but always evasiveness. Both of these are poison to a thriving marriage.

The D-word—divorce—is as difficult for some women to contemplate as the A-word—adultery. Why should they divorce? women wonder. To do what? Move on to another philanderer? Why trade one mistake for another? women ask themselves. "I might as well stay with my current husband, because *all* men cheat," is a frequently voiced sentiment.

Most of the women I interviewed were thoroughly committed to making their marriage last, despite their husbands' infidelities. Many women really do believe in marriage and are willing to work on their relationship with their husband, even though many of them could be considered to be "re-arranging deck chairs on the *Titanic*," in that their marriage is bound to sink sooner or later.

For some, standing by their man is the choice they make, and they focus their attention on making life as manageable as possible within the confines of an adulterous union. Other women decide to go off and build a new life. Women always have choices. We all create our own opportunities and we are never without options. Never stop believing in your ability to forge your own life, with or without a man by your side.

Marriage as the Status Quo

Human beings are, to a certain extent, creatures of habit, and marriage is certainly habit-forming. Even those people who divorce tend to marry again. Marriage provides routine and stability in an otherwise chaotic world. Many men realize this, and it explains why many don't want to leave their wives even though they also have girlfriends.

Women will seemingly try any sort of arrangement or affectionate ac-commodation before they decide to divorce a philandering husband. For women, marriage at its best provides a safe harbor from the often harsh realities of life. However, when a woman is being attacked from within the confines of her own home, which is what happens with adultery, then the warm and fuzzy security of home may not be as beneficial as it could be.

THE HUMILIATION FACTOR

$\mathcal{W}$omen talk of the humiliation they feel when they learn their husband is seeing another woman. That humiliation is made even worse if the woman was the last to know. In many cases, friends know before she does when a woman is being betrayed by her husband, and often it is with one of her friends that her husband is having the affair! This compounds the hurt and humiliation a woman feels upon the discovery of infidelity.

Women who have been betrayed report feeling "not good enough to keep him interested." A woman must ask herself: *How much humiliation can I stand? What is more humiliating for me: staying with a cheating husband or being by myself? Am I losing myself in a marriage of lies?*

In one way or another, each of us will suffer humiliation at some point in our lives. The only way to deal with it is to raise our heads high and get on with life. If your husband is humiliating you by cheating on you, ask yourself these two questions: *What's the worst thing that can happen to me if I stay? What's the worst thing that can happen to me if I leave?* A man's infidelity will always get you down, but it doesn't have to destroy you.

In order for a woman to continue to live in an adulterous marriage, she must disengage herself emotionally to the point where she can no longer feel the rage her husband's adulterous behavior causes her. The problem is, by disengaging her feelings in an attempt to ward off negative emotions, she is also limiting her ability to feel *positive* emotions. By trying to hold back her feelings of anger and betrayal, she is shielding herself from the warmth and love she is seeking in her marriage. Is staying in an adulterous marriage worth closing off joy from your life? By tolerating a philandering spouse, are you giving yourself up in the process?

IS AN ADULTEROUS MARRIAGE REALLY BETTER THAN NO MARRIAGE AT ALL?

$\mathcal{W}$omen wonder what their chances are of finding another man they could love, who would love them in return, and, most importantly, be faithful.

Some women decide to pursue a new life, while others choose to stick by their philandering husband and make do as best they can.

Many men believe that extramarital sex is no big deal. And, surprisingly, some women aren't upset by infidelity. They have generally resigned themselves, albeit reluctantly, to the fact that men will cheat. But these women are in the minority; it is generally very difficult for a woman to tolerate adultery if she wants a truly happy, intimate, and enduring marriage. Long-term infidelity is fundamentally incompatible with a truly intimate, thriving relationship. It is very difficult to be truthful when one is busily covering one's tracks with deceit—which is what's required to keep infidelity afloat.

Sex is easy to find, but good relationships are more valuable. Most important of all in a partnership are *respect* and *caring*. These are the ties that bind. It is virtually impossible for two people to feel close to each other—to be soulmates—when one of them is consistently lying to the other. Infidelity cracks even the most sturdy of marital foundations.

Too many women give up their interests, their careers, other opportunities—in fact, often themselves—in order to remain in a relationship with a man who won't even give up an affair! When you start acting differently, when you start acting like a bitch, when you start hating yourself, you will know you have stayed too long with your philandering man. When you become bitter, distrustful of others, and negative, you have stayed far too long. You may have to give up your marriage to save yourself.

Many women feel they must stay with a man who strays because they have no other alternatives. They feel financially vulnerable, emotionally numb, and socially ostracized. However, tolerating adultery requires time and energy—energy that would be better spent on improving *your* life.

Obviously, women need to consider practical financial issues when deciding whether to stay or leave an adulterous marriage. Obtaining an education and developing a career will be your best lifetime bet for financial security. The less you must depend on a man, or a marriage, the happier you will be. If you have your own job and money, you will have more options than women who are totally tied financially to a man.

The women I interviewed who have divorced philandering men voiced few regrets other than the time they had wasted:

- *I wish I had left the first time he cheated on me. By staying through five of his affairs, I'm afraid he thought he could treat me like dirt. I like myself so much better now.*

- *I can't believe I stayed with him as long as I did. My only regret is that I didn't leave him sooner.*

You don't have to let your life slip away while waiting for your husband to decide what happens to you. *You* are in charge of your *own* life. You have choices and options; you need only decide to pursue them.

TAKE NOTE

- You must trust your gut instinct about whether you should stay or leave your philandering man. It is no use asking your mother, friend, coworker, or any other person for advice because it is *you* — and you *alone* — who must endure the situation.

- If you are able to thrive in your life while married to a cheating husband, then perhaps staying will work for you.

- If you have physical and emotional complaints, and are always moody, perhaps trying to tolerate a cheating husband is not the course for you.

- Some women find a way to tolerate a straying husband. However, many women who stay with men who stray means locking themselves in their own private hell.

- Life is too short to waste. You must make each day count for *you*.

Part 3

THRIVING IN LIFE AFTER A HUMILIATING BETRAYAL

Chapter 11

THE AFTERMATH OF INFIDELITY

I want my life back.

—*Monica Lewinsky on her twenty-fifth birthday, July 23, 1998
quoted in Time, August 10, 1998*

*H*ow could he have unprotected sex with someone he doesn't

even know?

—*Wife of an unfaithful man*

*S*ex changes *everything*.

—*A philandering husband*

EXTRAMARITAL AFFAIRS—THE "GIFTS" THAT KEEP ON GIVING

Talk to anyone who has ever been involved in a triangle affair during their marriage and most will tell you that while there may be some sexual highs, there are no real winners in the aftermath of affairs. Affairs tend to be gifts that keep on giving—all too often, unwanted gifts. In the aftermath of an affair, almost everyone gets hurt in one way or another, whether emotionally, sexually, personally, or professionally. Perhaps the best infidelity movie of all time, *Fatal Attraction*, showed graphically that while a married man's fling may be over, his nightmare may just be beginning.

Some people do concern themselves with the possible consequences of their extramarital sexual activities; far more act without thinking about the impact their actions will have on their spouse and family. They want to be "swept away" and not ponder the consequences or possible problems. In fact, the desire to avoid problems is one reason cited for why many men get involved in affairs in the first place. They see their participation in extramarital affairs as a way to get away from the dreariness, the domesticity of everyday marriage—worrying about the mortgage and the kids—and to give in to their desire for uninhibited sex and a narcissistic need for attention.

Affairs may offer an antidote to the tedium inherent in some marriages, but at what emotional and financial cost to all involved? Who wins? Who loses? Does a short-term gain override a long-term loss? Many people don't ponder such tough questions until after their affair has been discovered and has wreaked havoc on their marriage and their life. The truth has a way of coming out eventually.

There Is No Such Thing as Safe Sex—only Safer Sex

If information is power, then what you don't know *can* hurt you. And these days, what you don't know could even *kill* you.

PROTECTING ONESELF AGAINST STDs

Women worry about catching a sexually transmitted disease (STD) from their hsuband if they continue to have sex with him while he is also sexually involved with another woman. Yet the women also worry that if they do not have sex with their man, then he will feel justified in having sex with other women. However a woman behaves, she feels she has a lot to lose. She worries that she will either lose her man to another woman or gain a sexually transmitted disease.

Fears about STDs are realistic. When a man strays, he may be putting himself and his wife at risk for an entire range of diseases. According to an October 16, 1997 study by the Center for Disease Control and Prevention, reported in *USA Today*, forty-five million Americans — one in five — carries the virus that causes genital herpes! The report also claims that 91 percent of people do not even know they have the disease, and *genital herpes rates are highest for people with multiple sex partners.*

Millions of innocent, monogamous women are being infected with sexually transmitted diseases by having sex with a straying husband. A woman must decide for herself if the benefits of remaining married to a philandering man are worth risking her health.

Many men do not use condoms when they have illicit liaisons. A sex survey conducted by *Philadelphia* magazine in December 1992 found that 57 percent of men and women don't discuss safe sex with a new partner prior to sex. A similar poll conducted in 1996 by EDK for Burroughs Wellcome Company, reported in *USA Today* showed that 40 percent of men never discuss their sexual history before starting a new sexual relationship; 31 percent of women don't discuss their sexual history.

There was a time when men had extramarital sex mainly with prostitutes or professional girlfriends, and they worried about the diseases they could spread to unsuspecting wives. These days, whether a man is caught with his pants down in a hotel room in Miami, the Hamptons, or Beverly Hills, chances are he's not wearing a condom. When a man has sex with a woman during a one-night fling, caution is often discarded in the heat of the moment. Some men and women don't consider it cheating or adultery if it "just happens," if it isn't premeditated. And to many people, "premeditated" means using condoms. Therefore, many otherwise intelligent people don't practice safer sex because to do so would imply that they had "planned" to have sex, and in their mind, that would constitute adultery.

Even with the risks involved in extramarital sex, some downright reckless sexual behavior is pursued, and many men and women take those risks in order to gain reassurance from someone other than their spouse that they are sexually desirable.

I interviewed one married man who had a one-night fling while away at a business conference. In the morning, he found the woman had left the room before he awoke. Not only had she taken his wallet, including his cash, credit cards, driver's license, and his wife's business card, but she had also left him a shocking message written on the bathroom mirror in her lipstick: "The joke is on you. AIDS."

The man was frantic. Was she trying to tell him she was HIV-infected? Was she going to call his wife and spill the beans? Was she for real? He immediately regretted his actions of the night before and wondered why he had ever been so naive as to risk *everything* just for an orgasm with a stranger.

I was astounded by the number of women who wrote to me about contracting a sexually transmitted disease from their philandering partners. Herpes was the most common STD mentioned. In one case, the woman's husband accused *her* of sleeping around and infecting *him*, when they both knew he had had several affairs and flings while she had remained faithful. Over and over I heard tales of men not using protection with their other women, while their innocent, unsuspecting wives continued to have sex with them. In this day and age, there is no excuse for reckless sexual behavior.

A philandering man's wife should worry *a lot* about STDs. The *New York Times* reported on July 31, 1997, that of the AIDS cases reported in New York City between 1980 and 1996, 49 percent of the women aged thirty to thirty-nine had contracted AIDS from sex, rather than from drug use or blood transfusions. The same article claimed that more and more AIDS cases are developing in people aged over fifty. (Part of the problem, researchers say, is that some doctors are age-biased and don't think older people have sex; thus such people aren't being monitored for symptoms of STDs such as AIDS.)

One sixty-four-year old man cited in the *Times* article recalled that after one episode of infidelity in a thirty-two-year marriage, he came down with several illnesses, including viral meningitis and pneumonia. It took his doctors until his third hospital stay to ask him about his sexual history. They then diagnosed him with AIDS.

According to Dr. Mark Johnson, an infectious disease specialist interviewed in the *New York Times* article, women "are at an increased risk of AIDS if they have passed menopause and . . . see no need for birth control. Many of these women are totally unsuspecting of their husband's extramarital dalliances." One sixty-one-year-old woman, who began dating men in her upper-class social circle after the end of her twenty-three-year marriage, now has AIDS. She told the *Times* interviewer, "You don't know the sexual history of anyone. Not anyone. You may think you do, but you don't."

There really is no such thing as safe sex—only *safer* sex. People lie about their sexual history all the time. Even when those involved in extramarital affairs use condoms, there is always the risk of condom breakage. When you engage in extramarital sex, you not only endanger yourself; you also endanger the health and life of an innocent party—your unsuspecting and trusting spouse.

Research has already established that a man's infidelity may place his partner at an increased risk of AIDS, herpes, gonorrhea, and other sexually transmitted diseases. Now new research reported in the December 1996 Sex & Health column of *Glamour* magazine links human papilloma virus—genital warts—to a woman's heightened risk of developing cervical cancer. If you are a woman looking the other way while your mate is having sex with other women, you may want to snap out of your denial *now*, as your health may depend on it.

Dr. Keerti Shah of Johns Hopkins University School of Medicine, who with colleagues N. Munoz and F. X. Bosch conducted the research published in the *Journal of the National Cancer Institute* reported in *Glamour*, has found that if a husband has multiple sexual partners and contracts the human papilloma virus, his wife is five to nine times more likely to develop cervical cancer than a woman whose husband has no other sexual partners. In addition, the risks of developing cervical cancer increase significantly depending on the number of extramarital sex partners the man takes. Basically, the more extramarital sex partners the man has, the more likely he is to contract the virus—which can lead to an increased risk of cervical cancer in his wife.

According to this same research, a man's exposure to another common sexually transmitted disease, chlamydia, also significantly increases the woman's risk of cervical cancer. Since both human papilloma virus and chlamydia usually pose few symptoms in the early stages, many men will not know they have contracted an STD.

A woman pulling the wool over her eyes, or putting her head in the sand as a way of ignoring a man's infidelity may suffer tragic physical and emotional consequences. If you are staying with a philandering man, and having sex with him while he is also having sex with other women, you must think carefully about your decision to continue doing so, as your physical health is at risk.

"LOVE CHILDREN"

More than a few men have been shocked when a current or former mistress informs him she is pregnant. Some of the men order the women to abort; but many women decide to keep the child—much to the man's dismay. After all, many of them already have a "first family." When news of an affair reaches a man's wife, she is usually livid. If she receives news of a pregnant mistress, or one with a child by her husband, it usually spells disaster all round.

Wives do eventually learn of the other children. It may take years, or even the death of the husband, but it is *never* welcome news. In the case of some of the women interviewed for this book, it spelled the end of the marriage—or of the illusion of marriage, with the couple staying together but leading separate lives.

When a man fathers a child with his lover, it will be a continuous, negative reminder to his wife of his philandering. The child will be a living, breathing sign of his other life—a life she most likely does not want to acknowledge or participate in. A love child makes it harder for the wife to deny the existence of another woman.

If other women are time bandits, then other women who bear illegitimate children can be major time and money sinkholes. If a man decides to be involved in his illegitimate child's life while remaining married, time, energy, affection, and money will all be diverted away from his primary relationship.

WHEN AFFAIRS TURN UGLY . . . AND THEY OFTEN DO

I once heard someone say that *all* affairs end badly, or why else would they end? Some affairs, it seems, have a particularly cruel and painful aftermath for one, two, or all the people involved. Several years ago in Manhattan, a respected judge was convicted for harassing his former lover, a socialite, after she ended their affair. The harassment was so severe it ended the man's career, landed him in prison, and is paving the way for new antistalking laws in New York.

Even a seemingly innocent cyber relationship can tip a jealous spouse over the edge. In January 1997, the *New York Post* reported that a radio talk-show host in Philadelphia sent flowers to a friend he frequently chatted with on the Internet, because she sounded down and he "wanted to brighten her day." Several days later, the woman was slashed to death, allegedly by her husband.

The police reported that the woman had seven male friends she corresponded with on the Internet and had allegedly had a rendezvous with one of them, though not the radio host. The police speculated that when her husband saw the flowers, it was the last straw. Several people who wrote to the *New York Post* sympathized with the husband, saying that men and women can't be "just friends." "I believe there had to be something else," one wrote. "Men just don't send roses unless they want something."

It seems that any attention to a woman can provoke some men, who may practice a strict double standard of sexual behavior: *I can, but you'd better not!*

CAREERS SINK

$\mathcal{M}$ore than a few rising careers have been halted in their ascent, and some have downright crash-landed, when extramarital affairs were revealed.

In July 1997, the president and chief executive of the Salt Lake City Winter Olympic Games 2002 organizing committee resigned amid allegations that he bruised and restrained his wife during an argument over another woman. The man had labored since 1985 to bring the Games to the city and now found his career and life in shambles when he acknowledged "emotional ties" to an unnamed woman.

Similar tales surface regularly in the media. Whether they are photographed leaving a woman's apartment or kissing an underage girl in a public park, or seen fondling a woman in a hallway outside a study, men put their personal and professional lives on the line when they engage in extramarital affairs. Whether the affair is recorded on videotape, audiotape, or a photographer's camera, the news generally is revealed. A picture or a letter speaks louder than a thousand denials.

Taking It to Court

In a dozen American states, and in some countries of the world, a person can sue for "alienation of affection"; that is, they can seek monetary damages from the person who robs them of their loved one. In an August 1997 case, a North Carolina woman was awarded $1 million against the woman she claimed had "stolen" her husband of nineteen years. The man divorced his wife and later married the Other Woman.

SURVIVING THE AFTERMATH

$\mathcal{T}$here is always an aftermath to extramarital affairs. Like the damage from an explosion, there is collateral damage. The aftermath of an affair may vary in severity, but usually there is human carnage in the form of emotional pain and suffering. Sexually transmitted diseases, divorce, career collapses, and financial ruin—all in the name of extramarital sex. Rarely are there any winners when infidelity is involved, and there are always some losers. Only the people involved can determine if it was all worth it.

Whether a woman stays for the short or long term with her straying husband, she will be a part of the wreckage of his affair(s). How long she will decide to subject herself to the abuse an adulterous union usually inflicts depends on personal, social, and financial reasons. But sooner or later, most women will begin to ask themselves hard questions about their husband's adultery. If a woman is ready to break through the denial of her husband's affairs, she will begin to ask herself if it is really in her best interest to stay with a man who strays.

Every relationship—whether with a friend, a business colleague, or a romantic partner—entails compromise and sacrifice. A woman must decide for herself whether the trade-offs involved in marriage to a philanderer are worth the personal price she will have to pay.

TAKE NOTE

- The cornerstone of extramarital affairs is their unpredictability. "You just never know" what will happen during—or after—an affair.

- There are seldom positive outcomes for romantic triangles. Marriages end, careers sink, illegitimate children can arrive on the scene, finances are drained, and STDs can haunt for a lifetime.

- Think long and hard before engaging in an extramarital affair, because if you go for it, nothing in your life will ever be the same again.

- Extramarital liaisons rarely have happy endings for anyone involved.

Chapter 12

INFIDELITY UNDER THE SPOTLIGHT: LIFESTYLES OF THE FAMOUS AND UNFAITHFUL

. . . . *How* much more poetic it is to marry one
and love many.

—*Oscar Wilde*

193

STARS UNDER THE SPOTLIGHT

$\mathcal{F}$. Scott Fitzgerald once said of the very rich, "They are different from you and me." Indeed, the rich are different—they have more affairs! So too do celebrities, politicians, and sports stars. Movie and television stars and other famous faces are notorious for their behind-closed-door actitivies. If it is difficult for the average adulterer to keep an extramarital affair a secret, imagine the difficulties for people who live out every move amidst cameras.

It is little wonder that most celebrities suffer a "fear of the tabloids." It is tough enough to keep a marriage thriving in the best of times; but for people who live their lives on the public stage, it is almost impossible to keep intimate relationships private. Each and every encounter with a member of the opposite sex, however innocent, is discussed and dissected, or at least whispered about loudly. If every time you talked to a member of the opposite sex, you were photographed together and written up in the newspapers as "secret lovers," it would be enough to cause ripples in even the most solid marriage.

Men and women living in the spotlight face particularly difficult times when the media focuses on their romantic activities. Yet the population at large has an almost insatiable and voyeuristic fascination with the extramarital escapades of the rich and famous. When a famous person cheats on their spouse, or is cheated on, it is big news to the public. The celebrity who is being betrayed probably feels the same pain as any other person, only they are forced to live out their hurt and humiliation in the glare of klieg lights.

Women are like magnets to male celebrities, sports stars, politicians, and successful businessmen. With such temptations, famous men are often unfaithful, and because of intense public interest in their personal lives, they are much more likely eventually to get caught. Making *any* marriage work is a hard task. For the rich and famous, it's even more difficult because the usual stresses on a relationship are compounded by constant intrusions from the prying public and press.

While the stories of celebrities and their sexual liaisons could fill an entire library, that is not the focus of this book. Celebrity infidelity is interesting as it relates to the images and messages it sends to average Americans, who usually look to the famous as role models.

Several famous people have confronted infidelity under the spotlight while their marital unions remained intact. Many women have been publicly humiliated by a famous philandering husband. People wonder how such women cope with their hurt and betrayal, while at the same time maintaining dignity and composure in public. And everyone wonders why and how these women stay with men who have strayed so flagrantly and so publicly.

The following examples of women publicly betrayed and their reaction to their situation are really only the tip of the iceberg. Any person who operates in the public arena—and that includes the spouse of the famous person—generally conducts his or her public and media appearances with the maximum of stage management. This means that every move is carefully calculated to project the image the individual or couple wants to project to the public. Did they hold hands—did they touch—did she flash him a cold shoulder? These types of questions scroll through our mind every time we look at a person or a couple in public, and especially when the people involved are experiencing a crisis. Reading body language is a powerful tool for determining what is really going on between two people. However, no one can ever know what a marriage between two people is *really* like.

Our attempts to guess about and to understand why a woman stays with a man who strays are based upon our own feelings about marriage, trust, men, and infidelity. Until a betrayed wife speaks out publicly about how she copes and why she stays married in the face of adultery, we can only imagine what is going on behind the doors of her bedroom.

Interviews with women in similar circumstances, but without the glare of public scrutiny on their marriages, can offer information about how and why someone in Hillary Rodham Clinton's position has endured long-standing rumors of infidelity by her husband, yet has stayed by and closely supported her husband through an exceedingly embarrassing and, one must suspect, humiliating experience.

Jane's New Life

In an April 1997 *Vanity Fair* article entitled, "The Royal Couple—Ted Turner and Jane Fonda," Jennet Conant reported that for years Jane Fonda had looked the other way when it came to her former husband Tom Hayden's alleged affairs. However, when he allegedly became involved with a thirty-two-year-old and refused to stop seeing her, it was reportedly the last straw for Fonda. She spoke of her anguish in an interview with *Ladies' Home Journal* in 1989: "I've never felt this kind of pain. It leaves you raw and vulnerable."

Every woman, young or old, rich or poor, is wounded when her husband betrays her. Being a star with a million-dollar face and figure is no insurance against a straying husband. As Fonda, now happily married to Ted Turner, founder of CNN, told *Ladies' Home Journal*: "When you're faced with something that painful, you have two choices. You can go down, go under — just cave in out of the fear of what it means to be single again. Or you can say this is to open a door that I've never even thought of opening."

These are words for every woman to heed. Whether you are a highly paid executive, a million-dollar model, or a housewife, coping with infidelity is difficult, but it is no reason to give up on yourself or your hopes of improving your life. Perhaps a better you, and a better relationship or marriage, is just around the corner.

The Mick:
Does Jerry Still Have Sympathy for Her Devil?

Nothing is more humiliating than forgiving his infidelitites.
— JERRY HALL

Photos taken just months ago of stunning supermodel Jerry Hall and her Rolling Stone hubby, Mick Jagger, showed the two looking blissfully happy as they flitted between London and the South of France, with baby Gabriel in tow. These images betrayed tabloid tales of Mick and this year's model. According to USA Today *and other newspaper reports in December 1998, the Mick was spotted with alleged former lover, model Carla Bruni. He's also been linked with a Brazilian model.*

Their marital saga has long been played out on the world stage. In the intelligencer column of New York *magazine for December 1996, Jerry was described as sporting a new diamond-and-ruby-encrusted pendant. According to the article: "Whenever Mick gets his hand caught in the cookie jar, Jerry* gets a new piece of jewelry, and it has to be more expensive than the last one. If it isn't, she threatens to file divorce papers."

It has been widely reported that for years Hall looked the other way as Jagger allegedly dallied. But when he reportedly took a particularly strong interest in one model, with whom he allegedly had a year-long affair, Hall allegedly rang the Other Woman and said: "Leave my man alone!" She then took her story to the media. As she told the Daily Mail (London) in 1996: "I can confirm that Mick and I are separated, and I suppose we'll get divorced. I'm in too much pain for this to continue any longer."

If Hall had a strategy, it worked, temporarily at least: she and Jagger got back together and the rage and pain were suppressed. However, most emotions eventually give vent, and Hall expressed some in an interview with Texas Monthly magazine in 1995. Hall blamed their problems partly on her own postpartum depression, saying she had lost her usual "sense of humor" about her husband's philandering. All she would say of Jagger's responsibility for their marital problems was, "He was very badly behaved."

These latest reports on the Jaggers indicate that Mick and Jerry are not getting satisfaction.

As the case of the beautiful model and the aging rocker so poignantly illustrates, being tall, rich, and beautiful, and the mother of a man's children doesn't spare a woman from the heartache of infidelity. Even a lovely woman can be caught in the dilemma of what course of action to follow when confronted with an unfaithful mate: Either love him and stay with him, and try to accept and tolerate behavior one despises; or leave him, even though you love him and don't want to raise children without their father. These fundamental questions face every woman whose life is touched by infidelity, regardless of her status in society.

EXECUTIVE PRIVILEGE

Although your typical executive, mogul, or politician does not have the same cachet as a celebrity or rock star, successful men are still greatly sought after and vigorously pursued by women every day. There is something very alluring to many women about a man in a suit, especially if he is wealthy.

Some of the stories I heard while researching this book could give a whole new meaning to the business reference "getting in bed together." One man with interests far and wide employs an assistant whose sole responsibility is to coordinate prostitutes for himself and his executives. And he maintains an apartment specifically for the illicit liaisons. While this might seem like the ultiimate perk for some men, others may see it as a form of blackmail-in-waiting should they ever wish to leave the employ of their mercurial boss. At least one of the men who had parted company had photos of his trysts mailed to his wife.

With frequent travel and lots of disposable income, corporate chiefs are among the men who practice serial philandering. Their wives are often aware of their dalliances. Although they don't like them, they stay married, and funnel their rage and energy into being the best of the corporate wife brigade, trying to show their husband how crucial they are in his success and his life. These betrayed women, their resentment clearly evident, play the role of the ultimate Mrs. Big.

Covering for the Big Man

Wives are not the only people who makes excuses for the errant ways of some corporate honchos. Executive assistants regularly field calls from "other women" and the wife, juggling their bosses' schedule so the two never meet. It is amazing the treasure trove of material the secretaries of this country keep in the name of holding on to their jobs or in choosing to be loyal to their boss.

Lower-level employees are not the only ones keeping mum to help the Big Man. One man quit his position as finance head of a private concern because he would not cover up the expenses for several girlfriends' and the wife's luxury cars, wardrobes, and apartments, which came from company expenses.

Judging by the number of people I spoke to, the practice of protecting the male boss from his wife and detractors, while smoothing his extramarital affairs, is more common than we care to acknowledge. Such protection also appears in the now famous Starr Report—*The Report of the Independent*

Counsel to the U.S. House of Representatives. The way President Clinton's secretary, Betty Currie, signed Monica Lewinsky into the White House after she ceased working there is pretty common behavior around corporate America when the boss is playing around.

When it is the secretary who is involved with her corporate leader, the affair gets very messy indeed. In this case, the secretary must lie to the wife to cover up the boss's affair, while at the same time trying to let the wife know about the involvement to further her own interests and break up the marriage. Many women are aware that a secretary can play a role in keeping her in the dark about her husband's business and romantic affairs. This is one reason why many times there is tension between the two. With so much sex and lies going on among the corporate elite of this country, it is a wonder anything other than funny business is accomplished in executive suites and hallways.

PHILANDERING POLITICIANS

Sex. Sin. Scandal. The Classics Never Go Out of Style.

—AD FOR *MELROSE PLACE*

Celebrities aren't the only people bed-hopping under the glare of strobe lights. Politicians are also notorious womanizers. Even as they espouse "family values," many politicians are conducting illicit affairs that could jeopardize their marriage and career. Women married to politicians are usually photographed smiling and holding the hand of their powerful partner. After all, if a woman has devoted much of her life to her husband's political career, and his career goes down, she goes down along with it. Behind closed doors is another story, however, and many political wives are probably breaking the good china in fights over their man's extramarital sexual affairs.

Power and Sex

Henry Kissinger once said that "power is the ultimate aphrodisiac," and in the eyes of many women, a politician is the epitome of power. Even if most career politicians are far from wealthy, there is a perception that they are sex and power personified. Thus, many politicians are "babe magnets," greatly sought after by women of all persuasions and ages, including White House interns!

With so many women flinging themselves at them, many politicians find the allure of a liaison too tough to turn down. After all, many successful men view philandering as a perk of their professional life. With so much young flesh on offer, even a happily married man may be lured into taking a lover.

Pity the poor politician's wife. She must conduct herself with the utmost discretion, yet is often dragged into a scandal because her husband can't keep his zipper closed and his hands to himself. Most political wives, like millions of other women, choose to stand by their philandering partner.

Some of the more infamous cases of recent political marriages publicly humiliated by infidelity continue to fascinate us. And always, we scratch our head and ask in amazement: "*Why* is she staying with him?" How does she get in bed each and every night with a husband she knows warmed (and in some cases, is continuing to warm) another woman's bed? How does she continue to smile when all the world knows the details of her husband's dalliances? We are baffled by the ability of some betrayed women either to live in denial, or to delude themselves about the sexual indiscretions of their husband, or to make excuses for their adulterous spouse, or to stand by his side and smile while saying how proud they are of their husband.

HOW SOME PUBLICLY HUMILIATED WIVES HAVE COPED WITH INFIDELITY

Monkey Business

Back in 1987, presidential hopeful Gary Hart taunted the press about his rumored philandering and issued them a challenge: "Follow me around. If anybody wants to put a tail on me, go ahead. They'd be very bored."

What the reporters from the *Miami Herald* found is now part of political folklore. Photos of Mr. Hart cavorting aboard the *Monkey Business* off Bimini with one shapely young woman named Donna Rice graced the pages of *People*, and Ms. Rice was featured on the cover. That dalliance cost Hart his presidential bid. The marital union of Lee and Gary Hart survived his rendezvous with his destiny, and they are still married today. Friends quoted by *People* in September 1998 say they have "never seen them happier."

In the wake of "Donnagate," Lee Hart stood stoically by her husband and has been rewarded by having her marriage remain intact. At the time of the scandal, loyal wife Lee stunned people by declaring that "if it doesn't bother me, I don't think it ought to bother anybody else."

Like millions of wives, Lee Hart chose to stay with her man. Still, it must have been difficult when a porn video was made mocking her husband's indiscretion, especially with characters in the movie named "Donna Nice" and "Gary Hard." The heart, it seems, has its own reasons for doing what it does — in compelling women to stay when their man strays. And Lee made a choice that she believes suited her.

Dreams Turn to Nightmares

As with most extramarital affairs, the aftermath often lives on indefinitely, and painful reminders of an illicit liaison can resurface over and over again, rubbing salt in still tender wounds. Such is the case with former Secretary of Housing and Urban Development Henry Cisneros. A September 7, 1998, *People* magazine story, "Surviving Infidelity: How They Cope, Why They Stay," describes the saga of Henry Cisneros. While mayor of San Antonio in 1988, Cisneros was involved in an affair with a political fund-raiser. When the affair became public, the Cisneroses initially separated, and wife Mary Alice filed for divorce. They reunited, however, and they are still married.

Like a recurring bad dream, though, remnants of Cisneros's affair resurfaced last year when he was indicted for allegedly obstructing justice and making false statements about payments to his former mistress before they ended their affair in 1991. Whether the Cisneros marriage will endure this latest twist, no one knows. The story illustrates that extramarital affairs entail lying, and that lying can come back many times over to haunt.

Like so many women in her situation, Mrs. Cisneros has not spoken publicly about how she has coped with the aftermath of her husband's affair. *But no individual, and no marriage, is ever the same after an affair.*

The Politician and the Prostitute

Members of the British Parliament regularly embarrass themselves with their sexcapades, and then blame the newspapers for their problems. One of the most salacious political scandals unraveled in the midst of the 1996 Democratic National Convention in Chicago. And it only tangentially involved Bill Clinton . . .

The spotlight was on President Clinton's closest political strategist at the time, Dick Morris. Morris resigned from his position amid allegations of his year-long affair with prostitute Sherry Rowlands. What stunned people most was the revelation by the call girl that Morris allegedly let her listen in on phone conversations he had with President Clinton.

The very-married Morris spent his weekdays working in Washington, D.C., and his week nights trysting with Rowlands. All the while Morris's wife of twenty years, Eileen McGann, lived and worked in Connecticut. Rowlands had reportedly been Morris's "regular" for a year.

Eileen McGann, who is an attorney, was in the dark about Dick's double life. However, when another scandal broke, Ms. McGann could no longer look the other way. In addition to learning that Rowland and Morris had an ongoing thing, Eileen also had to confront the truth of Dick's duplicity: he had had an ongoing affair for many years with still another woman in Texas, with whom he had a daughter.

After the scandals broke, Morris's wife stoically stood by him. Greeting the press in the yard of their Connecticut home in late August 1996, McGann said they were going to buy a new puppy, which they hoped would help them heal.

McGann was criticized for defending her husband and standing by him. Many people—the press as well as ordinary citizens—expressed dismay as to why an educated, financially independent career woman, with no children to worry about, would stay with such a flagrant adulterer. Like many millions of woman in this country, Morris's wife stayed loyally with her husband probably because she loved him and did not want to walk out on him or the decades she invested in their marriage.

Still, her decision was baffling to many. Here was a woman who was in a position to tell her cheating husband to get lost, while at the same time her profession, lifestyle, and financial standing would remain intact. Yet she stayed. This confused many people because some men and women alike think women only stay with an adulterer out of financial dependence. This is too simplistic an explanation, as the Morris example illustrates. Eileen had the resources to leave her philandering man, but initially at least, she chose not to. Why? I imagine for the same reasons millions of other women tolerate distasteful aspects of marriage: L-O-V-E. A love for her husband and a reluctance to give him up, even though he has done a very naughty and hurtful thing.

Months later, Eileen McGann did leave her husband. And what became of her Dick? Ironically, he went on to become a political analyst on the FOX Television News Channel, offering up commentary on President Clinton's sexcapades.

At last report, Eileen McGann and Morris had reconciled, then separated again, then reconciled again. Who knows how the volleyball game will eventually end. Like an affair itself, there are no real rules for "after-the-affair." After a long marriage, the Morrises, like most couples, have had their share of ups and downs, and letting go of the dreams of a shared future is hard for many women to do. As McGann told *Time* in August 1996, when she first learned of her husband's betrayal: "When you've had a long relationship, even when you're hurt, you can integrate all the good times with the bad for a complete picture."

Roy the Roamer

If the media spotlight on February 6, 1998, had not been focused on Bill Clinton's emerging "Monicagate" scandal, more attention might have been paid to the admission by the Colorado governor and chair of the Democratic National Committee (DNC), Roy Romer that he had, according to *Time*, (February 16, 1998), a long-term "very affectionate relationship" with his former deputy chief of staff, B. J. Thornberry, who now works for the DNC. After photos of Romer caught in a "six-minute kiss" with the woman he had previously denied having an affair with were about to be published, he finally revealed: "I'm trying now to say, there is a very good, close relationship with this friend." At a press conference, Governor Roy stood beside his wife of over forty-five years, Beatrice, known as Bea, as he explained that he had told her about B. J. "from the beginning," and assuring us that the relationship "has not affected our marriage or our family." Several of their seven adult children also participated in the press conference.

Mrs. Romer has not spoken publicly about her husband's relationship, nor did she back in 1990 when the first rumors of an affair began circulating. She is quietly, loyally staying with her husband and family.

But just *how* is she getting on with her life, knowing her husband's "friend" works with him at the Democratic National Committee? According to a friend quoted in the article in *People* magazine cited earlier, "Surviving Infidelity: How They Cope, Why They Stay," Bea is "going to go through this marriage literally for better or worse"; it added that she "got through the ordeal with the help of Prozac."

At the time of his confession, Governor Romer offered these comments, cited in *Time*, February 16, 1998, about his relationship: "The connection to B. J. is not a sexual relationship, as people know it, but it is a very affectionate relationship. Affair is a word you have to interpret."

It can't be easy for Bea Romer, or for any woman, to hear those words and not be hurt by them. Yet for personal reasons known only to herself and possibly her family, Mrs. Romer is standing by her man. She has invested over forty-five years of her life to her marriage to Roy, and she mothered seven of his children. These are strong incentives for a woman to remain with a man, even when he has disappointed you. Then there is L-O-V-E. Every woman I interviewed for this book told me that one major reason they wanted to stay with their husband, even though he was unfaithful, was because they loved their husband. Perhaps women do many things in the name of love and men do many things in the name of sex. One thing seems apparent these days: Even when a woman is cheated on, and whether or not she lives in the public spotlight, she will often fight for her husband and her marriage.

Political Wives Are Human, Too

While we all wonder how betrayed women can stand by men who so flagrantly and publically betrayed them, we should also ponder this: How long will the cheating husband stand by *her* side? Many women who have remained loyally committed to their adulterous husband, and to their marriage, end up divorced by him at a later date. This is a question few people ask, and even fewer wish to think about. After all, it smacks of unfairness. Who wants to think of a betrayed yet loving and devoted wife being dumped for someone else? Not many people. But it is a question that all women staying with straying men must honestly ask themselves.

Much more than "just sex," extramarital affairs are, at their core, about lying and deception. And living long term with a deceptive and evasive man can be "crazymaking" for a woman and her self-esteem. Whether a woman lives a private life or one under the constant glare of the public spotlight, she must be true to *herself* and make a choice for the future of her marrriage that benefits *her*. After all, if her husband continues to philander, he is *not* thinking of her feelings or valuing their marriage.

Another Day, Another Scandal

It's not illegal . . . but my wife and I—and I hate to tell you this— but my wife and I were separated three times.
— REPRESENTATIVE DAN BURTON,
QUOTED IN *TIME*, SEPTEMBER 14, 1998

Just when you thought it was safe to read the newspapers again, there it is— yet *another* politician confessing an extramarital affair. Confessions are exceptionally rare, and it is not surprising that they only seem to happen when a tawdry secret is about to hit the headlines.

In September 1998, Indiana Republican representative Dan Burton decided to announce to the *Indianapolis Star and News* newspaper that he carried on an illicit affair in the 1980s—which resulted in an illegitimate son. His wife knew—and in true political wife fashion, stood by him. They remain married today. And in December 1998, Representative Robert Livingstone confessed that he had been unfaithful to his wife! But how will these women feel now that the entire world is in on their secret? Will they continue to stand by their man after suffering the private pain again, and now public humiliation? Probably. If a woman stays when the secret is first disclosed, she is likely to continue to stay. Why? The appeal of their husband and family—as well as their life as they know it—are factors weighing heavily in the minds of all women who have to try to come to terms with infidelity and its aftermath.

SMART PRESIDENT, FOOLISH FONDLING

"... is it too much to expect the President of the United States to resist some of the [sexual] temptations thrown his way?"
"The ladies just go wild over him."
—EXCHANGE BETWEEN KATIE COURIC AND THE REVEREND BILLY GRAHAM ON *THE TODAY SHOW*, MARCH 6, 1998.

Extramarital sexual scandals, rumors, and allegations have long been part and parcel of the political landscape, and they continued into the administration of President William Jefferson Clinton. The Bill Clinton–Monica Lewinsky story is both ordinary and extraordinary at the same time. It is a classic tale of a middle-aged, married man who has an extramarital fling with a young, flirty woman, who he says makes him feel young.

There is an exchange of affection, gifts, phone messages, late-night sexually charged phone calls, a Valentine message in the newspaper, and a special memento saved from an intimate encounter the two shared. It is the story of an insecure woman looking for validation. A woman who, like millions of other women, wonders why a man won't call her when he says he will, or why he doesn't spend more time with her.

The Bill and Monica story underscores the secrecy, lies, and emotional ups and downs implicit in any extramarital affair. It is the saga of sexual encounters on the sly and under the roof he shares with his wife and his country, and worries about being found out. It is the story of sex behind closed doors while the wife is out of town. It is the story of a vivacious girl who falls unexpectedly in love.

It's a story of the tears and despair a woman feels when her married lover ends their affair. It is the tale of a distraught woman who tells eleven people about her affair, one of whom has an affinity for audiotape, while promising her lover she's being discreet. It is the drama of a wounded girl watching her lover attend public events with his wife. It is the melodrama of an idealistic girl who wonders if her lover will leave his wife for her. And it is the sad tale of a woman who allegedly threatens to expose her lover and their affair unless he sees her again.

This is a tale of a sexually aggressive young woman, and of a middle-aged man struggling with his sexual appetite, trying to be faithful to his wife, and chiding himself when he slips up. The Bill and Monica yarn is a story of a man who had it all and took a risky gamble where he could have lost it all. And this is yet another sad chapter in a loyal wife's marital nightmare.

Yes, the story of Bill and Monica has been lived out before by many and will be lived out again. But what makes this episode so special, so desperate, is the identity of the man it involves: William Jefferson Clinton, president of the United States, husband, father, leader. This story will be seen in reruns for many years to come for all the characters involved—even though it is a most disappointing tale.

For all its familiarity, we are still fascinated by the story of Bill and Monica, the president and the intern half his age. But most of all, we wonder about Hillary, the third person in this assorted triangle.

Queen of Dignity—or Denial?

For nearly a quarter of a century, Hillary Clinton has loyally defended her husband, Bill Clinton, and their marriage, through a variety of scandals. She once again rallied to his side after the Lewinsky allegations surfaced in January 1998, telling Matt Lauer on *The Today Show* on January 27, 1998, that "the only two people who count in any marriage are the two that are in it."

As the scandal heated up, Hillary staunchly went to bat for her husband,

and her approval ratings soared to their all-time high of 59 percent in September 1998 according to *Time*. Through everything, Hillary has been her husband's devoted partner. But why does she continue to support him?

Hillary Clinton has been a lightning rod of controversy for many people, for a long time, and never more so than in the Lewinsky scandal. Many people have accused her of being a power-hungry feminist, who stayed in a loveless marriage because she wanted a political voice. Others, less cynical, have seen her as a dutiful spouse who cares deeply for her husband.

So who is the real Hillary? Is she the Queen of Denial, who sticks her head in the sand and looks the other way so she can tolerate an unfaithful husband? Or is she the Queen of Dignity personified, fully aware of her man's philanderings, hurt and pained by them like the rest of us, but keeping the ultimate stiff upper lip? Is Hillary human, we wonder, as we think of Bill and Monica alone together in the Oval Office? And if so, why isn't she crying and screaming over Bill's wandering hands?

"What did Hillary know, and when did she know it?" has been a fiercely debated topic. When did Hillary find out the truth about Monica and Bill? What, exactly, did she know? Did she/does she know about the cigar trick? We are all preoccupied about what she knew about Bill's infidelity and when she knew it because we want to figure out how to judge Hillary. We figure if she knew back in January 1998, then she lied to us on *The Today Show* and *Good Morning America* when she said "These allegations won't be proven true," and maybe we won't think highly of her. If she truly just found out the dirty details of Bill's dalliances a few days before his televised confession on August 17, 1998, then we figure she was misled like the rest of us, and we will feel sorry for her.

Regardless of what she knew when, the important point is that Hillary Clinton once again stood by her husband's side in what must have been the most humiliating ordeal of her life. And many people showed their support for her handling of the situation. After Bill's televised confession her approval ratings reached their highest levels since entering the White House.

Like the story of Bill and Monica, Hillary's is one of the most familiar in the book: the betrayed wife who is cheated on repeatedly, and decides to stand by her man. Again and again.

Why Does She Do the Full Wynette?

Whenever a man strays, people wonder if his wife knows. The next thing they wonder is, *why* is she standing by him? Even though millions of women stay married to straying men, most people still marvel when a woman in the public eye is betrayed—and doesn't punch her husband out before the television cameras. A practiced politician like Hillary Clinton is not about to wear her emotions on her sleeve about her husband's betrayal. Of course she will feel denial at first; most women do. Then come anger and rage, mistrust, and for some people, acceptance and forgiveness. But when a woman lives in the public eye, she is expected to show us her full range of private emotions, even though few of us would want to display ours before the American public.

Many betrayed women take to their beds for weeks; others go about their everyday business without blinking. The range of emotions a person displays when they learn of their husband's betrayal is a very individual and private matter.

The overwhelming emotion most women feel toward their cheating husband is anger; yet many women direct their rage at someone other than their partner—the "other woman," a "vast right-wing conspiracy," a tabloid, a videotape, almost anything or anyone in order to avoid blaming the husband. Most women find it too threatening to direct their anger at their husband, even though they often feel like doing so. Instead, they lash out at everyone else.

So, why does Hillary stay with Bill? She stays with him for many of the same reasons most women stay with men who stray: L-O-V-E. Love for her husband, her daughter, her family, her lifestyle, and yes, love of her position as first wife and first lady. For a woman who has spent half of her life standing by her husband and her marriage, giving them up would not be an easy decision. Bill Clinton is part of Hillary's life, and she his. You don't break up a partnership like that without a fight.

Hillary Clinton is at once like the majority of women and unique. Many women tend to place a priority of having a successful marriage and a happy family life, and many do not throw that away over another woman.

Why Does Hillary Stay?:

- Personal reasons: Such as "I love him," I love my daughter, I love my family, I love my role as first mate. I've invested my life in him and us. I don't want to hand him over to another woman.

- Social reasons: There are less opportunities for women over fifty in the dating market than there are for men. Women do not want to have to face the shark-infested dating pool as many women see it. Other women will line up for a divorced man even if he is a philanderer, so many married women fight the competition every step of the way. For women in general, there are less career opportunities available as they age. Yet for Hillary Clinton, her professional opportunities are broader now than ever. But socially? Men still hold the advantage.

- Financial reasons: Many women are partially or totally dependent on a husband for financial support. Hillary Clinton has long been the family breadwinner, so she's not staying with Bill for his money.

Looking more closely at the Clinton marriage, it appears that Hillary has stayed with Bill because of shared goals, a deep friendship, real affection, and an appreciation of what they have achieved together. No woman — first lady or first-grade teacher — would want to toss those things aside without thinking long and hard about doing so.

Of course, in the wake of the Lewinsky scandal, the Clintons face a tough patch ahead for a long time. The beauty of a marriage is that two people commit to working together through the good times and the bad, and infidelity is definitely a bad time. But it doesn't have to mean one partner jumps ship.

Facing infidelity, living with a man who has betrayed her, is a difficult situation for any woman. To know in the abstract that your husband has been sexually intimate with another woman is bad enough; but to know all the details is much more difficult. Hillary Clinton said on *The Today Show* in January 1998 that she copes by "boxing things off" and by "taking a deep breath."

Detractors of Hillary Clinton say that she is an "enabler" — that by staying with her husband and essentially letting him get away with affairs, she unwittingly allows the adulterous marriage to continue. Some people maintain that she "colludes" with Bill—that she tolerates his flings and in return she gets the status of being his wife.

The truth is, everyone, in one way or another "enables" and "colludes" every day in order to get through life dealing with other people. We all trade off desirable things for less desirable aspects of every relationship we are a part of. Hillary and Bill Clinton are no different.

> *She's upset because he's messed up their presidency.*
> —ELIZABETH DREW ON MSNBC TELEVISION, SEPTEMBER 11, 1998

If a woman—any woman, first lady or not—stands by her man, her job, her family, her co-presidency, or whatever, it is her choice. She is the one who will live in the situation, so it is really no one else's business whether she stays with a man who strays. There is a part of all of us, however, that once—just once—would like to see a betrayed first lady call a taxi up to the White House and waltz out with her suitcases, just as the network correspondents are doing their nightly babble from the White House lawn. What ratings that would garner—not to mention a collective exhale from millions of women hoping to see an unfaithful man get public punishment!

Hillary Clinton is a well-educated and attractive woman, a brillant public speaker, and a role model for many. But the choices she makes in her personal life are not meant to be based on whether they will be good role-model choices for other women. We look to outstanding, successful women to see how they "do it all"; but their choices are their own, especially their marital decisions.

By maintaining a dignified silence during the rougher patches in the Lewinsky ordeal, Hillary Clinton received praise, in part because many women could, for the first time, identify with her. A vulnerable woman is often viewed as more approachable, and more likable, than a woman who is as tough as nails. Blind loyalty to a man and a marriage is not wise; but thoughtful, considered loyalty is admirable in the world today.

Hillary Clinton has stayed married for years with a man who is a magnet for sex rumors. Through it all she has held her head high and declared her support, her love, and her forgiveness for her husband. Her critics call her a doormat and wonder where she left her dignity. Other people are impressed by her resilience.

You're looking at two people who love each other. This is not an
arrangement or an understanding. This is a marriage.
—BILL CLINTON TO STEVE KROFT ON 60 *MINUTES*, JANUARY 27, 1992

Whatever the very private, very individual reasons why Hillary stays with a man who strayed, it appears to have worked for her. She has all the resources a woman needs to walk away from a marriage, and yet she has stayed—and stayed. Is she a saint or a sucker for doing so? Only she can be the judge. Just because a woman stays for now doesn't mean she's staying forever. Hillary Clinton did what most betrayed women wished they could do: she got mad, got glam, and landed on the cover of *Vogue!*

There's Something About Bill

Whenever a man strays, people automatically ask if his wife is going to leave him. After Bill Clinton's flings with Monica in the West Wing, seemingly everyone was asking, "Will Hillary Leave Bill?" And if not, why not—what's wrong with her? they wondered. The question we should ask is this: *Will Bill Stay Married to Hillary?*

After all, it was Bill who alluded to Monica Lewinsky, according to her testimony in the Starr Report, that he was uncertain whether he would remain married after he left the White House. Was that because he thought Hillary would leave him—or because he's planning to leave her? Many philandering men have eventually left wives who have loyally stood by their man. Will Bill be one of them? Or will Hillary beat him out the door? Only the two of them know for sure. After an affair, there is no telling what will happen.

Many people, myself included, would have liked her [Hillary] to
hurl her husband's boxer shorts out on the Truman Balcony
for getting us into all this.
—MARGARET CARLSON, *TIME*, AUGUST 10, 1998

Many people who are questioning why and how Hillary stays with Bill after her most recent betrayal are also telling how much they would like to see Hillary walk out on Bill. They don't seem to realize that for her to walk out on him, she would also be walking out on the only life she has known for nearly twenty-five years. That's not easy to do—not impossible, but not desirable.

Regardless of what other people think of a couple, ultimately their opinion doesn't matter because they aren't in the marriage. As amazing as it may be for some people to comprehend, Hillary probably still loves Bill. Even good men do make miserable mistakes. And sometimes, lots of them. It is Hillary alone who must decide if a series of mistakes adds up to a pattern, and if so, whether that is the kind of marriage she wants for herself, and the kind of model she wants for her daughter, Chelsea.

As one man interviewed for this book said to me, **"Infidelity will be with us until the end of time."** Then, so too will women who stay with men who stray.

What Hillary Clinton—and women everywhere in her situation—must ask is: *Am I standing up for myself while standing by my man and my marriage?*

Whether a couple lives their life together in the glare of the public spotlight or not, dealing with the aftermath of an affair is a harrowing experience. Only Hillary and Bill Clinton know whether they will be able once again to nod in agreement with the statement Steve Kroft said to them in that now infamous *60 Minutes* interview during the 1992 convention: "I think most Americans would agree that it's very admirable that you . . . have stayed together, that you've worked your problems out. . . ."

From the White House to Your House

If adultery isn't okay in my house, why is it okay in the White House?
—DON IMUS, MSNBC TELEVISION

Bill strayed, and Hillary stayed. But who knows what lies down the road? Together today does not necessarily mean together tomorrow. The sex thing—and the dishonesty thing—are not easy to cope with. A man may be at a woman's side; but the important thing is that he is *on* her side. If any man, whether sports star or celebrity or president, cheats on his wife and lies to cover it up, he's *not* on her side.

Fighting for a marriage is admirable, but so is fighting for oneself. No one can ever really know what goes on between two people, nor can one speculate what will happen when infidelity touches a marriage. But there is one thing certain about infidelity: there are usually no winners in the affairs sweepstakes.

With Adultery, You Just Never Know!

> *I know in my heart that she loves him. And I know in my heart that he loves her. They are a great team. You don't break up a great team and a strong family for a mistake. I think they'll stay together because of Hillary.*
> —ROGER CLINTON ON CNN'S *LARRY KING LIVE*, AUGUST, 1998

A FAMILY AFFAIR

> *French politicians can sleep in peace. And with whomever they please.*
> —ROGER THÉROND, *PARIS MATCH*

> *Yes, I have an illegitimate daughter. So what?*
> —FRENCH PRESIDENT FRANÇOIS MITTERAND

In 1994, at age seventy-seven, French president François Mitterrand was hospitalized for his second operation for terminal prostate cancer. After his two grown sons by his wife, Danielle Mitterrand, left the hospital, his "second family" arrived: his longtime mistress, Anne Pingeot, and their daughter, twenty-year-old Mazarine.

After Mitterrand was discharged from the hospital, he reportedly headed to a hospital to visit his loyal wife of nearly half a century who was recovering from open-heart surgery. Several months later, in November 1994, *Paris*

Match magazine ran a cover photo of Mitterrand with his arm on his illegitimate daughter Mazarine's shoulder, as they were leaving a Paris café.
The headline read, "A *Moving Story of a Double Life.*" The revelation,
which in France was a big deal because of the country's tight privacy laws,
hardly seemed to matter to the politicians, journalists, or others who had
long known Mitterrand to be a "dedicated womanizer," as the *Sunday Times*
(London) once referred to him.

Political commentators in France were allegedly alarmed, however, that
government quarters had reportedly occasionally housed the president's "second family." At the time, Danielle Mitterrand remained silent and seemingly
supportive of her husband's adulterous double life. After his death, however,
she spoke out in 1996 to the *Times* (London): "I was married to a seducer.
I had to make do. That's part of life. What woman can say, 'I've never been
cheated on'?"

HELL HATH NO FURY LIKE A WIFE AND A MISTRESS SCORNED!

England's Ninth Earl Spencer—known as "Champagne Charlie" to his
friends and the brother of Princess Diana to the rest of us—has been in the
news for more reasons than his speech at Diana's funeral. When Spencer
spoke out about newspapers and their editors in his moving speech at West-
minster Abbey in September 1997, few people knew of the earl's own press
headlines.

After newspapers sported stories such as "Cheating Spencer's Letter to
his Lover" (*Daily Mirror*, November 26, 1997), the public became aware of
Earl Spencer's love life. In a sensational divorce hearing, his estranged wife,
Victoria, accused Spencer of bedding twelve women during the months she
spent at a private London clinic being treated for bulimia and alcohol abuse.
To the earl's surprise and shock, his former lover, Chantal Collopy, spoke
of their affair, backing Victoria's claims of adultery. Ms. Collopy also pro-
duced copies of the love letters the earl had written to her behind his wife's
back. Ink, it appears, is as incriminating as audiotape. Just hours later, the
Spencers reached a financial settlement and divorced.

Even though Victoria Spencer, the mother of the earl's four children, had stayed married to him regardless of his alleged infidelities, she ended up divorced anyway.

Unfortunately, there is no way to tell what the outcome of an affair will be. Even though a woman stays with a man who strays, this does not guarantee that their marriage will endure.

PAIN IS PAIN, HUMILIATION IS HUMILIATION

Whether a woman is from Beverly Hills or the Bronx, Greenwich or Galveston, or the White House in Washington, she will be hurt and humiliated by her husband's betrayal. Neither fame, fortune, nor beauty can insure against a partner straying. In fact, celebrity and glamour seem to invite infidelity. A unique combination of love, affection, shared memories, family, devotion, and a common goal for a future together seem to be the factors that see many women through a marital crisis brought on by their husband's adultery. Living with infidelity is not easy, especially if the dirty details of the affair are broadcast worldwide. And saying one is going to stand by one's man in the wake of his infidelity is far easier said than done—especially when trying to tolerate that philandering man in the full glare of the world spotlight. But for a man and a woman determined to be together—to make their partnership permanent—nothing seems impossible. After all, isn't that what "for better for worse" is really all about?

TAKE NOTE

- Many celebrities, executives, sports stars, and politicians engage in extramarital liaisons. That doesn't mean it is the right thing to do. It most certainly is *not* if you want to have a happy marriage. You don't have to follow the lead of public figures.

- If we closely observe the behavior of public personalities, we can learn much about what works—and what doesn't work—in relationships. By paying attention, we can often avoid similar problems in our own lives.

- No one remains unscathed in the aftermath of infidelity—especially people living in the public spotlight.

- The way we judge a woman in the public eye for staying with a husband who betrayed her will tell us a lot about our own beliefs on infidelity. Pay attention to how you lash out at certain people and not at others. You are sending yourself a message about what you think is—and is not—acceptable behavior in a marriage.

- Most women—famous and otherwise—stay married to men who have betrayed them. This may be good for some women; but for others, it is not in their best interest. Every woman has a choice of staying or leaving. You do have choices. Decide what you want— and who you want. Then fight for it. But know when to stand up for yourself—first!

Chapter 13

WOMEN'S MOST FREQUENTLY ASKED QUESTIONS ABOUT MEN'S AFFAIRS

Why do men stray? Because they can?

—*A betrayed wife to her husband*

$\mathcal{I}$n my career working with the media, I am constantly quizzed about human behavior. Often, the questions come from women about men—specifically, "Why do men cheat on their wives?"; "What can a woman do to prevent her husband from having an extramarital affair?"; And "How can a woman get her man back from the Other Woman?"

These are not easy questions to answer, because every person, couple, and situation is unique. Still, there are common issues involved in infidelity. The following questions have been put to me time and time again. Not everyone will agree with my answers; but then, there *are* no easy answers to the very difficult questions that infidelity raises. It is hoped that these questions, which you have probably pondered many times, will help you to assess whether or not you should stay with your straying man.

WOMEN'S QUESTIONS

WHY IS HE CHEATING ON ME? WHY WON'T HE STOP FOOLING AROUND WHEN HE KNOWS HOW MUCH IT HURTS ME— AND OUR MARRIAGE?

If your husband continues his affair(s) even after you have confronted him about the pain you are experiencing as a result of his behavior, then he is blatantly disrespecting you and your marriage.

Don't waste your time pondering the futile question of *why* he is straying. Even *he* may not fully understand why he has affairs. The point is, he is being unfaithful. He is being duplicitous. He is lying to you—the person with whom he is legally joined. You may never understand why he does what he does, but you *do* know that his behavior hurts you.

The question you should ask yourself is: *What am I going to do about my philandering husband? Am I going to stand by him while I betray myself?*

In this day and age, affairs not only harm you psychologically; your physical health is at stake as well. If you know your spouse is sleeping with other women, or, as is increasingly common, another man, and you continue to have sex with him, you *must* protect yourself from disease. More importantly, you must make time for yourself away from your marriage for a few days in order to distance yourself from it and look at your husband's behavior, so that you can decide what your next steps will be.

You must ask yourself: *Am I better off with him or without him? Am I better off married to a man who lies to me daily* [and that is what an affair is], *or will I be better off on my own so that I might find a man who will respect my feelings and share my desire for fidelity?*

WHAT CAN I DO TO GET HIM TO GIVE HER UP?

You can start by banishing any notion that you can change your partner's behavior in any way. You cannot convince him to stop an affair. He will do what he wants to do. If you try to influence him unduly it may backfire, as he will think you are trying to control him and he may increase his philandering.

You aren't helpless, however. You can change *your* behavior, and in doing so, he will react differently toward you. Like the seesaw in a playground, when one end moves, the other end moves, too. But there is no guarantee that, even by changing *your* behavior, your husband will give up the Other Woman.

The more time and energy you focus on yourself, making *you* the best person you can be, the less upset you will be about your husband's errant ways. If you channel all your efforts into him and try to outdo the Other Woman, you are likely to feel even more miserable. Although the temptation to compete with the Other Woman is often great, if you let it consume you, your anger will bury you alive.

Rather than waiting around and wasting your valuable time hoping he will change, you need to determine if you really want to be married to a man who cannot be trusted. You need not act immediately; but you should pursue your own interests and make plans for your own future—a future that may or may not include your straying husband.

Change is difficult even for people who *want* to change. Have you ever tried to give up a behavior such as drinking coffee, smoking, or shopping? We are, quite simply, creatures of addiction and habit. A man may find it extremely difficult to give up his philandering. Usually a person can successfully make a difficult behavior change only when they are dissatisfied with themselves. Many men enjoy their affairs, see nothing wrong with them, certainly don't want to give them up—and especially not on orders from their wife!

If a man is to make a fundamental behavior change such as giving up womanizing, he usually must first experience some other sort of change. He may become ill, lose a parent or other close relative, suffer a business setback, or experience some other significant event that makes him take stock of his life and make a conscious decision to clean up his act. Even then, it may be difficult for a man who is used to womanizing to wean himself off his old behavior. As more than one man has told me, "Once you've strayed, you always stray."

A philandering husband will change only when—and if—*he* wants to change. Do you want to wait out your marriage while he decides?

How long should I wait for him to make up his mind? He keeps going back and forth between me and his girlfriend, and it is killing me. I don't want to push him away, but what am I supposed to do—hand him over to her?

At some point you will know that you have waited too long. When you start hating yourself and acting like a raving bitch, you have waited longer than is good for you.

Too many women wait too long, and end up without a husband anyway. Men who want to get divorced, get divorced. Men who want to stay married, stay married. If your husband is serious about leaving you for the Other Woman, he will do so. If he wants it both ways—you and a lover—he will keep the triangle going for a very long time because he has exactly what he wants.

If you are waiting for him to make up his mind, you may be in for a long wait. As long as you hang around and let him have a wife and a lover, he probably won't take any action to end the affair. You may need to set a deadline in your own mind—and stick to it! You need not share it with him, because if you don't act by the deadline, he will know you won't back up your words with actions, and your threats will thereafter be meaningless. Your behavior in not going through with your threats to leave or divorce him will indicate that he can have you *and* other women. Is that the message you want to give him?

Decide whether or not you want to stay with your husband, even if that means living out the rest of your marriage as part of a triangle. If you decide to stay under those conditions, learn to live with it. It will be extremely difficult, but millions of women do it, albeit bitterly and with great emotional cost to themselves. If you don't want to stay with a strayer, make plans for your departure and your new life without a cheating husband.

You must ask yourself: *How can I feel close to a man who constantly lies to me? Can I—and do I want to—live day after day with a duplicitous man?* Your heart (and stomach!) will tell you your answer.

If you do decide to stay with a straying husband, and you really don't feel good about yourself for doing so, then you are betraying yourself. You are likely to grow to dislike yourself. Gradually, your self-confidence and self-esteem will crumble, and you will feel less and less good about yourself and about life in general. Is this how you want to spend the rest of your life?

SHOULD I GIVE HIM AN ULTIMATUM? SHOULD I SPY AND SNOOP IF I SUSPECT MY HUSBAND OF CHEATING ON ME? SHOULD I CONFRONT HIM?

If you strongly suspect your husband is cheating on you, then you have every right to try to find out the details of his infidelity. Information is power. The more you know, the better prepared you will be for whatever decision you choose to make about your marriage. Apart from your marriage, your emotional and physical health are at stake. If you have a solid reason to suspect that your husband is betraying you, you have every right to do all you can to learn the truth. Hiring a private investigator or a "decoy" service is better than trying to snoop yourself.

If, by following your man, looking at receipts, or using other means, you confirm that your husband is having an affair, it doesn't mean you have to confront him or leave him immediately, or even leave at all. You don't have *to do anything*, if you don't choose to. Just knowing what he is up to behind your back will make you feel better. Yes, knowing can be liberating.

Too many women say they don't want to know if their husband is having an affair. This is usually because, if they know, they feel they may have to take action. As they don't know how they will react or what they would do in such a situation, they avoid it. *It is in your best interests to take your head out of the sand and snap out of your denial.* Learning that your husband *is* cheating on you will often relieve you of the burden of thinking you are going crazy, especially if you have confronted your husband in the past and he has denied it. Knowledge will help you in the long run to deal with a painful situation. Pretending it doesn't exist won't make the affair disappear.

If you decide to confront your husband about his affair, be sure to do so after you have worked out your feelings about the affair and decided whether you want to stay and work on the marriage. Be prepared for your husband to deny his philandering, blame you, or even to walk out.

Ultimatums are tricky, and I advise against them. Many people react to a quasi-threat by digging their heels in even further. Instead, make up your *own* mind about how you wish to proceed; then live your plan. Your partner will observe your behavior, which will speak louder than any words you might utter. If you start going about your business and getting on with your life, he may find you more appealing than if you act like a clinging wallflower, even though all you probably feel like doing is crying over your ordeal. Often, the more you try to grasp on to something, the harder it pulls away. There is strength in loose ties.

Many women believe that by hiring an investigator to spy on their husband, they are betraying him and violating his privacy. If this describes you, banish this thought! If your husband is cheating on you, he is betraying *you* and violating *your* privacy by risking passing on to you all sorts of diseases and subjecting you to humiliation.

The most important thing is to stay true to your beliefs, and to act in a way that will increase your good feelings about yourself. If your husband is having an affair, he is not respecting your feelings or your marriage, and *you* need to treat yourself well by acting in your own best interests.

WHO SHOULD I TURN TO FOR HELP? IF I CAN'T TRUST MY OWN HUSBAND TO TELL ME THE TRUTH, WHO CAN I TRUST?

When you are being lied to by someone you love, you end up feeling very cynical about people — and life. It is very painful to learn that your husband is cavorting behind your back, and then lying to you to cover up his actions. It is even worse when everyone else finds out about the Other Woman before you do. Who can you confide in? I don't suggest you run to your parents. Parents often will encourage a woman to put up with terrible behavior by the husband, because of the lifestyle the husband can provide for their daughter. I also don't suggest confiding in your best girlfriend. Your friend may even be the woman your spouse is having his affair with!

In times of trauma, you can only be certain when trusting *yourself*. Make some time for yourself — go away alone for a day or two and think over your situation. Go for a walk with a tape recorder and pour out your emotions. You will find it incredibly cathartic, and you won't have to worry about anyone betraying your trust. At the same time, you will be exercising, which is vitally important when you are under stress.

Most women care more about what others think than they do about their own inner voice. When you find out your husband is cheating on you, the only person you can trust is yourself. Be good to yourself. Think of yourself. Do what pleases *you*, for a change. Only *you* know what is best for your situation. What anyone else thinks isn't important. Any decisions you make should be your own. You are the one who must live with them.

Many women seek professional help when confronted with the trauma of an unfaithful husband. This may be helpful to some people and harmful to others. I know of several women who saw psychologists to help them deal with their pain. One woman was told by the psychologist, "What's wrong with you? *All* men cheat. Why can't you accept it?" The woman was crushed. Instead of being helped, she became nearly suicidal. If you decide to seek professional help, find out the beliefs of the therapist before deciding on therapy with a particular professional. Some therapists are against adultery, some condone it. You must know the point of view of your therapist, and be in agreement with it, for them to be able to help you.

You are better off trusting your own gut feelings. You are really the *only* expert on yourself and your marriage. If you use your intuition, you won't let yourself down.

Stop, look, listen, proceed—with caution!

If you allow yourself time alone to think about your marriage, and about what you expect and want from it, you will find the answer that suits you. It may take time, and it may be painful, but it is up to you to make your own decision—a decision you are comfortable living with. So many women are used to deferring to their husband, or to some other authority figure, when making decisions that this may be the first big decision they make alone.

HOW CAN I COMPETE WITH YOUNGER, MORE ATTRACTIVE WOMEN WHO WORK WITH MY HUSBAND AND WHO ARE ALWAYS AFTER HIM?

Men will always turn their head for, and be turned on by, young, attractive women. You cannot control women throwing themselves at your husband. You can only hope that your husband will look but be smart enough not to touch.

Unfortunately, there is really no way directly to compete with young and beautiful women. They will always be with us. There is only one alternative to aging, so all of us face advancing years; but we can still make the most of what we have. Living well—and looking good—are the best forms of revenge!

There are certain times in a marriage when a man may be more susceptible to the advances of another woman. While a wife is pregnant, or shortly after childbirth, are particularly vulnerable periods for a man to begin or resume an affair. Also, when he hits middle age, suffers financial or professional setbacks, or achieves more success, infidelity may begin or increase.

His just being around attractive, provocative women who pay attention to him will increase your husband's chances of starting an affair. None of these things has anything to do with *you*. Some things in life are beyond our control. We hate feeling helpless, but at times we *are*, in terms of controlling another person's behavior. Focus on your interests and goals; that way, you will have less time to worry about who your husband is taking to bed.

Other women making passes at your husband should not really be the issue of concern for you, because women will always try to poach a man from another woman. The important point is how your husband reacts when offered a come-on. Does he go for it? Does he say no? Does he say, "I'm flattered, but I'm married to a wonderful woman"? Women should be most concerned about whether or not their husband will respect his marriage vows and do the right thing by them. Other women will always act like other women, but many married men will act like gentlemen and turn away a predatory woman.

I STILL LOVE MY HUSBAND, BUT SINCE I LEARNED ABOUT HIS AFFAIR I SOMETIMES FEEL LIKE I HATE HIM. HOW CAN I FEEL LOVE AND HATE AT THE SAME TIME?

Love and hate are different sides of the same coin, meaning that you still care enough about a person to be moved emotionally by them. We don't feel anger toward a person we don't care about. Many people believe that hate is the opposite of love. Not so. You can only feel hatred for someone if, at some level, you still care about them. The opposite of love is indifference. When you cease to care about a person, you feel neither love nor hate for them. You are, quite simply, no longer moved by them.

When you are feeling hurt by your husband's infidelity, you are angry with him and may feel that you hate him. But, at times, you will also feel love for him. You are displaying *ambivalence*, the cornerstone of feelings — being tugged in two directions simultaneously. These ambivalent feelings are what keep you in the relationship. Although you may feel anger and hate toward your husband, you will also remember the good times and his loving ways. This back-and-forth thinking is often what keeps women in a marriage with a straying husband.

Many people have selective memories about their relationships. They stop themselves from thinking too much about the bad times, and instead cling to the good memories and hang on in the hope that the good times will return.

The reason so many women are devastated when they learn of their husband's infidelity is because they love their spouse. The only time a person can casually accept the infidelity of a partner is when there are no longer feelings of love present. Indifference to a partner and a relationship is a shield against hurt. Indifference is a protection against emotion. One neither feels happy nor sad. When one is indifferent, diffident, or disinterested, one simply feels nothing. Only when a marriage is nearly lifeless will a man or woman cease to care that their beloved is bedding another.

If your husband is betraying you, let yourself feel anger and hatred toward him. You are hurting, and you need to release your true feelings in a constructive way. Beat up a pillow, scream, shout, run, walk, dance. But beware of what you say to him, because you can't erase spoken words. Think before you speak. Write him a nasty letter, but don't mail it. The act of writing it will help you to vent in a constructive way, and you will feel better. The point is to let out your rage without hurting yourself, him, or the relationship.

Don't worry about feeling anger—you are angry because you care. Like the weather, many couples go through four seasons of feeling in one day! In the course of even an hour, you may feel like divorcing your husband, then marrying him all over again. The emotional ups and downs you are experiencing are a natural reaction to a traumatic and upsetting event—the sexual betrayal by your loved one.

We all get upset over the threatened loss of a love object: we fear the loss of someone we love. We fear abandonment, and the humiliation of having someone else chosen over us. Such feelings torment all but sociopaths, who cannot feel for anyone but themselves.

As time passes after the discovery of your husband's infidelity, and as you begin to deal with the problem, your erratic feelings should subside. Unless, of course, you are living with a long-term philanderer. Wild mood swings will likely be a part of your existence should you opt to live with long-term infidelity. You will either become indifferent to your husband, and therefore not care that he is unfaithful to you; or you will continue to love him deeply, and therefore will always be angered and hurt by his philandering.

You must ask yourself this: *Am I better off with a man I love but who angers me constantly when he cheats on me, or will I be happier off the emotional roller coaster?*

IF I STAY WITH MY HUSBAND AND TAKE HIM BACK AFTER HIS
AFFAIR, HOW WILL I EVER BE ABLE TO TRUST HIM? HOW DO I
KNOW HE WON'T CHEAT ON ME AGAIN?

This is one of the toughest questions any woman faces. Trust is a necessary factor for a long-term, happy, thriving relationship. If you can't trust your marital partner, who should have your best interests at stake, then who can you trust?

After trust has been broken, which is what happens in the aftermath of infidelity, it is difficult to rebuild without the cracks threatening constantly to topple the foundation of your marriage. If you decide to stay with your partner, you must try your best to trust him. Give him the benefit of the doubt. Or, as one of the messages in my fortune cookies instructed me to do: "Trust him — but still keep your eyes open!"

A broken trust is often difficult to repair, but it can be done if both parties work hard at it. He must stick to his word, and you must know that he is sticking to it. Unfortunately, however, there is no way to "affair-proof" any marriage. And sadly, men who have one affair most often have a second, third, and so on. More men than I can count told me that once they had an affair, there was no turning back. They simply derived so much "buzz," or thrill, or sex from them that they wouldn't stop having them, even if they were found out.

A woman whose husband has cheated on her once will always be looking for signs he is cheating again — or still. Living with such uncertainty can wear her down emotionally and physically. When you are investing your energy in keeping tabs on him, and on the women you think he is seeing, you have no time or energy left for yourself and *your* life.

Even if your husband assures you that you are "number one," and that even if he cheats on you, he will never leave you, you will still worry about being left. And justifiably so, for too many men do end up leaving their wives. Though the number of men who divorce is low compared to the number who philander, the more affairs a man has, the more likely it is that the marriage will ultimately end in divorce.

As I've said earlier, I know of many cases where women stayed with unfaithful husbands for twenty or thirty years, only to be dumped eventually anyway. These women gave up the best years of their lives, and the best of themselves, for men who continually cheated on them.

If you don't trust the man you get into bed with each night, and with whom you may share a home, children, money, and yourself, you must seriously ask yourself why you are staying in the relationship. There are other ways to live. Only you can decide to be happy and to take the steps to make the best life possible for yourself.

You will never be able to control whether other women try to "borrow" your husband. Assume they will, because babes can often be bitches. What is important is that your husband will pass up the invitations to infidelity and be true to you and your marriage.

Monogamy is important to some men. Tell yourself that some men *do* stick to their marriage vows. Many men—good men, successful men, nice men—are faithful to their wives. It is important to remind yourself that *not all men play around*. Regardless of what your husband, other men, women, or society implies, real men *do* say no to affairs.

There are many agonising questions women have to ask themselves about infidelity. None is more difficult than whether a woman is going to stay with a man who philanders, or leave him and begin a new life for herself. Women stay with straying men for a variety of reasons. Yet the decision to do so, and then to live with that decision and with long-term infidelity, proves to be a difficult if not impossible feat for many women to endure. Unless his affair was a one-time mistake.

WHAT EVERY WOMAN WANTS TO ASK HER HUSBAND: IF YOU KNEW I WOULDN'T PUT UP WITH YOUR STRAYING, WOULD YOU STILL HAVE AFFAIRS?

Amazing as it may sound, many couples don't even discuss infidelity before they marry. I know scores of men and women who have never broached the topic. That's the wrong way to handle a relationship. If you tell each other while dating that you hate cigarette smoke and cookie crumbs in bed, then you should also discuss the "messy" stuff, like what will happen if either one of you sleeps around. Men avoid "relationship talk" like the plague, and women are afraid to tell their true thoughts about philandering men, fearing the man will bolt before she has the ring. She may fantasize about what she would do with the cutlery if he strays, but she is likely to keep her thoughts to herself.

It is important to a relationship, and a marriage, for a man and a woman to discuss issues of great significance to them. If you are a woman who will walk out the door if your man unzips his pants for another woman, your man needs to know where you stand on the issue. Likewise, if you are a woman who will allow "a little adultery" — an oxymoron to me. (For example, some women "allow" their men oral sex with other women, rationalizing that only penetration constitutes true adultery!)

Whatever your thoughts are on adultery, your man should know where you and he both stand on the issue. Women who set their standards high, and don't compromise them, often get what they want. Men know they mean business. "Unzip for the blonde and you're toast" may sound crude, but it has a way of getting a man's attention. Men like women who are self-confident and respect themselves. Stick up for your beliefs, because you must look yourself in the mirror each morning and be comfortable with your beliefs, priorities, and actions. Decide your priorities regarding infidelity, and then live them.

Many men want to fool around and, like a little boy, try to get away with as much as possible. But also like a little boy, they want to be disciplined. They want to have limits defined, and they look to their wife to enforce them.

If you know you will walk out the door the minute you learn of your husband's affair, let him know ahead of time how you feel. Perhaps it will keep him from straying. Don't count on it; but be honest with him about your feelings from the start of the relationship.

Some women will forgive a man for one affair, figuring he made a mistake and won't do it again. Some women even forgive twice, rationalizing that once is a mistake, twice is a coincidence. And, amazingly, some women even forgive a third time. Each time a woman "forgives" her man for his infidelity, she is giving him the message that it's okay for him to stray, and that she will still stay with him even though she is hurt and doesn't approve of his behavior. Over time, he may lose respect for her and even resent her. He will figure she doesn't think much of herself if she accepts shabby treatment from him.

Before you decide to stay with a straying man, ask yourself if you want to play second fiddle to his affairs, and if you really want him to think it's okay to treat you like a doormat. Of course, many women have good reasons for staying with a straying man. However, the dilemma women face when doing so is that there is no insurance against eventual divorce anyway. There is no insurance against infidelity and no antidote to adultery.

Drawing the line on unacceptable behavior is different from issuing an ultimatum. By delineating what behavior is acceptable to you, you set the tone of a relationship from the start. Some women tell men up front that they won't stand for infidelity. The men know these women mean business, and they are less likely to stray, because they are well aware of the real consequences to them if they do. If a man is dead set against fidelity, he has a chance to leave the relationship early on, because he knows he won't get away with it with this particular woman.

One man I interviewed told a woman he once dated that he would not respect her if she tolerated his straying. He wanted to respect her, and therefore tried not to betray her. It was more important to him to be with a woman who thought highly of herself, and who wouldn't overlook infidelity, than it was for him to be able to fool around with other women.

Think highly of yourself and demand respectful treatment from everyone in your life. If you only expect the best, you have a much better chance of getting it. At the very least, you will be happy with yourself.

Many women wonder if their husband would still have cheated on them if they had made it clear to him from the start that they wouldn't tolerate infidelity and would be straight out the door if he cheated on them. Many men I spoke with said their wives didn't have the resources—either financial, social, or emotional—to leave the marriage even if they wanted to. Some men even seemed to delight in the torture their infidelity caused their spouse, knowing she was dependent on the marriage for her identity as well as financial stability.

MEN'S QUESTIONS

*I*llustrating the vast gulf between men's pursuit of extramarital affairs and their wives' general disapproval of them, I am rarely asked questions about infidelity by men. When I am asked, the two most frequent questions are:

WHY CAN'T SHE UNDERSTAND THAT EXTRAMARITAL SEX DOESN'T MEAN ANYTHING? IT'S JUST SEX. IT'S A SHORT-TERM THING AND HAS NO EFFECT ON MY LOVE FOR HER OR THE MARRIAGE.

This question usually drives women crazy. And I have heard it so often in the course of researching and writing this book that I could scream a scream you would hear from California all the way to Australia!

Quite simply, women find it very difficult to believe that it's "just sex," because for most women, sex has meaning. Even single women who engage in one-night stands often convince themselves the sex means something and that a relationship will form. The number of women who have sex just for sex is not as great as the number of men who do so, so women rightly believe that there is indeed more to something than just sex.

Besides, wives wonder: "He has sex with me, so why does he need someone else?" Women believe that when their husband cheats on them, something is wrong with *them*. They think the Other Woman possesses something they lack. And they end up blaming themselves.

Married women wonder why a man will risk everything—love, marriage, family—for sex that "doesn't mean anything." What they have trouble comprehending is that many men want a nice wife, a happy family—and a guilt-free, hassle-free bit on the side. They want it all, without complications. They want the comfort and security of a loving wife, and the supposed excitement and thrill of an illicit sex life. Such men are selfish and immature. Like a small child, they want everything their way, and feel no concern for their wife's feelings.

Women want more than just sex. They want affection, romance, and a continuing relationship. Even women who say, "It's just sex," find themselves tripped up by their feelings. Just ask the millions of other women trapped in going-nowhere relationships with very married men.

Men need to realize that sex, and sexual exclusivity, mean a great deal to women. If they want a healthy, thriving, and happy marriage, then extramarital sex is not a good idea. Women need to understand that men are capable of separating sex from emotions. If he does have sex with someone else, it doesn't mean he doesn't love you. However, sex and continued interaction can lead to genuine affection being formed, so a woman has legitimate concerns about her husband's "just sexcapades" turning into something more, such as an intense emotional relationship that can undermine even a rock-solid marriage.

If you don't want to risk the spark becoming a flame, stay away from the situation creating the sparks: extramarital sex. Treasure your partner and your relationship. A solid relationship is much harder to find than "just sex," and in the grand scheme of life, it will bring you more lasting pleasure.

WHY ISN'T MY WIFE MORE INTERESTED IN SEX?

This is the second question I hear so often I want to grab some man by the collar and shout, "Foreplay!" The truth is, women *do* like sex, and they want it just as much as men do. It's just that we also like romance, as in touching, kissing, compliments, greeting cards, sexy lingerie, champagne, bath bubbles—and, most of all, attention.

Physiologically, women need more time to become sexually aroused than men do. A man can look at a woman in a short skirt crossing the street and be ready to pounce on her. The vast majority of women take longer than a nanosecond to become aroused, even by a stud muffin or a himbo (the male equivalent of a bimbo).

The key is attention. A man believes that if he takes out the garbage or washes the car, he is doing something nice for his wife. A woman thinks those sorts of things are "housekeeping," not part of sensuality. Women crave attention and displays of affection, such as touching and caressing. Women love sex, too, but they want some of the other stuff first. That's why it's called *foreplay*. Every woman wants to feel special before she can feel particularly sexual.

For a woman, sex begins outside the bedroom. Sexual stimulation is an entire way of interacting with her. It is nice phone calls, surprises, warm touches—not just when sex is around the corner, but as an end in itself.

Attention makes a woman feel like it is *her* you want, not just sex. And certainly not just sex with anyone—only with her.

Sure, women also love sex on the run—or "take-away sex." But more often they also want the complete gourmet platter. If men put as much time into wooing their wives as they do their extramarital affairs, they will have an eager marital sex partner in their wife—for life.

I often hear men say they began an affair because they were dissatisfied by the sex with their wife. How is having sex with a third party going to improve sex with your wife? You can only improve sex with your wife by paying more attention to your wife, not by turning to another woman!

Women like sex. Women love great sex with a man they adore. Women are more sexually responsive when they trust a man and feel safe, respected, and understood. And especially when they feel special and know their relationship is sexually exclusive. Focus your attention on the woman with whom you share your life, and you'll be amazed at how nourishing and novel your marital sex life can be.

TAKE NOTE

- No issue polarizes men and women more than the topic of infidelity. Many men tend to think adultery is no big deal; most women think it is a very big nightmare.

- Wishing infidelty away will not make it disappear.

- You must take care of yourself, because if your partner is deceiving you, then he is not putting your best interests forward.

Chapter 14

HAVE AN AFFAIR . . . WITH YOUR SPOUSE

A simple enough pleasure, surely, to have breakfast alone with one's husband, but how seldom married people in the midst of life achieve it.

—*Anne Morrow Lindbergh*

M ore marriages have been ruined by irritating habits than by unfaithfulness.

—*H. R. L. Sheppard, American clergyman*

IS INFIDELITY INEVITABLE?

$\mathcal{N}$early every day, news of yet another extramarital affair is revealed. Newspapers, magazines, television, and talk-back radio feature tales of straying spouses, most often men, leaving spurned wives despondent in their wake. Extramarital sex—infidelity—is common in our society today. It might even be called a growth industry. Most people will, unfortunately, have infidelity touch their lives. Either they or their partner will have an affair, or they know someone who is sexually and emotionally involved with someone other than their spouse.

Just because infidelity is prevalent, however, doesn't mean it is inevitable. Infidelity never "just happens." It takes motivation, opportunity, and planning to carry out an extramarital affair. Despite the complications and risks involved, each day more and more people break their marriage vows and bed someone other than their spouse. Careers stall, marriages crash, finances dwindle. Yet infidelity continues to increase, regardless of the very real negative consequences it inflicts on individuals, marriages, and families.

Whether or not monogamy is a natural state is constantly debated. Many men, and even many women, shudder at the thought of sleeping with only one person for the rest of their lives. But regardless of varying opinions on the subject, most people enter into marriage pledging fidelity and expecting it from their partner. *Monogamy need not be equated with monotony.*

ARE YOU BOTH GETTING ENOUGH . . . ATTENTION? AFFECTION?

$\mathcal{M}$arriage means different things to different people. So does sex. People couple up, have sex, and marry for a variety of reasons, and one can never totally understand what attracts two people to each other, or what keeps them together in spite of infidelity.

One thing people never seem to get enough of in life is attention. Everyone thrives on being liked and cared for, and most people blossom when they feel special. Many parents are totally inadequate at making their children feel loved and wanted. Parents are rarely taught relationship skills or parenting skills. As a result, most adults are walking around literally starved for attention and affection; and they have never effectively learned from their parents how to demonstrate love.

Men, in particular, are uneasy expressing emotions and being physically affectionate. Away from sport, many men are generally blank about how to show their emotions. With sport, enthusiasm and anger are readily displayed in a safe environment. Tender emotions toward women don't usually flow as easily, much to the disappointment of many women. To many men, sex *is* emotion. To most women, emotions set the stage for sex, which is why for many women to truly feel loved and to enjoy sex, they like to be warmed up with compliments and intimate talk.

Women often say that some men leave a lot to be desired in the romance department. Most women wish their mates would make more time for them. When women feel their partner isn't giving them enough time and attention, they will be outraged if they learn that that time is being spent on another woman! Happily married couples say time together is more important to them than great sex or lots of money. Still, most couples don't spend time alone together, and they need to. Time alone together makes illicit affairs thrive, and will do the same for a marriage.

While most people need and want attention, men and women have somewhat dissimilar ways of seeking and displaying attention and affection. Men often use sex as a way of expressing their emotions. Women more often use romantic gestures first, then sex. When a man or a woman feels they aren't having their expectations fulfilled for attention, affection, and sex, they may look to someone else for it. Even if sex is good at home, some people want still more sex, and still more attention, so they look for it on the side. They are empty vessels striving to fill their emptiness through sex and affection.

For many men, extramarital sex is as much about pumping up a faltering ego as it is about physical pleasure. Yet, no matter how much attention and love a woman may fawn on her husband, many men say they can only get that sought-after ego boost from another woman. When this happens, problems are likely to pervade the marriage.

If your partner wants to "supplement" the sex and affection he receives from you by seeking it from an extramarital partner, there isn't much you can do to change his mind. However, you can try from the start of your relationship to be as attentive to your loved one as possible. Obviously, it is healthy to pay attention to *your* needs and wants first, and then shower your partner with love and affection. Unfortunately, many people take their partner for granted, and this will eventually stifle and kill their relationship.

When a couple first marries, it is the time in the relationship when the frequency of sex and levels of attention are highest. What happens then? They become consumed by life — by their work and other activities, which can, and often do, expand to take over their day-to-day life and erode their love life.

Lovers, or Worn-out Parents?

Here is a typical scenario. A man and woman join together and forsake all others. The man goes off to work, and the woman may continue her career, but she generally also takes on responsibility for the domestic aspects of their lives — the cooking, cleaning, laundry, social director, etc. The man has gained a wife and a keeper as well as a second income. So now the woman has two jobs, and the man still has one.

He still goes on the road for work and kicks back in front of the television or attends a live sporting event. Not often enough does he spend quality time — sexual time — alone with his wife. While men complain all the time that women lose interest in sex, perhaps they should listen to the fact that women complain that men don't pay enough attention to them. For the wide majority of women, attention and physical touching and displays of affection are preludes to good sex.

Although it often takes two incomes for a middle-class family to make ends meet, even if a wife is employed for pay outside the home, her work almost without question takes second place to the man's. A couple relocates more often to facilitate his career growth than hers, and more effort is expended by both the man and woman on his work life, even when the woman also has a career.

A woman may be professionally educated and employed; yet after she has children she is still generally the one who shoulders all the child-care and household responsibilities. Even for couples with a nanny, it is generally the woman who organizes that child care. While more men than ever before are taking an active role in family life, women still shoulder the burden, even when employed full time. In this day and age, it is still a status symbol for a woman to stay at home and look after the children while her husband works to provide for the family. Many women believe they are privileged to be in such a situation, and many men feel enormous pride in being the primary breadwinner. Some men would never think of coupling with a woman who earns more money than they do, lest they would feel less of a man. The downside is, the man also controls the purse strings. When this happens, the wife is more like a dependant than an equal partner, and has few opportunities for advancement.

Mommy Madness

Motherhood must be the hardest job in the world; it is also one of the most controversial and least respected. Society implicitly tells women that it is their true destiny, yet it punishes them with little societal support in the form of benefits when they become a full-time mother. As a man's world expands with his career, a woman's world shrinks with motherhood. A woman all too often becomes totally financially dependent on her husband if she stays at home raising children. She has little contact with other male adults, and few chances for self-confidence-building activities in the world outside the home.

A marriage begins to suffer when a woman is too dependent on her husband for everything: attention, conversation, money, and support. Yet this is what still happens, even today, in many marriages. And when it happens, infidelity is usually just a phone call away. I hear men complain all the time about how their wives put all their attention on the children, at the expense of the marriage. Indeed, when a marriage is too child-centered, it will suffer.

Many men say their wives are more focused on the kids than on the marriage, and a substantial number of husbands say this "drove them" to have affairs. A marriage is the foundation for the entire family; therefore the couple must come first and the children second. After the children are raised and gone, a couple-centered marriage will still be strong and alive; a child-centered one may have broken up years earlier, or fallen victim to numerous affairs.

I know of so many cases where bright, attractive, educated, and talented women have married and literally lost themselves in motherhood. Their grooming slipped; they became uninteresting, having nothing more to talk about than their children; and they lost interest in everything around them. Men and women alike find it difficult to talk to women at parties who can only converse about children.

When a woman gives up her personal interests, career, and friends, moves to follow her husband's career, and becomes financially dependent on him—literally loses herself to him—what will she have left if he strays or leaves? Only herself, which will have become more withered during each passing year of a marriage that is based on dependency.

What can women do differently? They can stay employed—even part time, or in a work-from-home arrangement. They can develop their hobbies, obtain more education; they can participate in volunteer activities. They can decide to remain child-free. They can cultivate male friends, or accompany their husband on some of his business trips.

The partnership between a husband and wife must be a priority, for the foundation of the couple is the foundation on which the family rests. It is imperative for both men and women to stay interesting and desirable to one another after marriage, and to have a passion for their own interests as well as for each other. A husband and wife must be couple-centered first, and child-centered second.

TREAT YOUR SPOUSE THE WAY YOU WOULD A LOVER

Regardless of workloads and other pressing "life" matters, some couples do manage to keep the flame alive, even after many years together. How do they do it? It is really quite simple. And certainly much simpler than divorce—or infidelity! Couples with thriving marriages—marriages alive with laughter, love, and sex—do exist. When a relationship is a priority, we pay attention to it.

We all know of marriages that basically exist in name only. The man and woman can barely tolerate one another, and we wonder why they don't do each other a favor and divorce and seek a happier life elsewhere. We also know of couples who still cuddle and kiss in public after twenty years together. Such marriages exude comfort, caring, and companionship.

Individuals in vital, alive marriages make each other a priority—and time alone together a necessity, not a luxury. Marriages in which a man and a woman are best friends, lovers, and soulmates are the marriages we all admire, and the ones we should emulate.

It is not only the woman's responsibility to stay interesting and attractive after marriage; it is also the man's. Both parties need to work hard at maintaining their own identity, as well as developing the "couple" aspect of their marriage. Too many marriages become empty shells. Lonely coexistence does not make a marriage. In order to feed a marriage, a couple *must* spend time alone. People thrive on attention, and so do relationships.

When dating, men and women put a great deal of effort into their appearance and personal hygiene. The opposite often happens in marriage. They feel free to relax. But feeling relaxed and cozy isn't the same thing as letting one's standards of hygiene and grooming slip. Don't make the mistake of wearing old clothes around the house and saving your "good" outfits for special outings or work. Dress for your partner, not for strangers at work. *Don't "save the good china for company."* By this I mean, be your best self, every day, with your partner.

The reason so many men, and more and more women, are indulging in extramarital affairs is because that makes them feel great. They feel desirable and wanted. Someone they like is "using the good china" for them. Sex is a part of it, but so is all the stuff that goes with sex—the mystery, attention, and intimate conversation. People are unfaithful because they want someone to stroke their ego, as well as other parts of their body.

If you realize that you are complimenting other people more than your spouse, or your spouse is complimenting others more than you, it is time to rekindle your marriage by having an affair—with your spouse!

The most important four-letter word that has to do with sex is: TALK! A couple must talk to each other if they are to have a thriving marriage. Time alone together is essential. Happy couples spend lots of time together and *talk* about everything. Companionship and verbal intimacy seem to be the most important aspects of a happy marriage. However, criticism, contempt, withdrawal, and loneliness are all too often the cornerstones of marriage. According to the psychologist John Gottman in his book *Why Marriages Succeed or Fail* (1994), a marriage must have five times as many positive moments as negative moments if it is to be stable. Dr. Gottman's research also indicates that the two most basic ingredients for a happy marriage are love and respect. You must ask yourself this: *Is love and/or respect present if your husband cheats on you?*

ROMANCING THE SPOUSE

Both men and women say that their sex lives suffer after years of marriage. This doesn't have to be the case. In a new book on life after marriage, *Just Married* (1998), Barry Sinrod and Marlo Grey report that a full 67 percent of people say they had more sex before marriage. This may be related to another of the authors' findings: Seventy percent of respondents said they had gained weight since they met their spouses. Both men and women are equally guilty for letting their physical attractiveness slip after marriage. Love is wonderful in a relationship, but it usually also takes an appealing presentation to turn on a lover, both before and after marriage. Remember how you cleaned yourself up and dressed your best when going on dates? By doing the same thing after marriage, you are more likely to keep your sex life alive and thriving. We are all turned on by an appealing vision.

Treat your spouse the way you would the person you were beginning an affair with. Court them, dote on them, compliment them. If you are going to expend the time and energy, you may as well do it for your marital partner rather than a stranger!

Sex is really in the head, not between the legs. The brain is the ultimate sex organ and attention the ultimate aphrodisiac. If you spend at least one weekend every two months away alone with your partner, your sex life, mood, and marriage will improve. The more time you can spend away from home alone together, the better. Mini-honeymoons are wonderful.

I know of one couple who hadn't been away alone together in nine years. The husband confided to me that his wife wanted to go away for a weekend together, but he didn't know what they would find to talk about! While their marriage wasn't exactly on the rocks, the romance aspect of it had certainly crumbled. The marriage was ripe for an infidelity crisis. Couples simply *must* have time alone together if they are to remain close sexual companions and lovers.

Quite often the lure of an affair is the romance and escape from everyday rituals and routines. Fantasy is made up of hotel rooms, baths, champagne, crisp sheets, and no television or other interruptions. Make your marriage free of bedroom boredom. Get out of the same old bedroom more often. Hotels are great for romance. Just like an affair!

Extramarital affairs allow for the pleasurable diversions that have often been lost in a marriage. With an extramarital affair, you don't have to live every day with your lover, so you actually appreciate them more. In a fantasy romance, you can have an intimate partner without real life intruding. You can actually improve your own marriage by fantasizing about having sex with another partner. Have an affair in your fantasies, then use that energy to enhance your real-life relationship. Many men and some women have told me that fantasizing about having an affair was often better than the affair itself, and had none of the potentially damaging side effects of straying.

No man or woman can resist being the center of attention, being thought of as number one by someone they care about. Women, in particular, are suckers for intimate attention. It is the rare person who can ever receive too much attention.

Rekindle the flame in your marriage regularly. You will both be surprised at how thrilling an affair — with your spouse — can be. There are nine keys to enhancing the relationship:

FUELING THE FLAMES OF ROMANCE: SHOWING AND TELLING

Attention	Caring	Touching
Affection	Cuddling	Talking
Appreciation	Calling	Teasing

Take-Away Sex and Event Sex

Life intrudes, and sex too often gets put on the backburner. Take-away sex is wonderful when *some* is better than *none*. But for a real indulgence, make the time for event sex. Event sex is what you had before you were married. Event sex is *the* way to recapture the fun, shared laughter, and excitement you had earlier in your relationship, and it's the kind of fun and sex that draws millions of men into extramarital affairs.

Everyone wants more sex. And more affection before, during, and after sex. More kissing. An active partner. A willingness to try new things. More foreplay. Sex after orgasm. More consideration. More responsiveness. More communication. Companionship. Happiness. Trust. Fidelity. All these things are possible in marriage, but they have to be worked at. If you funnel your energy into achieving them with your spouse, you won't be throwing your time away, as you would be if you direct your attention away from your spouse to chase an illusive affair.

Alone, Yet Together

In addition to spending quality time alone together, a man and a woman also need lives of their own. Married couples should strive to allow time alone for each person, as well as time together for shared experiences. Everyone needs a life away from the marriage.

Time apart from a spouse is as important as time spent together. Each person must nurture themselves, pursue their own interests and dreams. The real challenge in a relationship is for each partner to develop themselves as individuals without growing apart from the spouse. Solid marriages are made when the two people in the relationship grow individually as well as together as a couple.

Some time apart is healthy. You learn about yourself, and you actually do appreciate your partner more after a few days away. Some absence *does* make the heart grow fonder. The psychological concept of novelty is what drives our appreciation for something temporarily removed from us. When we have something around all the time, we grow used to it, so we barely notice it any longer.

In an extramarital affair, contact is limited. You only see the person on their best behavior, and don't have to put up with hairs in the sink, or makeup all over the counter. You appreciate the good times together because they usually don't happen every day. You have a chance to miss the other person. In marriage, you get more sick of the person each day, rather than missing them more. That is why it is important to build into your life natural breaks from each other. Even a day away can do the trick to give you a chance to miss your partner—and him to miss you.

The dual needs of closeness and freedom operate in everyone, but some people need more of one than the other. Work on reaching an acceptable accommodation with your partner. Give him a chance to miss you—and you to miss him. Everyone needs some time and space to get over the annoying habits of their partner, only to later miss them and look forward to the reunion. And to appreciate the marriage rather than dread it.

In a real relationship, we must be ourselves as well as part of a couple. We are more interesting when we continue to develop who we are. When we have our own identity, we can contribute much more to our marriage. Extramarital affairs recognize the separate identity of each of the parties involved. Marriage should do the same.

A good marriage is nourished by the little things a husband and wife do for each other every day—the loving phone calls, the wink, the smile, the kind words. It grows from the attention you shower on your spouse, and the way you feel about them—and yourself—when you are with them. In sum, the qualities that make an affair exciting can also make a marriage sizzle.

TAKE NOTE

- There is no way anyone can "affair-proof" their marriage. If a man is going to stray, he is going to stray.

- Some men will stray no matter what—they will cheat regardless of how a woman looks.

- Good marriages can be weakened by a partner's infidelity. Bad marriages are rarely helped by infidelity.

- Turning to an affair will not improve your sex life with your spouse.

- Be the best you can be — physically, emotionally, spiritually, financially. Use "the good china" every day — not only for people outside your home.

- Make sure your marriage is couple-centered. Too much attention to children at the expense of your spouse can spell trouble for a relationship.

- Make each day with your partner count. Couples who are best friends as well as lovers are less likely to deceive their mate.

- Treat your spouse as you would a new lover.

- Make each other a top priority. Have an affair with your spouse — or someone else will!

Chapter 15

LIVING BEYOND BETRAYAL: GET A LIFE!

*I*n three words I can tell you all that I have learned about life:
It goes on.

—*Robert Frost*

*I*f you can't change your fate, change your attitude.

—*Amy Tan*

*I*f you're seeking revenge, you'll never get over it. I think that
the best thing is living well, letting go, going on.

—*Diane Keaton*

LOVE YOURSELF AND
LIVE YOUR LIFE

Sigmund Freud once said that people need both love and work to have a happy and emotionally healthy, fulfilling life. Indeed, both men and women say they want a solid relationship and an interesting and financially reward- ing job. One of the great challenges of life is achieving these goals.

When infidelity enters the picture, both the personal and the profes- sional lives of all those involved can be threatened. A woman is particularly vulnerable if she is financially dependent on her husband and her marriage. Virginia Woolf pointed out that "A woman must have money and a room of her own." What a woman really needs is a life of her own!

A common thread in many women's lives is their near-total dependence on their husband for virtually *everything*—identity, social status, financial stability. When women discover their husband's infidelity, one of their first reactions is to worry about the possible loss of their lifestyle and the very roof over their head. Yes, even today.

What every woman needs is *"stick-it money"*—her own income—which will enable her to leave an uncomfortable situation, such as a philandering husband and a sham of a marriage, whenever she chooses to do so. A woman needs to be financially independent of her husband. The security this pro- vides will allow her to walk away from a relationship that has turned phys- ically violent, emotionally abusive, or intolerable because of her husband's cheating. "Stick-it money" gives a woman the freedom to say, "I'm not will- ing to take this anymore," and to move forward with her life.

When a woman has a life of her own, she can say to her husband, "I can't forgive you—I can't forget your infidelity. I'm out of here," and actually follow through with her threat. She will have money, a job, separate friends; in short, she will have other options that she can exercise if her husband treats her poorly and she doesn't want to take it any more. And if she stays married, she'll be happier with herself and more interesting to her partner.

Being a wife and a mother are very worthwhile life choices, but they are not stable professions. Being a wife and a mother should be side paths along the road of life; the main road of every woman's life must be paved with her own interests and her own income. *Every woman needs a life to call her own.*

> *The best is yet to be.*
>
> — ROBERT BROWNING

WOMEN AND MARRIAGE: BED OF ROSES OR BED OF THORNS?

𝒟ecades of research indicate that married women suffer depression and other emotionally based difficulties at twice the rates of men and employed and/or single women. One reason for this is that a married woman who is a housewife has few avenues in which to grow as an individual, and often feels helpless, powerless, and dependent on her husband for her livelihood — indeed, her basic identity. When such a woman discovers her husband is unfaithful, she feels trapped.

Most women are encouraged to believe that marriage and motherhood are the most important roles they will ever have. It is little surprise, then, that marriage falls short of many expectations. If one enters into something with unrealistic expectations, then the realization that even a happy marriage is a mixed bag can lead to feelings of despair.

Women end up feeling betrayed many times over: when they realize marriage may not be all they hoped for; when they are faced with their husband's infidelity; and when they are forced to deal with their loss of identity and the need to rebuild it on their own.

A woman's belief in herself is everything. Why should she give up everything for a man who won't even give up a girlfriend?

A LIFE OF ONE'S OWN

*If we did not look to marriage as the principal source of happiness,
fewer marriages would end in tears.*

—PSYCHOLOGIST ANTHONY STORR

Perhaps more women are getting the message that a life of their own is their only guarantee of security. Many women these days consider a career and friends as the most important and rewarding aspects of their lives. Women are realizing that their life is in their own hands, and that they can shape a happy and fulfilling life by focusing on a career, regardless of their marital status.

Marriage and motherhood will continue to be a priority for the majority of women. However, it is time more women realized that domestic bliss is not incompatible with a career and a life of one's own. Interests apart from home and husband may be the most important ingredients for women's emotional well-being—and for a fulfilling marriage.

When people have multiple interests and roles in life, they are psychologically better off. There seems to be a mechanism in us that thrives when we have many roles to fill. Each role brings us diversity and interaction, and with it the chance for us to enhance our self-confidence.

When marriage is a side path on the road of life, rather than the goal to which all directions lead, women have the opportunity to continue developing their own identity. A woman who has her own interests, who is self-confident, and who likes herself, is, in all likelihood, a better marriage partner. A woman with a life of her own is not as vulnerable to the ebbs and flows of the sea of marriage.

For all couples today, infidelity is likely to intrude on the marriage at some point. Under any circumstances, infidelity is painful, and it is worse for a woman if she has no alternative but to stay with a man for financial reasons, as many millions of women are forced to do. As one "first wife" told me, a woman needs a career of her own and money of her own.

Even women are judgmental of other women who aren't employed outside the home. Most of us find people more pleasing to speak with when they have something interesting to say. And that means they have to have things happening in their life—activities other than caring for children and cleaning the house. Men, too, appreciate women who are interesting companions.

Some women are interested in careers; but the vast majority of women, even employed women, think marriage and children are important responsibilities. The difficulty with a total focus on the family at the expense of work is that it puts women in an extremely tenuous position, financially and psychologically. Women need to think about their own interests, and that includes some consideration of work and career as a way of enhancing their financial and emotional freedom.

Moving forward with life does not always have to involve divorce — just a solid commitment to an individual goal. Tending home and children is not enough to fulfill many women these days. And the more interests and roles a woman has, the happier and psychologically healthier she is.

> *Married men face pressure to earn money, but they don't face*
> *what married women do: an internal demand to "give up" their*
> *own goals and become selfless.*
>
> — DALMA HEYN

MOVING YOUR LIFE FORWARD

Get an education. Obtain a job. Change jobs. Find a hobby apart from your spouse and kids. Develop new friendships. Pursue activities on your own. Solitude is a growth experience. Rediscover the you your husband fell in love with. Set a challenge and goals for yourself.

You will be amazed at how much better you will feel about yourself when you set yourself the challenge of achieving something. It will give you a brighter attitude and a purpose in life apart from your marriage. Think of yourself for a change. If *you* don't take care of yourself, who will?

CAN MEN AND WOMEN, WHEN ONE OR BOTH ARE MARRIED, *REALLY* BE FRIENDS WITHOUT SEX GETTING IN THE WAY?

When a person marries, they don't automatically become hermetically sealed off from one half of the human race. It just feels that way sometimes, especially for women. It isn't considered proper for married women to be overtly flirtatious. Yet when married men flirt, they are considered charming. Men who flirt are just being nice; a woman who flirts is "looking."

The sexual double standard has ramifications for married people as well as single ones. It isn't often one sees a married man having lunch with a married woman who isn't his wife, his secretary, or his business partner. When a man and a woman who are married to other people are seen having lunch, drinks, or dinner together, the rumor mill goes into overdrive. It is assumed they must be having an affair. Jean-Paul Sartre said that "The association of a man with a woman always has sexual implications." Society has yet to acknowledge that men and women can, and do, have the desire and the right to socialize with married members of the opposite sex without either spouse being present; and more important—contrary to what Sartre believed—without "the sex thing getting in the way."

Whenever a married man helps a woman other than his wife find a job, or advances her career, or dines alone with her, people assume an affair is going on. It looks bad only because men and women are assumed to be sexually motivated, rather than motivated to seek interesting companions regardless of their age, career position, or marital status.

I recall meeting a man I thought was very interesting, and who worked in a field similar to mine. When I commented to a friend, who also knew the man, that I was going to ask him to lunch to learn more about him and his work, she nearly choked on her wine. "Invite his wife, too," she advised. As I wasn't particularly interested in talking to his wife, I didn't see why I should invite her. I had no designs on the man; I simply thought he would be interesting to talk to, and lunch was a convenient way of doing so.

If more men and women were allowed to have friends of the opposite sex, they would have some of their needs for attention, compliments, variety, and companionship met without pressuring their spouse to fulfill all of those needs. Everyone needs to have friends, so why are married adults supposed to have only friends of the same sex?

Many people see opposite-sex friends as threats to their marriage. Ironically, a marriage is more threatened by an affair if men and women *don't* have platonic friends of the opposite sex. It is natural for both men and women to seek attention from, and the company of, other men and women throughout their adult life. If they cannot have innocent friends of the opposite sex without raising the ire of their spouse, then an affair may be more likely to happen. A woman can and should live on the fringe of many men's lives — that doesn't mean you have to have sex with them! Male friends enrich a woman's life and her self-esteem.

JUST FLIRTING . . . OR?

No matter how happily a woman may be married — it always pleases her to discover that there is a nice man who wishes that she were not.

— H. L. MENCKEN

Flirtation and fantasy are the safest sex one can have these days. Flirtation makes all the parties involved feel better about themselves. Everyone needs attention, and playful, harmless flirting can fit the bill. Supplement the attention from your spouse with interaction with other men. Adult women in general have too limited contact with men. Use each encounter with men to keep your social skills polished and your flirtations fed.

In real life, more women are having affairs than ever before in history. Their main reason in doing so is to seek attention and emotional intimacy. So many women are tired of being treated as a piece of furniture, or of having to compete with the television or sport for attention. They simply turn their passion to other men. If even a generally loyal woman is left wanting more from her husband, eventually she will turn elsewhere to fulfill her emotional and sexual longings.

Women who stray say they have affairs to feel good about themselves; to feel attractive and cherished again; and to feel that their life and their body aren't being wasted. Many of these women say they are totally disillusioned with marriage. While they enjoy the security of a home base and children, generally they feel emotionally neglected and empty. They are seeking a relief from boredom, as well as something else—an indescribable something that they believe is missing in their life.

If you are a woman staying with a man who strays, you have probably thought about having an affair of your own. By advising you to "get a life," I'm not suggesting you get a *double* life! Obviously, some women benefit from the emotional boost an affair gives them; but a woman who has a "revenge" affair just to get back at her husband will rarely find that it brings her comfort.

The most difficult aspect of infidelity is that there are no guarantees how it will all turn out. You just never know when you will really fall for someone you thought you were seeing "just for sex," and you never know when a third party will want to ruin your marriage.

Before you get involved in an affair, ask yourself these questions: *How will it end? Is an affair better than a divorce? Are you willing to risk your marriage by having an affair?*

WHAT SORT OF LIFE IS BEST FOR YOU?

If you create a life of your own along with your marriage, you will have a better chance of being happy with your life, your spouse, and your marriage. And, if your husband is inclined to be unfaithful, you will be in a better financial and emotional position to consider your options rationally and realistically.

There are back-stabbers, liars, and cheaters everywhere. The world can be a cold, cruel place, and marriage and the family are meant to be our buffer against that world. A spouse should have your best interests at heart. If you live with a man who is unfaithful to you, you are being persecuted from within your own home. Is this how you want to spend your life? Can you survive—and thrive—in this situation?

If your marriage depends on your tolerating your husband's infidelity, you must ask yourself if your spouse and your marriage are worth sacrificing your emotional well-being. Facing up to infidelity can make you stronger. If you expect the best from those around you and refuse to accept less than respectful treatment, you may just get what you want.

Divorce is not a dirty, four-letter word. For many women, it has been a liberating experience, and they have gone on to lead happy and successful lives. In fact, some women would never consider remarriage, because they feel a husband would limit their career progress and control their life choices.

You can love a man and yourself at the same time. You do not, and should not, have to give up *you* in order to be married. It is difficult to live your own life when you are worrying about your husband being in bed with another woman. If the role of second fiddle doesn't suit you, then decide whether you want to change your life. If you fundamentally believe in monogamy, and you can't bear to share your husband with other women, then perhaps marriage to a philandering man is not for you. However, if sexual exclusivity isn't high on your list of traits desired in a marriage partner, then maybe you will find it easier than most women to stay with a straying husband.

Only you know the answer to the most important question you will ever face: What type of life is best for me?

It is never too late to be what you might have been.

—George Eliot

TAKE NOTE

- Only *you* are an expert on your life. Only *you* know what sacrifices, compromises, and trade-offs are worth making for your marriage.

- Never forget that you make your own opportunities in life. Don't ever think you have no options. You do.

- The single most important thing you can do for your emotional well-being is to have interests, income, and friends separate from your marriage.

- Living with a philandering husband is possible for some women. You must decide for yourself if that is how *you* really want to spend your life.

Epilogue

I have learned much over the last years. From now on I am going to own myself and be true to myself. I am going to be me.

—DIANA, PRINCESS OF WALES

The untimely death in Paris of Diana, the Princess of Wales, in 1997 highlights just how brief life can be. Our time is precious and fleeting, and each day is a treasure to be valued and enjoyed, not simply endured. Diana's death was made even sadder by the fact that for years she was married to a man who loved another woman. She stayed with her husband and tried to improve her marriage, but she ended up divorced anyway. She gave up valuable years of her life to a man who claimed he had never loved her. And just as she seemed finally to be happy and to be getting on with her life as a single woman, that life was taken from her.

MAKE EACH DAY COUNT!

While researching this book, I heard many women complain that they were in marriages like Diana's—unhappy marriages devoid of affection, filled with acrimony and adultery. These women elected to stay with a straying man in the hope that, if they wait long enough, he will one day be monogamous. I also heard stories of women who gathered the courage to leave philandering men. They all said their only regret was they *stayed too long*.

Many women who stay with men who stray end up getting dumped anyway. After giving up years of their life to philandering men, they find themselves out in the cold. Standing by a straying man is no guarantee he won't leave—or that he will change. Lying, deceitful, philandering men seldom become trustworthy, loving, monogamous husbands. In the meantime, many women are frittering away their lives on men who won't even give up an affair for them.

Several women I interviewed spent the better part of their life standing by men who philandered throughout their entire marriage, and ended up being divorced by their husbands so that they could marry a younger woman. These long-suffering wives were left with few financial resources, and even less confidence and self-respect.

While personal reasons such as love and children, along with social and financial concerns, and even talk of "political or power partnerships," often compel women to tolerate a cheating husband, it is still, ultimately, the woman's choice to stay. Each day a woman stays with a straying spouse, she is depriving herself of the opportunity to live a better life. By standing by a philanderer, she is perpetuating her misery by sending him the message that it is okay to betray her.

As difficult as it is to stand up for oneself, if more women decided not to tolerate philandering men, men might be less inclined to betray women. By staying married to a man who is sexually and emotionally involved with other women, a woman is saying to her husband—and herself—that *her* feelings don't matter. That their marriage doesn't count. In colluding with her husband in his betrayal of her, she betrays herself.

Very often we get what we allow in relationships. Even though most women want a monogamous marriage, it isn't easy for them to take a stand against infidelity—and to enforce that stand. However, unless men know they have something to lose by their adultery, most of them won't respect a woman's wishes. How you treat yourself often determines how others will treat you. If you expect to be cheated on, and have low expectations of honesty from your spouse, then you will probably get what you expect. Don't compromise your beliefs. If you follow through on them, you will garner the respect you deserve.

Anyone married more than ten minutes knows there are ups and downs in marriage. But turning to a third party is no way to deal with marital problems. It solves nothing, and adds another complication that may ultimately ruin the marriage. If you are having marital problems, try to work them out with your partner, or seek professional help. If you are married, your responsibility is to do all you can to improve your marriage without involving a third party. Focusing attention on one's *spouse* is the *only* way to improve a marriage.

Extramarital affairs are not just about sex, and they don't "just happen."

Affairs are about planning, lies, and deception, and attention and affection showered on someone other than one's spouse. At their most basic, affairs are a betrayal of trust. Once trust—the fundamental component of a happy marriage—is shattered, it is difficult to mend. Like a fine piece of crystal that has been broken and glued back together, it is never quite the same again.

Even if a woman stays and tolerates infidelity, a marriage is never the same after a betrayal is discovered. Women who stay with men who stray are living a life in limbo. The limbo is a dance, not a way of life. Once a woman decides she will no longer live her life in a holding pattern, she can more confidently move forward.

Sex is only a part of any marriage. However, women link sex with feelings of exclusivity and trust. Intimacy is vital for a happy, long-term, successful, connected union. One of the most important aspects of a thriving marriage is respect. When a man constantly deceives his wife by carrying on extramarital affairs, he is not respecting her. It is virtually impossible for a man and woman to feel close to one another on all levels, and to trust one another, when one party is lying to the other day in, day out, as affairs require them to do. Remember the White House finger wagging?

Just because illicit sex is offered to a man doesn't mean he has to indulge. Real men can—and do—say no to extramarital affairs. Far from being bland and boring, as society portrays them, faithful husbands realize the benefits of a thriving marriage and make a conscious choice not to fool around. They may flirt outrageously with women, but they draw a strict boundary around their marriage and don't give in to dalliances. As one enlightened man explained:

There is one thing I know for sure, and that is even if a red-hot babe comes after me, I'll turn her down. I've already gotten the thrill by her approaching me, and at the end of the day, there is no way she could measure up to my wife. Where would it lead to, anyway? What would be the point, other than a quick poke? Why bother?

There is simply no doubt that marriages are happier and more stable when a husband and wife are not running around deceiving one another in extramarital affairs. Moral and religious issues aside, relationships are happier and calmer when a man and a woman don't have to worry about adultery. As one monogamous man told me, "If you look once at an attractive woman, you are a man. If you look twice, you're an adventurous man. If you touch, you'll be a divorced man."

Many women told me they are afraid of being alone if they leave their marriage. Yet loneliness *within a marriage* is much worse than being alone. What could be worse than being married to a man who loves another woman? Is being with a man in name only *really* better than being free to pursue one's own dreams, or to be with a man who respects and loves you?

Many women believe that the worst thing that can happen to them is to have their husband become involved with another woman. In fact, the worst thing that can happen is for a woman to live a lie. Very often, staying and being betrayed is much more detrimental to a woman's self-esteem and overall mental health than leaving an untenable lifestyle. Constantly being around a person who lies, deceives, and evades questions will damage even a strong woman's self-confidence. Living with lying is bad for your mental, emotional, physical, and marital health.

Many women I spoke with used the term "deadened" to describe how they felt about their husband's dalliances. At a certain point in their husband's affairs, a part of them died and was closed off from their husband, they said. To protect themselves from continually being hurt, they had to let *all* their feelings die.

A woman confronts a terrible choice when her husband is unfaithful. She can try to look the other way and hope his affair will end soon. She can confront him, and risk losing him because he has been found out. She can stay and try to find a way to tolerate his philandering. She can have an affair of her own. Or she can decide she wants out of her deceitful marriage.

There is a collective cultural ambivalence about infidelity, which makes it difficult for women either to accept it or to leave their marriage. There is no getting past it: infidelity is a nightmare for most people to deal with. How women respond will depend on many factors. Relationships come in all shapes and sizes. Find the one that best fits *you*.

If there are three people in your marriage, you don't have to stay a part of the crowd. Your life is too short — and too valuable — to waste on a marriage in name only. There are many desirable, attractive, successful men in this world who want a happy marriage and who are *not* philanderers. It is up to you to decide whether you will stay with a man who strays, or move forward and build a new life. As Princess Diana told Martin Bashir in November 1995, "People think that at the end of the day a man is the only answer. Actually, a fulfilling job is better for me."

Appendix:
INFIDELITY MOVIES

$\mathcal{M}$ovies provide a wonderful opportunity for individuals and couples to explore relationship issues. By viewing and discussing movies, men and women can learn more about their own and others' behaviors, motivations, and deeply held beliefs. It is far easier for a couple to discuss the infidelity of two people they watch on a movie screen than it is for them to talk about their own infidelity or their feelings about a straying spouse. Yet, by talking about a movie, they are really communicating important information to each other, such as what qualities matter to them in a person, what they expect in a marriage, and what sort of behavior they will tolerate.

The following list of "infidelity movies" includes, in order of preference, those that I believe are among the best films ever made on the subject of adultery. If you suspect your husband is cheating on you, or you are looking for ways to open a discussion about adultery with your partner, these movies will show you how screen characters deal with a variety of issues.

By watching a selection of infidelity movies, you will become more aware of the major issues extramarital sex presents for people. Hopefully, you will then be better equipped to deal with infidelity should it ever touch your own life.

1. *Fatal Attraction* (a cautionary tale) (1987), D: Adrian Lyne
2. *Heartburn* (1986), D: Mike Nichols
3. *Until September* (1984), D: Richard Marquand
4. *Sliding Doors* (1998), D: Peter Howitt
5. *Something to Talk About* (1995), D: Lasse Hallström
6. *The Bridges of Madison County* (1995), D: Clint Eastwood
7. *Indecent Proposal* (1993), D: Adrian Lyne
8. *Too Beautiful for You* (1989-French), D: Bertrand Blier
9. *She's the One* (1996), D: Edward Burns
10. *The Brothers McMullen* (1995), D: Edward Burns

11. *Miami Rhapsody* (1995), D: David Frankel
12. *The Unbearable Lightness of Being* (1988), D: Philip Kaufman
13. *The Politician's Wife* (1995), British Broadcasting Corp. (*BBC Telefilm*)
14. *Presumed Innocent* (1990), D: Alan J. Pakula
15. *The First Wives' Club* (1996), D: Hugh Wilson
16. *Husbands and Wives* (1992), D: Woody Allen
17. *Scandal* (1989), D: Michael Caton-Jones
18. *Sex, lies and videotape* (1989), D: Steven Soderbergh
19. *Weekend with Kate* (1991-Australian), D: Arch Nicholson
20. *The Journalist* (1979-Australian), D: Michael Thonrhill
21. *The Prince of Tides* (1991), D: Barbra Streisand
22. *Body Heat* (1981), D: Lawrence Kasdan
23. *Crimes and Misdemeanors* (1989), D: Woody Allen
24. *Afterglow* (1997), D: Alan Rudolph
25. *Hope Floats* (1998), D: Forest Whitaker
26. *A Perfect Murder* (1998), D: Andrew Davis
27. *The Man Who Loved Women* (1983), D: Blake Edwards
28. *Shirley Valentine* (1989), D: Lewis Gilberg
29. *The Ice Storm* (1997), D: Ang Lee
30. *One Night Stand* (1997), D: Mike Figgis

Classic Older Infidelity Movies

1. *Back Street* (1961), D: David Miller
2. *Same Time Next Year* (1978), D: Robert Mulligan
3. *Diary of a Mad Housewife* (1970), D: Frank Perry
4. *A Change of Seasons* (1980), D: Richard Lang
5. *Bob & Carol & Ted & Alice* (1969), D: Paul Mazursky

References

Amende, Coral. *Hollywood Confidential: An Inside Look at the Public Careers and Private Lives of Hollywood's Rich and Famous*. New York: Plume/Penguin Books, 1997.

American Psychiatric Association. *Diagnostic and Statistical Manual of Mental Disorders—DSM III-R*. 3rd ed. Washington, DC: American Psychiatric Association, 1987.

Andersen, Christopher. *Jack and Jackie: Portrait of an American Marriage*. New York, William Morrow, 1996.

Applewhite, Ashton. *Cutting Loose: Why Women Who End Their Marriages Do So Well*. New York: HarperCollins, 1997.

Avna, J., and D. Waltz. *Celibate Wives: Breaking the Silence*. Los Angeles: Lowell House, 1992.

Bandura, Albert. *Principles of Behavior Modification*. New York: Holt, Rinehart & Winston, 1969.

Barreca, Regina. *Perfect Husbands (And Other Fairy Tales)*. New York: Harmony/Crown Publications, 1993.

Bar-Tel, D., and L. Saxe. "Effects of Physical Attractiveness on the Perception of Couples," *Personality and Social Psychology Bulletin*, 1, (1974): 30–32.

Baum, Geraldine, and Elizabeth Mehren. "Through It All, She Stands by Her Man," *Los Angeles Times*, September 12, 1996.

Baumeister, Roy. "Subjective and Experiential Correlates of Guilt in Everyday Life," *Personality and Social Psychology Bulletin*, 32, (1995): 1256–68.

Berke, Richard. "Clinton's OK in the Polls," *New York Times*, February 15, 1998.

Bermant, G. G. "Sexual Behavior: Hard Times with the Coolidge Effect," in M. Siegel and H. Ziegler, eds., *Psychological Research: The Inside Story*. New York: Harper & Row, 1976, pp. 76–103.

Bernard, Jessie. *The Future of Marriage*. New Haven, CT: Yale University Press, 1982.

Berry, Barbara Cochran, with Joan Parrent. *Life After Johnnie Cochran: Why I Left the Sweetest-Talking Most Successful Black Lawyer in Los Angeles*. New York: Basic Books, 1995.

Biddle Barrows, Sydney. *Just Between Us Girls*. New York: St. Martin's Press, 1996.

Bittman, Michael, and Jocelyn Pixley. *The Double Life of the Family*. Sydney: Allen & Unwin, 1997.

Blanchard, Paul. *Why Men Cheat and What to Do About It*. Tampa, FL: Luv Books, 1995.

Botwin, Carol, *Men Who Can't Be Faithful*. New York: Warner Books, 1988.

———. *Tempted Women: The Passions, Perils, and Agonies of Female Infidelity*. New York: William Morrow, 1994.

Brock, David. *The Seduction of Hillary Rodham*. New York: Free Press, 1996.

Brooke, James. "Governor Romer Says He Had 'Relationship' with an Aide," *New York Times*, February 7, 1998.

Bryant, T., and F. Leighton. *Dog Days at the White House*. New York: Macmillan, 1975.

Bushnell, Candace. *Sex and the City*. New York: Atlantic Monthly Press, 1997.

Buss, David. "Sex Differences in Human Mating Preferences: Evolutionary Hypotheses Tested in 37 Countries," *Behavioral and Brain Sciences*, 12 (1989): 1–49.

———. *The Evolution of Desire: Strategies of Human Mating*. New York: Basic Books, 1994.

Campbell, Christy, and Greg Neale. "Goldsmith Dies with Wife and Mistress at Bedside," *Daily Telegraph* (London), July 20, 1998.

Campbell, Lady Colin. *Diana in Private: The Princess Nobody Knows*. New York: St. Martin's Press, 1997.

"Can Your Marriage Survive an Affair?" *Daily Telegraph* (Sydney), March 18, 1996.

Carlson, Margaret. "With Women Like These," *Time*, August 10, 1998.

Cawthorne, Nigel. *Sex Lives of the Presidents: From Washington to Clinton*. New York: St. Martin's Press, paperback, 1998.

"Cheating Spencer's Letter to His Lover," *Daily Mirror* (London), November 26, 1997.

Clark, R., and E. Hatfield. "Gender Differences in Receptivity to Sexual Offers," *Journal of Psychology and Human Sexuality*, 2 (1989): 39–55.

Coleman, Fred. "French Views on British Sex Scandals," *U.S. News & World Report*, November 14, 1994.

Conant, Jennet. "The Royal Couple—Ted Turner and Jane Fonda," *Vanity Fair* (April 1997).

Cooper, Matthew, and Karen Breslau. "For Better and For Worse," *Newsweek*, February 9, 1998.

Culbertson, Frances M. "Depression and Gender," *American Psychologist* vol. 52 (January 1997): 25–31.

Davies, Nicholas. *Diana: The Lonely Princess*. Secaucus, NJ: Birch Lane Press, 1996.

Davis, Robert. "Study Takes the Mystery Out of Romance," *USA Today*, February 16, 1998.

Dion, K., E. Berscheid, and E. Walster. "What Is Beautiful Is Good," *Journal of Personality and Social Psychology*, 24, (1972): 285–90.

"Divorce in the 90's," *Sunday Telegraph* (Sydney), January 19, 1997.

Duffy, Michael, and Michael Weisskopf. "Devil of a Blue Dress: Taking the Wraps Off a Fashion Strategy," *Time*, August 31, 1998.

Dutton, Donald, with Susan K. Galant. *The Batterer: A Psychological Profile*. New York: Basic Books, 1995.

Eaker Weil, Bonnie. *Adultery: The Forgivable Sin*. New York: Hastings House, 1994.

Elias, Marilyn. "Marital Spats Sicken Wives, Not Husbands," *USA Today*, March 30, 1998.

Ellis, B. J., and D. Symons. "Sex Differences in Sexual Fantasy: An Evolutionary Psychological Approach," *Journal of Sex Research*, 27 (1990): 527–56.

Emery, Erin. "Protestors Focus on Fidelity," *Denver Post*, February 15, 1998.

Ephron, Nora. *Heartburn*. New York: Pocket Books, 1983.

Evans, Patricia. *The Verbally Abusive Relationship—How to Recognize It and How to Respond*. 2nd ed., Boston: Adams Media Corporation, 1996.

Faludi, Susan. *Backlash: The Undeclared War Against American Women*. New York: Crown Publishers, 1991.

Fielding, Helen. *Bridget Jones' Diary*. New York: Viking, 1998.

Fields, Jamie Schilling. "Our Fair Lady—Jerry Hall," *Texas Monthly* (August 1995).

"First-Ever Sex Survey: Sex in Philadelphia," *Philadelphia* magazine (December 1992).

Fisher, Helen. *Anatomy of Love: A Natural History of Mating, Marriage, and Why We Stray*. New York: W. W. Norton, 1992.

Flowers, Gennifer. *Sleeping with the President: My Intimate Years with Bill Clinton*. New York: Anonymous Press, 1992.

Foerstel, Karen, and Linda Massarella. "Bill's Through with Big-Mouth Friend Morris," *New York Post*, January 29, 1998.

Gibbs, Nancy, and Michael Duffy. "I Misled People," *Time*, August 31, 1998.

Glamour. "Is Society biased against single women?" (April 1997).

———. "Reader Survey: Is Society Biased Against Single Women?" (April 1997).

———. "Sex & Health: His Infidelity May Raise Her Risk of Cancer" (December 1996).

———. "Why Men Pay for Sex" (July 1998).

Glass, Shirley. "After Infidelity and Advice for Hillary," *Psychology Today* (August 1998).

———. "Justifications for Extramarital Relationships: The Association Between Attitudes, Behaviors and Gender," *Journal of Sex Research*, 29, no. 3 (1988): 361–87.

Glass, Shirley, and Thomas Wright. *Sex Differences in Types of Extramarital Involvement and Marital Dissatisfaction.* New York: Plenum Publishing, 1985.

Goldberg, Robert, and Gerald Jay Goldberg. *Citizen Turner: The Wild Rise of an American Tycoon.* New York: Harcourt Brace, 1995.

"Gossip Queens: Cindy Adams," *New York* magazine, November 4, 1996.

Gottman, John. *Why Marriages Succeed or Fail—And How You Can Make Yours Last.* New York: Simon & Schuster, 1994.

Graham, Caroline. *Camilla—The King's Mistress—A Royal Scandal.* New York: HarperCollins, paperback, 1994.

Graham, Katharine. *Personal History.* New York: Alfred A. Knopf, 1997.

Grant, Toni. *Being a Woman—Fulfilling Your Femininity and Finding Love.* New York: Random House, 1988.

"The Great British Sex Survey," *Sunday Mirror* (London), April 8, 1996.

Gross, Jane. "More AIDS Is Seen in People Over 50," *New York Times*, March 16, 1997.

Gurley Brown, Helen. *The Late Show: A Practical, Semiwild Survival Guide for Every Woman in Her Prime or Approaching It.* New York: William Morrow, 1993.

Hafner, Julian. *The End of Marriage: Why Monogamy Isn't Working.* London: Century, 1993.

Hagood, Wesley O. *Presidential Sex: From the Founding Fathers to Bill Clinton.* Secaucus, NJ: Citadel Press, 1996.

Halper, Jan. *Quiet Desperation: The Truth About Successful Men.* New York: Warner Books, 1988.

Handy, Bruce. "How We Really Feel About Fidelity," *Time/*CNN Poll, *Time*, August 31, 1998.

Hatfield, E., and S. Sprecher. *Mirror, Mirror: The Importance of Looks in Everyday Life.* New York: SUNY Press, 1986.

Hayes, Christopher C., Deborah Anderson, and Melinda Blau. *Our Turn: The Good News About Women and Divorce.* New York: Pocket Books, 1993.

Heyn, Dalma. *The Erotic Silence of the American Wife.* New York: Random House, 1992.

———. *Marriage Shock: The Emotional Transformation of Women into Wives.* New York: Villard, 1997.

Higham, Charles. *Rose: The Life and Times of Rose Fitzgerald Kennedy.* New York: Pocket Books, 1996.

Hill, E. M., E. S. Nocks, and L. Gardner. "Physical Attractivenss: Manipulation by Physique and Status Displays," *Ethnology and Sociobiology*, 8 (1987): 143–54.

"His Secret Family. France Learns of Mitterrand's Mistress and Love Child," *People*, November 21, 1994.

Hite, Shere. *Women in Love*. New York: Alfred A. Knopf, 1987.

———. *The Hite Report on Male Sexuality*. New York: Macmillan, 1981.

Indianapolis Star and News, "Dan Burton's Affair," September 5, 1998.

Isikoff, Michael, and Evan Thomas. "Monica's Story," *Newsweek*, February 2, 1998.

Jackson, Laura. *Heart of Stone—The Unauthorised Life of Mick Jagger*. London: Smith Gryphon, 1997.

Jacobson, Neil, and John Gottman. *When Men Batter Women*. New York: Simon and Schuster, 1998.

Janus, Samuel S., and Cynthia L. Janus. *The Janus Report on Sexual Behavior*. New York: John Wiley & Sons, 1993.

Johnson, Peter. "Scandal Coverage Gets Higher Marks in Poll," *USA Today*. August 26, 1998.

"Jones Lawyers Issue Files Alleging Clinton Pattern of Harassment of Women," *New York Times*, March 14, 1998.

"Jones Revised First Version of Clinton's Actions in Hotel," *Washington Post*, February 21, 1998.

Jong, Erica. *Fear of Flying*. New York: Signet, 1974.

Kay, Richard, and Christopher Levy. *Diana: The Untold Story*. London: Boxtree, 1998.

Kenrick, D. T., and R. C. Keefe. "Age References in Mates Reflect Sex Differences in Reproductive Strategies," *Behavioral and Brain Sciences*, 15 (1992): 75–133.

Kessler, Ronald. *Inside the White House: The Hidden Lives of the Modern Presidents and the Secrets of the World's Most Powerful Institution*. New York: Pocket Books, 1995.

Kinsey, A. C., W. B. Pomeroy, and C. E. Martin. *Sexual Behavior in the Human Male*. Philadelphia: W. B. Saunders, 1948.

———. *Sexual Behavior in the Human Female*. Philadelphia: W. B. Saunders, 1953.

Klein, Edward. *All Too Human: The Love Story of Jack and Jackie Kennedy*. New York: Pocket Books, 1997.

Klein, Joe. "An American Marriage—How to Explain Bill and Hillary Clinton?" *The New Yorker*, February 9, 1998.

———. "Primary Cad," *The New Yorker*, September 7, 1998.

Klerman, G. K., and M. M. Weissman. "Increasing Rates of Depression," *Journal of the American Medical Association*, 261 (1989): 2229–35.

Komarow, Steven. "Report Says General Had Affairs with Wives of Four Subordinates," *USA Today*, July 7, 1998.

Lacayo, Richard. "The Politics of Yuck," *Time*, September 14, 1998.

Ladies' Home Journal. " 'The Amazing American Woman Survey.' What Wives Will Forgive" (September 1998).

Laumann, Edward, John Gagnon, Michael Robert, and Michael Stuart. *The Social Organization of Sexuality: Sexual Practices in the United States.* Chicago: University of Chicago Press, 1994.

Laurence, Charles. "Hillary Still Dances to Tammy's Tune," *Daily Telegraph* (London), January 23, 1998.

Lawson, Annette. *Adultery: Analysis of Love and Betrayal.* New York: Basic Books, 1988.

Leen, Jeff. "A Powerful, Generous Mentor," *Washington Post*, February 20, 1998.

Life. "Affairs of the Heart" (August 1987).

McGrath, Ellen, G. P. Keita, B. Strickland, and N. F. Russo. *Women and Depression: Risk, Factors and Treatment Issues.* Washington, DC: American Psychological Association, 1990.

Malone, Andrew. "Victoria's Secret," *The Times* (London), November 30, 1997.

Manning, Anita. "Genital Herpes Infections Up 30% Since Late 1970's," *USA Today*, October 17, 1997.

Maraniss, David. *First in His Class: A Biography of Bill Clinton.* New York: Simon & Schuster, Touchstone, 1995.

Marie Claire. "Why Men Pay for Sex," (March 1997).

Markman, Howard, and Scott Stanley. *Marriage in the '90's. Special Report.* Denver: University of Denver Press, 1997.

Masters, William, Virginia Johnson, and Robert Kolodny. *Heterosexuality.* New York: HarperPerennial, 1994.

Mayerson, Charlotte. *Goin' to the Chapel: Dreams of Love, Realities of Marriage.* New York: Basic Books, 1996.

McCood, Sheridan. *Hollywood Lovers.* London: Orion Media, 1997.

Michael, Robert, John H. Gagnon, Edward O. Laumann, and Gina Kolata. *Sex in America.* New York: Warner Books, 1995.

"Monica and Bill—The Sordid Tale That Imperils the President," *Time*, February 2, 1998.

Morton, Andrew. *Diana: Her True Story—In Her Own Words.* New York: Simon & Schuster, 1997.

New Woman. "The Infidelity Report" (March 1994).

New York Times. "Attitudes about the Lewinsky Matter," *New York Times*/CBS New Poll, August 22, 1998.

"No More Mrs. Nice Guy," *Newsweek*, September 23, 1996.

Nolen-Hoeksema, Susan. *Sex Differences in Depression.* Stanford, CA: Stanford University Press, 1990.

O'Brien, Pamela. "The Love Life of an American Wife," *Ladies' Home Journal* (February 1993).

O'Neill, Nena, and George O'Neill. *Open Marriage: A New Lifestyle Choice for Couples*. New York: M. Evans, 1972.

Osborne, Claire G. *The Unique Voice of Hillary Rodham Clinton—A Portrait in Her Own Words*. New York: Avon Paperbacks, 1998.

Parrent, Joanne. *You'll Never Make Love in This Town Again*. Los Angeles: Dove Books, 1996.

Parrent, Joanne and Michelle, Lisa, Sophie, Jewel, Tatiana, and Jennifer. *Once More with Feeling*. Los Angeles: Dove Books, 1996.

Pearson, Allison. "I Did Not Have Fabric Interaction with That Man," *Evening Standard* (London), August 5, 1998.

People. "Angry and Hurt, But No Quitter," August 31, 1998.

———. "Surviving Infidelity: How They Cope, Why They Stay," September 7, 1998.

———. "Older Actors, MUCH, MUCH Younger Actresses," August 10, 1998.

Perlini, A. H., and S. Bertolissi. *What Is Beautiful Is Good: What Is Beautiful and Young Is Better*. Toronto: American Psychological Association, 104th Convention, 1996.

Peterson, Karen S. "Does Tying the Knot Put Women in a Bind?" *USA Today*, April 22, 1997.

———. "Million-Dollar Message from Ex-Wife, Jury," *USA Today*, August 8, 1997.

———. "Liaisons Test the Bonds of Marriage," *USA Today*, February 11, 1998.

Pittman, Frank. *Private Lies: Infidelity and the Betrayal of Intimacy*. New York: W. W. Norton, 1989.

Plimpton, George. "Whither Now, Princess Di?" *Cosmopolitan* (February 1997).

"Psychogossip," *Forbes*, July 1, 1996.

Quilliam, Susan. *Women on Sex*. New York: Barricade Books, 1994.

Reinisch, June. *The Kinsey Institute New Report on Sex*. New York: St. Martin's Press, 1991.

Reiss, Swan D., K. Anderson, and S. Thompson. *Redefining Monogamy: Sexual versus Emotional Exclusivity—The Implications for Sexual Health Risk*. Toronto: American Psychological Association, 104th Convention, 1996.

Richardson, Laurel. *The New Other Woman: Contemporary Single Women in Affairs with Married Men*. New York: Free Press, 1985.

Ross, Lillian. *Here But Not Here: My Life with William Shawn and The New Yorker*. New York: Random House, 1998.

Schickel, Richard. *Clint Eastwood: A Biography*. New York: Alfred A. Knopf, 1996.

"Sex and the Cosmo Girl—International Survey," *Cosmopolitan* (March 1996).

"Sex, Lies and Videotape," *Dateline NBC*, NBC Television, November 12, 1996.

Shah, Keerti, and F. X. Bosch. "Male Sexual Behavior and HPVDNA: Key Risk Factors for Cervical Cancer in Spain," *Journal of the National Cancer Institute*, 88 (1996): 1060–67.

Shah, Keerti, and N. Munoz. "Difficulty in Elucidating the Male Role in Columbia, SA, A High Risk Area for Cervical Cancer," *Journal of the National Cancer Institute*, 88 (1996): 1068–75.

Sheehy, Gail. "Hillary's Choice." *Vanity Fair* (February 1999).

Shipman, Claire. "Hillary's Hide-and-Seek," *George* magazine (September 1998).

Sigall, H., and D. Landy. "Radiating Beauty: The Effects of Having a Physically Attractive Partner on Person Perception," *Journal of Personality and Social Psychology*, 28 (1973): 218–24.

Sileo, C. C. *What You Should Know About Women and Depression*. Washington, DC: American Psychological Association, Office of Public Affairs, 1990.

Sinrod, Barry, and Marlo Grey. *Just Married*. Kansas City: Andrews McMeel, 1998.

Smith, Liz. "Bill's Marital Woes," *New York Post*, February 16, 1998.

Spring, Janet Abrahams. *After the Affair*. New York: HarperCollins, 1996.

"Spy Hard: Women Who Snoop on Their Lovers," *Elle* (Australian) (January 1997).

Staheli, Lana. *Triangles: Understanding, Preventing, and Surviving an Affair*. New York: HarperCollins, 1997.

Starr Report. Report of the Office of the Independent Counsel to the United States House of Representatives, September 11, 1998.

"Summertime and the Living Is Single," *New York Times*, August 4, 1996.

Tavris, Carol, and Susan Sadd. *Redbook Report on Sex*. New York: Delacorte Press, 1977.

Taylor, Richard. *Having Love Affairs*. New York: Prometheus Press, 1982.

Thomas, Evan, and Daniel Klaidman., "A Star's Fall from Grace," *Newsweek*, December 22, 1997.

Thompson, A. P. "Emotional and Sexual Components of Extramarital Relations," *Journal of Marriage and the Family*, 46 (1984): 35–42.

Time. "The Morris Mess—After the Fall," September 9, 1996.

———. "Just an Affectionate Guy," February 16, 1998.

———. "When Is Sex Not 'Sexual Relations'?" *Time/CNN* Poll, August 24, 1998.

———. "How We Really Feel About Fidelity," *Time/CNN* Poll, August 31, 1988.

———. "It's Nobody's Business But Ours," August 31, 1998.

Townshend, J. M., and G. D. Levy. "Effects of Potential Partners' Physical Attractiveness and 'Socioeconomic Status on Sexuality and Partner Selection,' " *Archives of Sexual Behavior*, 371 (1995): 149–64.

Trump, Ivana. *The Best Is Yet to Come: Coping with Divorce and Enjoying Life Again*. New York: Pocket Books, 1995.

USA Today/CNN/Gallup Poll. *"The Public Reacts,"* August 18, 1998.

USA Today. "The White House Can Finally Exhale," July 30, 1998.

————. "Lewinsky Felt Liaison Would Last," August 20, 1998.

————. "Scandal Dominates," August 27, 1998.

————. "Practice What We Preach?" September 3, 1998.

————. "Genital Herpes up 30% Since late '70s," October 16, 1997.

Vaughan, Peggy. *The Monogamy Myth: A New Understanding of Affairs and How to Survive Them.* New York: Newmarket Press, 1989.

W magazine, "Lady Diandra," (August 1998).

Walker, Lenore E. *The Battered Woman.* New York: Harper & Row, 1979.

Wallerstein, Judith S., and Susan Blakeslee. *The Good Marriage: How and Why Love Lasts.* New York: Warner Books, 1995.

Weitzman, Lenore. *The Divorce Revolution: The Unexpected Social and Economic Consequences for Women and Children in America.* New York: Free Press, 1985.

Young, Josh. "Bill Clinton's Grand Seduction,," *George* magazine, (March 1998).

About the Author

Debbie Then, Ph.D., an expert in social and media psychology, is a California-based writer and consultant specializing in relationships, women, beauty, and style. Dr. D, as she is known, received her Ph.D. in Education and Psychology from Stanford University, and is a member of the American Psychological Association and its Media Psychology Division, which advises magazines, newspapers, and television shows about editorial issues related to human behavior and psychology.